# RUSSIA
# REVISED

*By the same authors*

Living with Glasnost

# RUSSIA REVISED

## AN ALPHABETICAL KEY TO THE SOVIET COLLAPSE AND THE NEW REPUBLICS

### Andrew Wilson
### &
### Nina Bachkatov

ANDRE DEUTSCH

To the memory of Alain Oulman

First published 1992 by
André Deutsch Limited
105-106 Great Russell Street, London WC1B 3LJ

ISBN 0 233 98767 3

Printed and bound in Great Britain
by Hartnolls Limited

# CONTENTS

# FOREWORD

A few days after the abortive *putsch* of August 1991, the United States government told its map makers to stop their presses until, as an official put it, the new Soviet frontiers became a bit clearer. Across the world publishers of books must have wished they could do the same. The chain reaction that had started in 1985 was accelerating so fast that no one could keep up with it. It was like a film in a runaway projector; at any moment the celluloid had to snap.

It did, three months later, at Minsk – or more accurately Brest – where on December 8 three republics – Russia, Byelorussia and the Ukraine – decided to torpedo the Union by setting up a so-called Commonwealth.

As writers we were lucky. A year and a half before we had been in the middle of a conventionally planned book, to be called by our publishers *From Totalitarianism to Democracy*, when we realized that any attempt to make sense of the changing scene would be out of date before reaching the printers. The easiest thing would have been to put it aside till the pace slowed down or there was a break in the fog of events. But the urge to describe what we saw around us was irresistible, so we decided to gather up the thousands of facts in our notebooks and lay them out in a simple way that in due course might help others (and ourselves) to construct a coherent picture. The resulting book was published in France* three months before the 'days of August' and enjoyed a critical success. The coup, and then the dissolution, opened many windows, enabling us to enlarge its English successor with a great deal of additional material, not only about these events themselves, but also about the complex situation leading up to them.

For each of the thousand or so entries that follow in alphabetical order we had one of three criteria. Was the subject – person, organization, concept or statistic – an essential part of current events? Was it a significant or commonly used reference point from the recent past? Was it likely to be referred to in the near future? The first

*Les Nouveaux Soviétiques – de A à Z*. Calmann-Lévy, Paris.

criterion needs no comment. The second accounts for the inclusion of items such as Lenin's New Economic Policy, which, until the rout of Leninism, was regularly cited by Party apologists as a precedent for a Soviet 'market' economy. The third accounts for entries, usually economic or military, germane to the debate about the Soviet Union's successors.

Much of our material comes from our first-hand observations as Moscow-based journalists roaming through two continents and eleven time zones. In six years this has meant thousands of meetings with officials, as well as hours following newspapers and television. Our literary sources include the books listed on page 248. In addition we have made use of the BBC Daily Summary of World Broadcasts, the annual Military Balance and other publications of the London-based International Institute for Strategic Studies, and the last available edition of the Soviet Encyclopaedic Dictionary.

Although we have sought to be objective with facts, little that is written about the Soviet Union can be a simple record, and we make no secret of our occasional bias. We sharply disagree with much that has been written in the Soviet (and Western) press in the past few years, particularly the tendency to accept as a democrat almost anyone claiming that title.

In any case, the notion that 'democracy' *per se* can solve what used to be called the Soviet problem is simplistic. Democracy of a recognizable kind is an essential of any transition to a modern society. But only one essential. And to go on to equate democracy with a market-based economy is even more simplistic. There have been 'markets' in totalitarian countries and state economic controls in democratic ones. It is slovenly thinking to ignore the whole process by which Western democracy has been painfully built up over centuries.

*

To readers who may be tempted to use this as more than just a reference book, and to root among its entries for an insight into what is happening today, we have compiled a thematic index (see page 249). We also owe readers what our A-to-Z formula would otherwise preclude, a quick bird's-eye look at the chapter of history just ended and the new one just beginning.

For those on the spot, the birth of the Soviet reform movement in 1985 was a moment of great optimism. By the same token, the collapse of the Union after six years' struggle to reform it, was a disaster, leaving no one to care for the after-effects of the empire's implosion. Between the two events lay a time of perplexing contradictions falling, roughly, into four stages.

The first phase, covering 1985–87, was marked by the reformers' imperfect understanding of the hugeness of the task in front of them. For Gorbachev and like spirits at the Twenty-seventh Party Congress, the crisis of stagnation bequeathed by the Brezhnev era was mainly technological. The Soviet system needed restructuring (*perestroika*), but it would still be a Party system. *Glasnost* (openness) was a way to open up science. Problems would be solved by command.

Orders went out for 'quality control', 'shop-floor initiative', 'sobriety'. The goal – to bring the country into competitive relationship with the rest of the world – was new; but the method of reaching it scarcely differed from those of the past thirty years. Only about halfway through 1987 did the reformers realize that command would never produce the popular will needed for achieving their goal.

The next phase, lasting nearly a year, revolved around the 1988 Party Conference and included a return to the drawing board. Command had to be replaced by a system of incentives, and central planning by devolution, starting with the octopus-like Gosplan. To arouse political interest it was necessary to create new legislative bodies. The 1989 parliament set up as a result of hard-fought conference decisions was far from being fully representative (a third of the deputies were still Party nominees); but for the first time people could watch on television as their deputies asked awkward questions about things like the Party 'special shops' and illegal actions by the KGB. More importantly, parliament gave Gorbachev a new power base.

Incentives took the form of freedom to set up co-operatives and engage in joint ventures, to travel abroad and hold foreign currency. A new breed of citizen appeared – Adam Smith economists, company executives, heirs of the 1920s NEP men. Soon Western newspapers would be reporting the appearance of the first 'rouble millionaires'.

Outwardly it looked fine – especially when combined with the momentous changes that signalled an end to the Cold War. But within the walls of Soviet society reality was different. The masses whom Gorbachev had hoped to electrify remained trapped by inertia. People might crave for Western luxuries but they rejected any change that threatened their security. The economic transformation, which had been the starting point of *perestroika*, never caught up with the artistic and intellectual liberation that had been almost its by-product.

The next phase, covering the 1990 republic and regional elections, can now be seen as the time when the course of history shifted – away from the liberalization of the super-state, towards its disintegration in an anarchy of individual aspirations.

There were several reasons. One was the continuing economic decline. Another was the character of the elections, which were held in a much more emotional atmosphere than the Union elections the year before. The result favoured nationalist groups. And when these took on militant tones, Gorbachev, though still assured of a parliamentary majority, was thrown on the defensive. Instead of action he passed to *reaction*, against 'democrats' and nationalists on the one hand and Party hard-liners on the other.

In what was intended to be one of his famous 'balancing acts' he leaned toward the right. But this time the ploy went wrong. Caught in a cross-fire between militant nationalists and the 'forces of order', he found himself identified with the repressive actions of appointees like Kryuchkov and Pugo who were shortly to turn against him.

The fourth phase began when, too late, he pulled back and offered republics a new union treaty which, had it been offered two years earlier, would have been greeted with acclaim. As it was, he found himself isolated and almost without friends when the signing of the treaty was pre-empted by the 1991 *putsch*.

The train of events leading from the failed coup of August to Boris Yeltsin's political coup of December is sufficiently documented among the entries that follow and needs no elaboration here. What *is* needed is to recall how so many Western voices, now raised in alarm over the vacuum left by the disappearance of the Soviet Union, were only yesterday calling for its destruction.

*

The break-up of the Union in the way it happened was a stupendous piece of folly. Gorbachev made a number of tragic misjudgements. But he will surely be remembered as a giant brought down by pygmies. Nor was his downfall simply the product of his own mistakes, the obstruction of party die-hards, or the machinations of power-hungry rivals. The West, too, played an ignominious part in toppling him, while simultaneously loading him with Gorbification (*Time* 'Man of the Year' and other embarrassments).

It was Western economists who shouted from the sidelines that all that was needed to save the ailing economy was a leap into an instant 'market', when there was neither the economic infrastructure nor the popular work ethic needed for such a miracle. And it was the Western media (commonly fed by émigré political lobbies) which gave uncritical support to nationalist movements, when the urgent need was for cool counsel.

Indeed, were we to begin assigning blame for today's instability, we would begin not with the obstruction of the Party bureaucrats, which is well enough known, but with the intervention of outside bodies, such as the American Heritage Foundation, preaching that all that was needed to overcome Russia's crisis was to renounce communism, substituting one ideology for another.

The speed of events should teach one not to make predictions. Nevertheless, in the aftermath of Soviet collapse, it is possible to see a variety of ways in which the situation could develop. Nearly all are gloomy.

The first is in the area of the economy, where the worst-case scenario is that, even with Western aid and the hoped-for stimulus of free prices, neither food nor manufactured goods reach the market in time to prevent an explosion of social unrest comparable with that of 1917. Such an explosion would almost certainly lead to demands for a return to state communism, or to fascism – in any case an authoritarian regime.

The second is in the area of inter-republic relations, where the worst-case scenario includes the pursuit of narrow economic goals, grandeur, and the romantic dreams of national poets. Opportunities for mischief exist not only *among*, but also *within*, nearly all the new independent republics, as 'autonomous' communities clamour for their own independence, often with outside support.

A third kind of scenario can be written at international level, as the flux touches regions on the former Union's periphery. The Cold War has ended, but because of the Union's precipitate demise, it has been succeeded by a much more dangerous instability. On one hand there is a threat, perhaps already the fact, of nuclear proliferation, in terms of expertise and materials. On the other there is a seismic geopolitical problem.

If the five ex-Soviet Asian republics fall to Islamic fundamentalism imported from southern neighbours, yesterday's Iron Curtain could be succeeded by a new geopolitical fault line. Nor is Islam the only factor to be considered. Powers like China and Turkey can also be expected to be drawn into the vacuum.

Of course, there are also less pessimistic scenarios. According to one, within a reasonable time the market will establish itself, material wants will be satisfied, and (democracy following prosperity) the new republics will co-exist in a brotherhood of diversity. But, as this is written, there is not much sign that this will happen.

In such a fluid situation, writing about the ex-Soviet Union means battling with words. Newspapers use, for example, the word democracy. But what does 'democracy' mean in the Soviet context? Often no more than a slogan seized by rivals in the contest for power. For this reason we nearly always put words such as 'democracy' and 'democrat' into quotation marks. 'Autonomy', 'sovereignty' and 'independence' are among the words which demand this cautious treatment.

Nomenclature has also become a problem since independence. Nearly half the republics, and at least ninety towns, have changed their names. But for ease of recognition and historical continuity we initially use the old name, with the new one immediately after it (e.g. Kirghizia/Kyrgystan).

In the case of entries describing 'Unions', we have used the style 'Artists' Union', rather than Union of Artists – again, for ease of reference. And in transliteration from the Russian, we have tended, at the cost of offending purists, to use the spelling most familiar to Western newspaper-readers.

Finally, with one of the most important words in the book, we have followed William Safire – a writer with whom we profoundly disagree on almost every other account: the *putsch* was just that, i.e. an attempt that failed; not a *coup*, which suggests a successful take-over.

In addition to the sources already mentioned, we wish to acknowledge our debt to the friendship (and even more, the copy) of Moscow-based colleagues, particularly those working for the *Guardian*, the *Independent*, the *Financial Times*, the *Washington Post*, the *New York Times* and *Newsweek*, as well as a number of European newspapers. We must also thank the many Soviet and Western experts who have given us their time to discuss things we have written about – particularly Roy and Zhores Medvedev, Mikhail Gorbanevsky and Valeri Pogrebenkov. The views expressed here are, of course, our own.

Words with an asterisk against them have entries of their own.

Moscow, February 1992

# A

**ABACUS.** Universal calculator in use by shops. Symbol of attachment to the economic past.

**ABALKIN,** LEONID IVANOVICH (1930– ). Director of the Institute of Economics of the Russian Academy of Science. In 1990 – torn between caution, as recommended by the prime minister, Ryzhkov,* and haste, as urged by his professional rival, the economist Shatalin* – he defended a 'controlled' transition to a market economy.

**ABKHAZIA.** Ancient Colchis, since 1921 an autonomous republic* in Georgia. In 1988, 83,000 native Abkhaz, already feeling dominated by the 213,000 Georgians in the republic, grew alarmed at the rise of Georgian nationalism and began a campaign for self-determination. In April 1989, a wave of disturbances led to counter-demonstrations in Tbilisi,* where Georgian nationalists claimed that Abkhaz separatists were encouraged by Moscow. A second wave, in July, left eighteen people dead and 239 wounded. A blockade of roads and railways caused heavy damage to the economy, and the Soviet army had to rescue thousands of tourists stranded in trains. In August 1990, the republic parliament in the capital, Sukhumi, proposed talks about ending Abkhazia's 'forced integration' with Georgia. But positions hardened with the Georgian nationalists' win in the November elections. Divisions also appeared among the Abkhaz.

**ABM TREATY, 1972.** Cold War arms treaty that became everyone's text in the 'Star Wars' row. The original treaty restricted each side, the US and the USSR, to two ABM (anti-ballistic missile) complexes, consisting of interceptor missiles and radars. Each could deploy one complex round its capital and another to defend a group of offensive missile (ICBM*) sites. Under a revision of 1974, each side agreed to have only one deployment. The Soviet Union chose to defend Moscow, and the US an ICBM site in Utah. (The Americans later abandoned their system altogether.) Anti-missile technology was sceptically regarded by many scientific and military experts (see 'ABM-X-3'). In the mid-1980s the US accused the USSR of developing a second ABM radar at Krasnoyarsk;* Moscow eventually said it had been misled by its military, and dismantled it. In a key clause of the ABM treaty, later central to the 'Star Wars'* row, each side undertook not to develop space-based anti-missile systems. The

Reagan administration claimed that this still allowed 'research'.

**ABM-X-3** (NATO code name). Anti-ballistic missile system based on the Galosh interceptor missile, deployed round Moscow under control of the Air Defence Command.* At the time of its construction, officers of the rival Strategic Missile Command said resources would have been better applied to acquiring more offensive missiles. After an interruption in 1968, work was completed between 1971 and 1980, using updated components. Western experts say the system is now obsolete.

**ABORTION.** Common method of birth control (in the Soviet Union by surgical intervention) until the early 1990s, due to the lack of contraceptives. Although abortion is legal and theoretically free, in practice an anaesthetic can cost up to half a month's wages, and the omission of one's name from medical records may involve a further bribe. Abortion is officially available on demand until the twelfth week (the twenty-eighth, if a medical panel considers the mother to be in danger). Many abortions are performed illegally, either because the woman does not want her employer to know about the operation from a medical certificate, or because of the forbidding reception given patients at state abortion clinics. A doctor convicted of performing an illegal abortion risks two to three years' imprisonment. Since 1990 doctors have taken to providing women with IUDs after a second abortion (subject to availability).

**ABSENTEEISM.** Scourge of the economy. In 1990 absenteeism and work stoppages (for industrial or technical reasons) caused an average of 200,000 people to be absent from work – a year's loss of ten million work-days, a daily loss of three billion roubles, and an overall loss of 0.9 per cent of production.

**ABULADZE,** TENGIZ YEVGENYEVICH (1924– ). Georgian film director, famous for his film *Pokayaniye* (Repentance). The film was given its Moscow premiere in 1986 after being shown in Tbilisi. Described as a 'farce' by contemporary Soviet critics, it denounced dictatorship in the character of a central villain with physical resemblances to Stalin, Beria, Hitler and Mussolini. Though it was acclaimed at the Cannes festival, many Western audiences were puzzled by its abstraction and heavy symbolism. In the Soviet Union it inaugurated a period in which artists took the lead in telling the truth about recent history.

**ACADEMY OF SCIENCES** (founded 1724). Organization with a structure derived from Peter the Great. Until the break-up of 1991 the Soviet Academy of Sciences continued to play a central role in Union scientific, industrial, economic and social matters, with 17 divisions, 244 institutes and research centres, and 150,000 people engaged in all sectors of natural and social science. Academies of Science exist in all republics, including, since 1991, Russia. In the second half of the 1980s reforms were made with a view to ending the Soviet Academy's political manipulation, rejuvenating its membership, and increasing its usefulness to the nation. In October 1986 a secret ballot (the first in its history) resulted in the replacement of the elderly president, Anatoli Alexandrov (83), by Guri Marchuk (61). Other reforms included a 75-year age limit (causing 250 vacancies), four-yearly elections (from 1989) for the president and council, and bi-annual general meetings to elect new members. In 1990 a Presidential decree made the Academy independent of the state, gave it ownership of many state-owned facilities, increased its budget, and allowed it to work with institutions abroad. This last change caused a brain-drain, as specialists – particularly mathematicians and computer experts – on foreign secondment showed a reluctance to return home.

**ACCELERATION** (*uskoreniye*). Magic word in 1985–87. Coined at the Central Committee plenum of April 1985, *uskoreniye* joined *perestroika* and *glasnost* in a troika of concepts to defeat 'stagnation'.* First used to mean economic acceleration, it was soon applied to everything, even including culture.

**ACCIDENTS.** Happenings unknown to the Soviet public before 1986, thanks to censorship. Post-*glasnost* accidents have included: Chernobyl★ (23 April 1986); the sinking of the cruise liner 'Admiral Nakhimov' (September 1986); and the Bashkiria gas explosion that engulfed a train (June 1989), killing 575 passengers. Coverage of accidents by newspapers and television has moved on from reporting bare facts, usually with an accent on heroism, to the harsh exposure of responsible officials, often highly placed. Since the 1988 Armenian earthquake and the Bashkiria disaster, photo coverage has observed few limits. See also 'Submarines', 'Traffic', 'Work'.

**ACTIVIST.** Party evangelist carrying the word to the people and teaching discipline by sermons called *lektsiya*. Living in the catacombs since August 1991.

**ADAMOVICH,** Ales Mikhailovich (1924– ). Writer, deputy and spokesman for a Byelorussia traumatized by Chernobyl. In 1966 he was sacked from his job as a Moscow University professor for refusing to sign a letter denouncing his colleagues Sinyavsky and Daniel.★ While not supporting their political opinions, he said he was ashamed to be asked to join in their political extinction. Returning home, he amazingly received the support of Byelorussia's conservative rulers.

**ADIDAS.** Brand label on sports clothes signifying the wearer's modernity. Attachment immediately ensures a black market price, even if the garment itself is from a Soviet back-street factory.

3

**ADVERTISING.** Way to look 'Western' and give the illusion of consumer choice. In 1989 the first billboards appeared, in 1990 television commercials, in 1991 advertisements in the Metro and on buses and trams. Except for blocks provided by advertisers abroad, the first newspaper and magazine ads were primitive. But media of all kinds were looking to advertising to offset the often heavy cost of independence.

**ADZHARIA** (pop. 379,000). Autonomous republic of Georgia bordering Turkey and the Black Sea, with a problem similar to that of Abkhazia.* In 1991 President Gamsakhurdia* rushed through elections for its parliament without safeguards, as hitherto, for the representation of the (Muslim) Adzhars, who are in a minority vis-à-vis Georgians. The campaign was marked by violence culminating in the assassination of the local vice-president, Nodar Imnadze.

**AEROFLOT.** State airline, founded 1923, flying obsolescent planes with heavy fuel and maintenance requirements. Reorganized since December 1991 on a republic basis, the former Soviet commercial carrier is still far from achieving international standards of service, comfort and safety (in 1991 there were still no passenger oxygen masks). In 1988 deputy aviation minister Boris Panyukov, responding to Soviet press criticism, said that by 1995 the airline would have replaced much of its fleet with the more efficient Tu-204s and Il-96s. But at the beginning of 1991 it was on the verge of bankruptcy. Refused a government subsidy, and faced with a critical fuel shortage, it had to cut flights to Africa and Eastern Europe and triple the rouble price of international tickets. In 1991 Aeroflot's monopoly of the Soviet interior was broken by the opening of a number of destinations to Western airlines, and its external monopoly by a presidential decree authorizing preparations for an independent company, ASDA, to start competing in June 1992 with Boeing 747s and 767s from Vnukovo. In 1992, 'Air Russia', a joint venture of British Airways and Aeroflot, was due to start flying from Domodyedovo (see 'Airports').

**AFANASIEV,** Viktor Grigoryevich (1922–   ). Chief editor of *Pravda* (1976–88). On the eve of the 1988 Party conference he was shocked to find himself lumped with the 'old guard' whom the time had come to drop. Though he hastily wrote powerful editorials about the public's right-to-know ('so long as there is no giving away of state secrets'), he failed to save his job.

**AFANASIEV,** Yuri Nikolaevich (1934–   ). Intellectual political counterpart of Boris Yeltsin.* As keeper of the state archives, he led a campaign for rewriting Stalinist history and in 1988 helped to found Memorial.* Elected a deputy in 1989, he joined the Inter-regional Group.* In 1990, during preparations for the Twenty-eighth Congress,* he spoke in such violently anti-communist terms for the Democratic Platform* that Gorbachev called on him to choose where he belonged. He left the Party before the Congress opened and sought to form in the Democratic Forum* (later Democratic Russia*) the nucleus of a coherent opposition.

**AFGHANISTAN.** From 1979 to 1988 the scene of bloody fighting between Soviet forces and the *mujaheddin* (Islamic rebels against the communist government). Soviet losses totalled 14,000 dead or missing (12 per cent of deaths being from sickness or accidents). Under the 1988 Geneva accords, half the 116,000 Soviet troops were withdrawn by 15 August, the rest by 15 February 1989. Defying Western predictions, the Soviet-backed Najib government was still in power three years later, amid unresolved national divisions. For the Soviet army, Afghanistan was a hard lesson. Troops had to forget conventional tactics and learn new ones. But, like the Americans in Vietnam, they failed against a poorly equipped but determined enemy. (The worst year was 1984: 2,343 dead, including 305 officers.) After the war, problems arose with embittered veterans (*Afgantsi*), who formed clubs, and in places vigilante groups, to preserve old comradeships and instil civic morality. Sometimes the movement was welcomed by officials; but there were excesses. In 1991 groups of Afgantsi won honour by joining the resistance to the *putsch*.* In later official accounts of the war, it appeared that in December 1979 the Soviet forces had been sent into Afghanistan after only the most cursory discussion by the Brezhnev Politburo. According to Boris Yeltsin, only Brezhnev, Gromyko, Suslov and Ustinov* were present. In 1988 it was further officially conceded that the Soviet-backed Democratic Party of the Afghan People (DPAP) had ignored religious susceptibilities. (The sequence of events preceding the Soviet intervention was as follows: In 1978 the DPAP took power in a military coup; in December 1979, its leader, Nur Muhammad Taraki, was assassinated by a faction under Hafizullah Amin. In December 1980, Kabul asked for aid against Islamic rebels; Amin was mysteriously killed in a shoot-out with a Soviet KGB 'special anti-terrorist group' and was succeeded by Babrak Karmal, who arrived with the Soviet troops. In 1987 the hard-line Karmal was replaced by Najib, the head of the secret police, whom Moscow found more amenable to a settlement.)

**AFRICA.** Quicksand of Moscow hopes to endow the Third World with the blessings of the Soviet political model. Throughout the post-colonial period Moscow continued to swamp the continent with all kinds of advisers – until in 1987 *Literaturnaya Gazeta* called for the truth to be told about dictators like Idi Amin and 'Emperor' Bokassa. Such men were presented as inspired patriots, it said, without a word being uttered about their victims; and countries were shown as going from success to success when in fact they had been repeatedly shaken by coups and their economies were in ruins. By the end of the 1980s newspapers had started to expose acts of gross misgovernment by current leaders. See also 'South Africa'.

**AGANBEGYAN,** ABEL GAZEVICH (1932– ). Academician and reformist long before *perestroika*, and until 1991 one of Gorbachev's chief advisers. Born of Armenian parents in Tbilisi, Aganbegyan graduated from the Moscow State Institute of Economics and took an administrative post. In 1961 he moved to Novosibirsk, where he helped to found the Siberian branch of the Academy of Sciences. Twenty-two years later he used its house journal *EKO* to publicize Tatiana Zaslavskaya's* famous criticism of the centrally planned economy, the 'Novosibirsk Study'. In 1985, Aganbegyan moved to Moscow to head the Academy's economic section and its commission for the study of productive resources, where he argued the case for economic reform based on socialist principles. His stress on the need to avoid mass unemployment brought him into conflict with economists like Nikolai Shmelyev, who saw 'moderate unemployment' as a necessary work incentive. Though later somewhat eclipsed by rivals like Shatalin* and Abalkin,* he was chosen in October 1990 to synthesize rival reform plans in an economic programme put before the Soviet parliament. The 66-page document, 'Basic Directives', was approved in October by 333 votes to 12, with 34 abstentions. To critics of the programme's vagueness, he said that what mattered was to fix the general lines, leaving the republics* to decide the practical methods. The same year, in an uncharacteristically violent outburst, he accused Boris Yeltsin* of costing the country 'several billions of dollars every time he made a speech'.

**AGRICULTURE.** Lame duck of the Soviet economy, despite repeated attempts at reanimation. After collectivization in the late 1920s, Soviet agriculture devolved entirely on state* farms (*sovkhozy*) and collective farms (*kolkhozy**). In 1987–88 the law was changed to encourage sales from private plots* or 'surplus' collective farm output. The move was nullified by administrative harassment, lack of transport, and individual inertia. A new law in 1988 allowed peasants to take leases of up to fifty years. Another in 1989 permitted tenant farming. But despite a press campaign eulogizing the tenant farmer, few responded. Peasants were afraid of going back to the 'old days', and collective farm directors had no interest in arranging the granting of land leases, which had to be negotiated with the *kolkhoz*. In 1990 the sale of land was envisaged by the '500 days' Shatalin* plan, as in plans by some republics, but was excluded from the compromise eventually adopted by the Soviet parliament. In March 1991, no one had yet found a method of valuation. In 1990 agriculture engaged 19 per cent of the Soviet labour force (compared with 2 per cent in America) and took 17 per cent of national investment (half the value of delivered production). Devised by city experts unaware of the realities of the countryside, reforms over five years only widened the gulf between town and country, particularly when reformists confused peasants with 'reactionaries' – or when cities barred shops to non-residents, and peasants hit back by withholding food from the towns. In the autumn of 1990, faced with the deteriorating situation in the cities, the

Soviet government was obliged to appeal for international aid. Western countries, led by Germany, responded promptly with food, humanitarian aid* and credits. But everyone knew it was not the 2.3 per cent fall in production that was to blame so much as the system of distribution. Western aid faced the same problem. At the beginning of December 1990 only one-fifth of deliveries had been unloaded because of lack of trucks, drivers and storage. But Western governments wished to help Gorbachev stay in power in conditions of relative calm, and in 1991 the US sent a team of distribution experts to advise on methods of avoiding a repetition of the 1990 harvest disaster (see 'Grain').

**AGROPROM.** See 'Gosagroprom'.

**AGROPROMBANK.** Bank to help rural areas into a market economy with credits and technical advice. Its statutes were finally registered in September 1990 after it had been in existence for two and a half years, supposedly helping to finance peasant co-operatives. At the time of registration there were 3,500 shareholders (co-operatives, factories, state and collective farms). Reserves stood at 8 million roubles, making it one of the most powerful banks in any field. Its statutes make it open to participation by foreign banks, firms or individuals.

**AIDS.** Once-rare disease transmitted by foreigners, with the eventual help of Soviet prostitutes. Official figures speak of 26 cases detected in 1987 and some 1,500 in 1991. Of the latter total 77 per cent were said to be male homosexuals or persons having a 'disorderly sex life', 15 per cent drug addicts, 1 per cent children born to affected mothers, and 5 per cent cases hard to analyse. Foreign experts believe the figures are understated, but that the country has been kept relatively clear of the disease. Contamination is helped by shortages of disposable syringes, condoms,* needles and throw-away dialysers. The anti-AIDS campaign began in 1987 with the distribution of 5 million booklets, the setting up of a special centre at the Institute of Virology of the Academy of Sciences, a law forbidding sexual relations between known cases (penalty: eight years' imprisonment), and (briefly) obligatory tests for all foreigners applying for visas of more than three months.

**AIR DEFENCE COMMAND** (*PVO-S*). Branch of the armed forces created in 1955, with separate commands (1958) for anti-aircraft and anti-missile defence. In 1985 it was responsible for shooting down a Korean Air Lines passenger jet, killing 269 people; and in 1987 for failing to intercept Matthias Rust.* Its commander, General Aleksandr Koldunov, was dismissed the next day, together with the Defence Minister, Marshal Sokolov.

**AIR FORCE.** Most prestigious of the former Soviet armed services. For years 'pilots' topped boys' popularity charts. In 1991 the Air Force still had a strength of 420,000 men, including 290,000 conscripts, and about 4,335 combat aircraft. Over half (2,510) were forward ground-attack aircraft, and under half (1,825) fighters. There were 175 long-range, and 390 medium-range, strategic bombers. The principal long-range bomber was the Tu-95, the most advanced forward ground-attack plane the Su-24, and the latest fighter the Su-27.

**AIRPORTS.** Except for the Moscow international airport, Sheremetyevo-2, which was built by foreign contractors for the 1980 Olympics, Soviet airports remain mostly as they were in the 1960s, pens for passengers manned by teams of authoritarian women. There are four secondary Moscow airports (Domodyedovo, Sheremetyevo-1, Vnukovo and Bikovo), all lacking modern facilities. Many provincial airports consist of little more than a shed and a runway; but in 1991 an improvement was promised by the opening of a number of direct international services from airports like Kiev. In 1988, Sheremetyevo-2 (6.2 million passengers) was given a duty-free shopping centre jointly operated by Aeroflot and Ireland's Aer Rianta, and in 1990 faster customs procedures. The same year saw completion of an agreement on a £273 million plan to modernize Sheremetyevo, including the reconstruction of Sheremetyevo-1, to handle 15–18 million passengers a year, under joint venture of Aeroflot and Lufthansa. A similar plan exists for St Petersburg. At the end of 1991, 92 airports (over half the total) were closed by an aviation fuel shortage.

**AITMATOV,** CHINGIZ (1928– ). Kirghiz national writer and leading environmentalist. In 1986 he became a secretary of the Writers' Union,* in 1989 a Soviet parliamentary deputy, and in 1990 a member of the Presidential Council.* In November 1990 he was appointed ambassador to Luxemburg and replaced by Gubenko.* In 1986 he created a sensation with his novel *Plakha* ('The Executioner's Block'), containing an exposé of Central Asian corruption and drugs rings.

**AKHMADULINA,** BELLA AKHATOVNA (1937– ). High priestess of Russian poetry, endowed with a magic sense of language. In the 1970s this small, fragile woman was one of the few intellectuals with the courage to speak up about contemporary conditions. In 1979 she narrowly escaped expulsion from the Union of Writers for helping Aksyonov* to publish his 'independent almanac'. Ahead of others, she publicly applauded Nabokov* and called for publication of the works of Brodsky.* With Aksyonov, Yevtushenko* and Voznesensky,* she helped to form a group that epitomized the country's short-lived cultural liberation after Khrushchev's denunciation of Stalin. Once briefly married to Yevtushenko, she now lives in Moscow with her second husband, the painter Boris Messerer.

**AKHMATOVA,** Anna Andreevna (1891–1966). Major Russian poet of the first half of the twentieth century; a member of the acmeist movement, devoted to clarity and naturalness. Her works ceased to be published after 1922, on the ground that they contributed nothing to communism. In September 1986 *Ogonyek*★ published letters and poems of her dead husband, Gumilev,★ two poems of her own, and a collection of her letters to her brother-in-law, Sergei von Stein. Married for eight years, Akhmatova and Gumilev had a son, whose imprisonment under Stalin inspired some of her finest verses.

**AKHROMEYEV,** Marshal Sergei Fyodorovich (1923–1991). Former chief of the armed forces, once thought likely to become Defence Minister. Instead Gorbachev chose General Yazov★ and used Akhromeyev to project the new defence policies abroad, conspicuously taking him to top-level East-West meetings on arms control and disarmament. In 1988 Akhromeyev resigned in unclear circumstances generally attributed to his resistance to unilateral force cuts. Though he was subsequently named as Gorbachev's personal defence adviser, his departure signalled a decline in the influence of the General Staff. In August 1991 Akhromeyev committed suicide, hanging himself in his locked office on the third day of the *putsch.*★ There was no evidence to suggest his involvement. It was generally accepted that he died an honourable soldier, dismayed at the disgrace of the army and his country.

**AKSYONOV,** Vasili Pavlovich (1932– ). Leading writer stripped of his Soviet citizenship while visiting America in 1981, and given it back by decree in 1990. During the Khrushchev 'thaw' he helped to found a group of poets and other writers with Voznesensky,★ Yevtushenko★ and Akhmadulina.★ His early writings are filled with anguish at the imprisonment of his mother, Evgenia Ginzburg★. In 1979, his involvement in *Metropol*, a collection of writings by himself and twenty-two others, led to quarrels with the Writers' Union. In exile he used his talent for social observation to write about American society. His works were not published in the Soviet Union until the late 1980s, when his *The Isle of Crimea* became a best-seller.

**ALBANIA.** Prodigal son returned with the collapse of the Stalinist regime in 1990. After thirty years' separation Moscow and Tirana resumed diplomatic and trade relations. In 1991 an Albanian parliamentary delegation arrived in Moscow 'to help melt the ice'.

**ALCOHOL.** Opium of the people subjected in 1985–88 to an ill-conceived campaign of suppression. Not realizing that drinkers are the one solid Soviet pressure group, Gorbachev alienated the workers and peasants whose productivity the move was supposed to increase. Drastic cuts were ordered in wine and spirits production, and the 'sober citizen' depicted, in defiance of all tradition, as a 'real man'. The campaign foundered as a result of the excess (see *'Peregib'*) with which it was pursued. Ordered to set an example, officials entertained guests with mineral water and married off their daughters on fruit juice. In 1984–87 sales of alcoholic drinks dropped from 14.7 billion to 8.2 billion litres a year. The campaign cut crime and industrial accidents, and cleared the streets of drunks. But in three years the state lost 37 billion roubles, while the making of *samogon* (moonshine liquor) became a national industry. In 1985–88 there were 2 million convictions for moonshining. The strict regime caused a sharp rise in accidental poisoning. In 1987, thousands of people died from drinking bad spirits or substitutes. Among the latter were perfume (which had to be rationed), anti-freeze, insecticides, cleaning fluid, varnish and glue. On New Year's Eve 1987, a Moscow wine-shop had a record queue of 3,000. A major aim was to cut drunkenness at work. Workers found drunk at their work-places were forced to join the teetotal 'Sobriety Society' (at one point numbering 11 million members) or, on a second conviction, to undergo a cure. In May 1988 the press appealed for a relaxation of the campaign, and in 1989 the government called a halt. In 1991 the country still showed evidence of economic and social damage through the uprooting of vineyards and breaking-up of distilleries and even breweries.

**ALEKSEI II** (ALEKSEI MIKHAILOVICH RIDIGER) (1928–   ). Metropolitan of Leningrad and Novgorod, elected Patriarch in 1990 to succeed Pimen.* The election was made with unusual haste, suggesting deep division and an internal crisis in the Russian Orthodox Church. The new Patriarch faced problems resulting from the Church's internal *perestroika* and *glasnost*. Others were a tendency of some dioceses to place themselves under the jurisdiction of the (monarchist) Orthodox Church Abroad; a conversion offensive by the Catholic Church; and the growing politicization of Christians. Aleksei has himself since given an example of the last by involving the church in all possible public events. He strongly supported the return of Leningrad to its old name, St Petersburg. More ambiguously, he co-signed a public appeal for 'order' that was used to support the 1991 *putsch*,* while later presiding at ceremonies to bless the victory of 'democracy'.

**ALIYEV,** GEIDAR ALIYEVICH (1923–   ). Former Azerbaijan KGB chief whose 1967–69 anti-corruption drive attracted notice in Moscow. In 1976 he became a candidate member, and in 1982 a full member, of the Politburo. He was retained by Gorbachev despite rumours of having favoured his own clan during the clean-up. But soon after taking power, Gorbachev saddled him with responsibility for two notorious crisis fields – social services and transport. In 1987, after months of speculation about the cause of this disgrace, Aliyev retired on health grounds to Baku. His eclipse surprised Kremlin-watchers who had seen him as a possible prime minister. The Aliyev clan declined to accept his retirement and took its revenge by stirring up discontent and Azeri nationalism. In September 1990 Aliyev was elected to the Azerbaijan parliament as deputy for Nakhitchevan★ with 95 per cent of the vote — a development as disconcerting for the Azerbaijan Popular Front as for the Communist Party, which feared a split between an Aliyev faction and members following the first secretary, Mutalibov.

**ALKSNIS,** MAJOR VIKTOR IMANTOVICH (1950–   ). Leader of the ultra-conservative parliamentary group *Soyuz* ('Union'). In February 1991 he proposed the formation of a 'National Salvation Committee',★ and in March was the first to call in parliament for the resignation of Gorbachev because of his handling of the economic crisis.

**ALMA-ATA** (pop. 1.068 million). Capital of Kazakhstan★ and scene of the Soviet Union's first major ethnic riots on 17–18 December 1986 (2,401 arrests, 1,700 injuries, 90 criminal convictions, of which 46 were later quashed). The riots were blamed on a spontaneous anti-Russian outburst after the dismissal of the ageing Party chief, Dinmukhamed Kunayev, and his replacement by a Russian, Gennadi Kolbin. The findings of an inquiry, published in September 1990, pointed to general discontent resulting from social injustice and poor living conditions. When threatened with anti-corruption proceedings, Kunayev's circle complained of the 'foreign' nationality of the investigating judges. At the same time, it appeared that Ministry of Interior troops had made an ill-judged intervention, following a biased and panicky report to Moscow.

**ALMA-ATA AGREEMENT.** Treaty signed on December 21, 1991, establishing the Commonwealth★ in place of the USSR. Signatories were the presidents of eleven republics – the three signatories of the Minsk★ Agreement, the five Soviet Asian presidents (who had just met at Askhabad★), and those of Armenia, Azerbaijan and Moldavia/Moldova. The only absentees among fifteen former Union republics were the Baltic states and Georgia (which merely sent an observer). By a protocol to the Minsk agreement, all signatories were designated Commonwealth co-founders. Other protocols dealt in deliberately vague terms with military affairs, nuclear weapons, the setting up of co-ordinating bodies, and the transfer to Russia of the Soviet UN Security Council seat. The agreement's lack of precision about functions and structures reflected members' fears that the Commonwealth could be a disguised attempt to recreate a 'centre'. It also allowed members to avoid practical and technical decisions, which were postponed to a further meeting in Minsk. An earlier 'Alma–Ata agreement', on October 2, 1991, was to set up an 'economic community of sovereign states'. It was signed by eight republics out of the twelve invited by Nazarbayev,★ then out to make his mark as statesman. Abstainers were Azerbaijan, Armenia, Georgia and Moldavia/Moldova. Lacking a political basis, it was overtaken by the agreement of December.

**ALTAI.** South Siberian *krai*\* (population 2.7 million), with rich gold and diamond reserves. In 1990 it declared itself sovereign, then a 'special economic zone'\* within the Russian Federation.

**AMERICAN.** Pre-1986 synonym for all evil; post-1986 for all good. After the 1988 summit,\* uncritical admiration of everything American became epidemic. Newspapers opened their columns to Alices returning from a Wonderland of limitless shopping and opportunity. It was sophisticated to be able to compare 'Coke' with 'Pepsi',\* smoke native American (not Soviet-made) Marlboros, have Hollywood films on the home video, wear jeans and 'jokey' T-shirts. To aspiring emigrants, America, 'land of the free', promised quick assimilation, in contrast to Western Europe, where immigrants stayed life-long foreigners. For the young, it was the land beyond the rainbow, which Soviet governments, unable to give their own people a decent life, had always maligned. Even foreign-policy makers, while talking about a 'common European home',\* had dreams of a world ruled jointly with the other superpower, which would recognize the USSR as an equal.

**AMNESTY.** Spectacular gesture periodically allowing the righting of miscarriages of justice. In 1987 Gorbachev chose the 70th anniversary of the October Revolution to sign a decree offering an amnesty to political and religious prisoners (who had been excluded from amnesties on the anniversaries of 1967 and 1977). Among their offences were 'breaking the law on separation of church and state' (criminal code, Article 142), 'defaming the Soviet state' (Article 190), and 'anti-Soviet agitation and propaganda' (Article 70). Several of those freed, particularly nationalist and religious activists, were elected to parliament two years later.

**AMNESTY INTERNATIONAL.** Human rights organization long depicted as the instrument of foreign intelligence services seeking pretexts for interference in Soviet internal affairs. In 1989, in a gesture of reconciliation, Amnesty representatives were invited to Moscow by the Academy of Sciences, and their visit reported by the press. In November 1990 Amnesty opened a Moscow office to help communities form local branches and eventually set up a Soviet 'section'.

**ANARCHY.** Ghost returned from pre-revolutionary history to haunt any kind of public demonstration by showing the anarchist black flag. Its first appearance was in February 1990. A 'Confederation of Anarcho-Syndicalists' (chairman Aleksandr Shubin) publishes a newspaper called 'Obshchina', after the old-time village community.

**ANDREEVA,** NINA ALEKSANDROVNA (1932– ). Unknown teacher at Leningrad Technological Institute, rocketed to fame by a single letter to a newspaper. Her letter to *Sovietskaya Rossiya* attacking reform became the symbol, first of conservative reaction, then of Russian chauvinism. Headlined 'I cannot deny my principles', it appeared on March 13, 1988. The letter praised Stalin as the true upholder of Lenin who 'had raised the country to the rank of a world power'. It did not overtly attack *perestroika*, but rather the concepts of 'peaceful co-existence' and 'cosmopolitanism' (Stalinist code-word for Jews). It singled out the Jewish intellectuals Shatrov★ and Rybakov★ for denouncing Stalin and 'peddling so-called truth about the past'. For three weeks the letter went unanswered, most conspicuously in the Party newspaper *Pravda* – a lapse attributed to the absence from Moscow of Gorbachev, who had left affairs in the hands of his deputy, Ligachev.★ On Gorbachev's return, *Pravda* published a denunciation, and *Sovietskaya Rossiya* (whose staff had helped Andreeva write the letter) was obliged to print an apology. Shocking as it was, the letter merely echoed what many people like Andreeva were saying under their breath. In June 1991 she founded the Leninist Labour Party, uniting former members of the Communist Party who disagreed with 'revisionism'.

**ANDROPOV,** YURI VLADIMIROVICH (1916–1984). Underestimated precursor of Gorbachev's revolution. Although his years as KGB chief (1967–82) made him deeply suspect to most Western commentators, Andropov's influence on events was decisive and positive. From the mid-1970s, he used his position in the Politburo to bring on new men (Gorbachev, Ryzhkov); to start corruption proceedings against Brezhnev supporters; and, as General Secretary (November 1982), to institute new norms of efficiency. From September 1983, when he was immobilized by a fatal kidney illness, Gorbachev became his agent in state and Party business. He died the following February.

**ANGOLA.** Burdensome client, finally got rid of in May 1991 when Moscow and Washington joined forces to bring about a peace settlement between the Soviet-backed MPLA and the CIA-backed Unita rebels. Moscow was the MPLA government's chief arms supplier during sixteen years of post-independence fighting; it also paid Cuban troops to fight its war by proxy. More than 300,000 people died in the fighting.

**ANIMALS.** Unprotected species till 1988, when the Russian parliament instituted six months' gaol for persistent cruelty. In the 1980s, Moscow in particular saw an exponential growth of dog-ownership. Helped by subsidized meat, dog shows encouraged the keeping of dogs in crowded apartments. In 1990 shops displayed the first Soviet pet food, when food for people had almost disappeared. Later, pets abandoned as a result of price increases formed packs of fierce strays. A rural council near Sverdlovsk offered priority in the queue for household supplies to anyone bringing in 'fifty or more' stray dogs.

***ANONIMKA.*** Russian word for the police state's stand-by, the anonymous letter. Portrayed as a device to help citizens expose crime without risk of retribution, it became a sore of post-revolutionary society. In 1988 a decree on 'processing' denunciations laid down that, to be considered, letters must give the sender's name and work-place. Revealingly, liberal newspapers, though aware of the *anonimka*'s odious aspects, detected in the requirement a bureaucratic way to discourage protests. Such was the popular state of mind.

**ANTI-CRISIS PROGRAMME.** Economic programme agreed in principle in May 1991 by ten republics (excluding Georgia, Moldavia and the Baltics). It envisaged: the restoring by 1992 of 1989 production levels; an energetic transition to a market economy; a broad disposal of state property; moves to attract foreign capital; a cut in state spending; guaranteed transition to rouble convertibility; and the suppression of foreign currency transactions within the USSR, from the following January. After many vicissitudes it was finally adopted on a one-year working basis three months before the Soviet collapse.

**ANTI-SEMITISM.** Centuries-old sickness reactivated by the shock of reforms. In the 1980s, the prominence of Jews among the urban intelligentsia caused ultra-conservative intellectuals to speak of 'the genocide of Russian culture and national morality' by 'Jewish masonry'. Despite Jewish emigration★ the disease continued, inspiring the Pamyat★ society. Among ordinary people, anti-semitism is more simply due to jealousy of the many Jews who have chosen to remain in the country and are active in co-operatives and private professions opened up by economic reforms. In the Baltic states, Moldavia and the Ukraine, anti-semitism is perpetuated by a reluctance to revise national history — to take account of pogroms★ and the participation of popular elements in the holocaust. Nationalist demonstrations have included slogans that liberal intellectuals prefer not to see — like (in Vilnius), 'Lithuania for Lithuanians. Poles back to Poland, and Jews to the crematoria!', and (in Lvov) 'Death to the Judaeo-communist anti-Christ!' On May Day 1991, 3,000 people took part in an anti-semitic demonstration in Leningrad.

**ANTI-ZIONIST COMMITTEE.** Body set up in the 1960s to flatter Arab client states. Purporting to draw a distinction between Jews and Zionists, it mostly achieved the opposite. It ceased activity with the normalization of relations with Israel. One of its last public acts, in 1988, was to publicize the return of a group of Soviet Jewish emigrants disillusioned with life in the United States.

**APPARAT.** Body of officials administering Party organizations. Not necessarily a pejorative term, unlike *apparatchik* (a member of the *apparat*). In 1990 the Central Committee voted for cutting the numbers of the *apparat* throughout the country. After the 1991 *putsch*★ the *apparat* was dissolved by the government decree suspending the Party's activities.

**APRIL.** Association formed in March 1989 to break the monopoly of the Writers' Union; handicapped by including a number of second-rate writers in search of publishers, but strengthened by well-known founder-members including Tatiana Tolstaya, Rybakov,★ Yevtushenko★ and Anatoli Pristavkin.

**AQUARIUM.** Leningrad rock group, clandestine in Brezhnev's time, reaching national status in Gorbachev's. In 1991 it was still in the charts, despite age, including that of its star, Boris Grebenshchikov. Longevity is shared by two other groups with similar origins, Kruise★ and Kino.

**ARAL SEA.** World's fourth largest inland sea, steadily disappearing. It once received the full flow of the Amu-Darya and Syr-Darya rivers. The water of the Syr-Darya no longer arrives at all, being tapped for cotton irrigation, while the Amu-Darya delivers only 1–2 cubic kilometres per year. In thirty years, accelerating over the last five, the level of the sea has dropped thirteen metres, the volume by 60 per cent, and the surface area by a third. The original coast and ports are now 10–40 miles from the water. The fall has destroyed valuable fisheries and produced a salt concentration of 15 grams per litre. Experts estimate that by the year 2000 the Aral will be only a salt-lake and by 2010 will vanish entirely. Winds carry clouds of salt and dust 300 miles long by 30 wide, depositing 15–75 million tons on adjacent land annually, destroying agriculture and threatening the survival of a small people, the Karapalkaks. Accompanying climate changes have caused excessively hot summers and prolonged winters. Projects to save the Aral have engaged leading intellectuals and ecologists. In 1991 plans included a further cut in cotton★ cultivation and reducing evaporation from irrigation canals, to secure an annual inflow of 8.7 cubic kilometres, later rising to 20 cubic kilometres. Ecologists remain sceptical.

**ARBAT.** Old street in central Moscow, the first to become a pedestrian precinct, in 1986. Heavily restored and dubbed 'our Montmartre' because of the junk artists, it has also become a kind of 'speakers' corner' where tourists take occasional soap-box oratory as a sign of *perestroika*. Part-time prostitutes, drug peddlers and drop-outs now congregate in a street where in 1987 the KGB staged its last heavy-booted action against refuseniks.★

**ARBATOV,** ALEKSEI GEORGYEVICH (1951– ). Policy analyst, like his father (see below). In 1988 he was attacked by the military, and, surprisingly, by the Foreign Ministry's *Journal of International Affairs,* for proposing drastic cuts in the armed forces. Arbatov argued that, because of escalation, a small number of nuclear weapons was enough for deterrence and that conventional forces could safely be reduced. The proposal was far from extreme. Other civilian analysts (Zhurkin, Maraganov and Kortunov) have argued for complete denuclearization.

**ARBATOV**, GEORGI ARKADYEVICH (1923–   ). Director of ISKAN,* where, before serving Gorbachev, he participated in the analysis of foreign policy options under Brezhnev. Though cynics accuse him of an over-smooth transition, Arbatov has the respect of many Western analysts who see him as having helped to prepare policies only later adopted under *perestroika*. In late 1991 he emerged as an adviser to Yeltsin.

**ARBITRATION.** Standard form of settlement for legal disputes between ministries and public entities (later extended to include private firms). It has gained importance with moves towards a free market. In December 1990, Veniamin Yakovlev, Minister of Justice and newly appointed president of the arbitration court, said arbitration would be needed to ensure a harmonious hand-over of ministerial powers in the period of transition.

**ARCHIVES.** Centre of a tug-of-war between keepers of secrets and historians bent on filling in 'blank spots'. Jealously guarded by ministries, the military, the KGB, the Party and other 'collectors', archives were fair booty in the power game between new non-communist republics and the Kremlin.* The destruction of KGB archives (such as happened in a fire in Tbilisi* in 1990) could remove awkward evidence of links between the old security apparatus and newly arrived politicians. The archives of the Soviet Communist Party were guarded by the Marxist-Leninist Institute on behalf of the Central Committee. They were held in sixteen centres attached to institutes of Party history, and in 153 regional centres. After the *putsch** they became, like the KGB archives, a source of conflict between the republics and the centre. The argument was settled by Yeltsin, who at the end of 1991 transferred them to a Russian centre headed by Vladimir Kozlov.

*ARGUMENTY I FAKTY* (Arguments and Facts). Weekly publication of the Znaniye (Knowledge) Society, originally designed to provide Party propagandists with background material, but now devoted to answering readers' questions. In five years (1985–90) the formula raised its circulation from 1.4 million to 25 million. Its 1991 circulation (22.7 million) was still the country's highest. In 1990 the editor-in-chief, V. Starkov, narrowly escaped the sack for publishing a popularity poll in which Mikhail Gorbachev was unplaced.

**ARMED FORCES.** In the autumn of 1991 the Soviet armed forces still numbered 3.9 million, including 2.5 million conscripts, 490,000 men in railway and construction units, and 530,000 transferred to the Army from the KGB* and the Ministry of the Interior.* But in September the Defence Ministry announced plans for a reduction to 2.5–3 million over the next one and a half years. Reductions were foreshadowed when in 1988 the high command and Warsaw Pact leaders proclaimed a new doctrine of 'Sufficient Defence'.* At the UN General Assembly in December 1988, Gorbachev announced a unilateral reduction of 500,000 'by 1991'. Under it, six armoured divisions in East Germany would be withdrawn and disbanded, contributing to a total withdrawal of 5,000 tanks and 50,000 men. Other reductions, in European Russia, would bring the total cut to 10,000 tanks, 8,500 artillery pieces, and 800 combat aircraft. About half the programme had been completed when, towards the end of 1989, communist rule in Eastern Europe suddenly collapsed, leading to the end of the Warsaw Pact* as a military organization. At the request of new governments in Czechoslovakia* and Hungary,* the Soviet Union agreed to withdraw all its forces from these countries by mid-1991. But the Polish government provisionally asked for the 50,000 troops in Poland to remain. In May 1990, yielding to demands for German re-unification, the Soviet Union undertook to withdraw the last of its 390,000 men on East German territory by the middle of 1994. In return, Bonn promised 7.8 billion Deutsche Marks towards the building of quarters for them in the Soviet Union, and to pay their interim stationing costs. It was at first agreed to remove Soviet forces from Poland within the same period, but the limit was later advanced to mid-1992. In November 1990 the cut in Soviet armed forces strength was written into the CFE Treaty,* leaving Moscow's stated goal as the withdrawal of all foreign troops from Europe by 1996 and the worldwide closing of all foreign military bases by the year 2000. See also 'Army', 'Navy', 'Air Force', 'OMON', 'KGB'.

**ARMENIA** (pop. 3.28 million). South Caucasian republic between the Black and Caspian seas, made independent ahead of its own timetable by the Soviet collapse of 1991. Its population was long one of the most homogeneous in the USSR: 88 per cent Armenian, 5 per cent Azeri (before 1988), 2 per cent Russian, and 2 per cent Kurdish. Traumatized by the 1915 massacre of 750,000 to 1.8 million Armenians by Ottoman Turks, the Christian Armenians' fear of extermination by their Muslim neighbours was revived by the 1988 Sumgait* massacre and tension with Azerbaijan over Nagorno-Karabakh.* Moscow's rejection of Armenia's plea for the enclave's incorporation caused an upsurge of nationalism. After peaceful demonstrations under a responsible leadership, nationalism took a violent turn in reaction to Sumgait, the 1988 Spitak earthquake and the arrest of leaders of the active Nagorno-Karabakh committee. Elections in 1989 ousted the republic's corrupt communist leaders and set off a fever of independence. By early 1990 Armenia was on the verge of civil war. The civil authorities no longer recognized the right of intervention by Soviet troops, who had been involved in exchanges of fire with Armenians. Local factions formed armed groups to defend frontier zones and attacked Azeri villages and Soviet military convoys. Full-scale intervention by Soviet forces was only narrowly averted after Levon Ter-Petrosian (a former member of the Armenian National Movement, elected president in August 1990) obtained two months' stay while the Armenians themselves impounded illegal arms and a parliamentary commission brought all 'self-defence' groups under a single authority. In December 1990 Ter-Petrosian went on to get parliamentary approval for a year's special powers 'to bar the way to anarchy'. But trouble returned the following year when Armenians attacked Soviet troops, and MVD troops raided Armenian villages in Azerbaijan, allegedly killing fifty people in arms searches. The republic faced an unprecedented energy crisis in the winter of 1991–92, when Azerbaijan shut the gas pipeline crossing its territory and stopped rail traffic. The blockade brought Armenia's industry to a standstill and obliged it to reopen the Medzamor nuclear power station, closed for environmental reasons. This reminder of the republic's vulnerability led Ter-Petrosian to adopt a pragmatical approach towards participation in the Commonwealth* and even to make overtures towards Turkey.

**ARMY.** For years a rallying point for patriotism and expression of national unity, going back to the Civil War (1918–21). But morale, which had triumphantly survived Stalin's purges (1937–38, see 'Terror'), gross unpreparedness at the start of the Great Patriotic War* (1941–45), and the bitter experience of Afghanistan* (1979–88), was severely tested in 1990–91 by the hurried withdrawal of forces from Eastern Europe. Lack of proper quarters, hostility from ethnic minorities, and the contempt of the younger generation for uniforms, were further blows to morale and prestige. In 1991, before the disintegration of the Union and the creation of republic armies, Soviet ground forces numbered 1,400,000 men, including 1,000,000 conscripts. There were 195 divisions in various states of readiness (75 per cent at full strength). Relations with Gorbachev had often been strained as he moved to bring the military under tighter control. At the same time, beginning with the Rust* affair, there was public discussion of military shortcomings. Reports in the press spoke of *dedovshchina*,* corruption, alcoholism, 'lazy' and 'arrogant' officers, and obsessive secrecy preventing any serious military journalism. The army was also accused of neglecting soldiers' welfare. In 1986–89 there was an average of 4,000 non-combat deaths each year, one fifth of them suicides; and in 1990 280,000 service families were living in conditions described by Marshal Akhromeyev* as 'disgraceful'. Another sore was the increase in ethnic tensions with local communities, seized on by conservatives and nationalists alike. In the Baltic republics and Transcaucasia, troops were called 'an army of occupation' and denied social services; at the same time conscripts from the Baltic and some other republics complained of harassment and acts of brutality by fellow soldiers. Younger officers, particularly members of 'Shield',* used political contacts to call for reforms, including moving to an all-volunteer army. But no decision was taken to change the system of military service* until after the 1991 *putsch*.*

**ART COLLECTOR.** Species of citizen long dubbed 'profiteer', now a 'philanthropist' invited to make donations to the Cultural Fund.* Also the victim of serious crime* in a country inexperienced in the protection of private property. Many collections began in the 1950s when works were scattered among owners who knew nothing of their worth. The rewards of collecting boomed with *perestroika* – and Sotheby's.*

**ARTISTS' UNION.** Creative union least touched by *perestroika*. In 1987 it re-elected its president, Valentin Sidorov, just after he had made a speech extolling realism as 'the only form of art able to express the truth about "contemporary life",' and one which 'certain forces' wanted to destroy. As examples of 'complete strangers to the spirit of the Revolution', Sidorov instanced Malevich and Kandinsky. Revolted by such outpourings, some artists took the earliest opportunity to work part of the time abroad, their foreign exchange earnings enabling them to ignore the union. The rest continued living as parasites, or else on the bread-line. In 1991 the membership of the union was 22,700.

**ASHKHABAD.** Capital of Turkmenistan (pop. 400,000), scene of an agreement by five Asian republic leaders, meeting on December 12–13, 1991, to join the Slavic Commonwealth created at Minsk.* Their initially hostile reaction to Minsk caused fears that they would set up an opposing Muslim 'commonwealth'. The split was prevented by Kazakhstan's Nazarbayev,* who proposed that they should join the Slavs on condition that they were all registered as co-founders. They were also influenced by their dependence on the more developed Slav republics for economic support and industrial imports.

**ASIA AND PACIFIC REGION.** Upgraded foreign policy field since 1986. The switch began with high-level Ministry staff changes. A China expert, I. Rogachev, and an Indo-China expert, B. Chaplin, were appointed deputy foreign ministers for the region, where Moscow's main allies were Vietnam and Mongolia (both Comecon members) and North Korea, the other socialist countries being Laos and Kampuchea. On his appointment as Foreign Minister, Edvard Shevardnadze set up a new bureau for relations with the socialist Asian states. The move was seen by some Western analysts as an attempt to set up an Asian political organization to counter American efforts. But it soon gave way to a more pragmatic policy, spelled out to party secretaries for ideology at a meeting in Ulan Bator in March 1988, when class conflict was de-emphasized. The first result was the development of trade, then full diplomatic, relations with South Korea,* which the Soviet Union saw as a possible substitute for Japan in helping its industrial development, particularly in Siberia. In April 1991 a new Directorate for General Problems of the Asian and

Pacific Region was set up under Aleksandr Losyukov. See also 'Afghanistan', 'China', 'Cambodia', 'North Korea', 'South Korea', 'Japan', 'India', 'Iran'.

**ASIAN REPUBLICS.** See 'Central Asia'.

**ASSASSINATION/POLITICAL TERRORISM.** Rarely considered possibility in the Soviet Union until on November 7, 1990 a 38-year-old unemployed Leningrad locksmith, A. Shmonov, harmlessly fired a shotgun during the October Revolution Day parade in Moscow's Red Square. The conservative *Sovietskaya Rossiya* described him as a supporter of the left-wing 'Democratic Union'★ movement. The reformist *Komsomolskaya Pravda* said simply that he was an 'anti-communist'. In 1991 a rash of terrorist incidents, including train bombings, occurred in the Transcaucasus, and a scarcely less bloody series of incidents in the Baltic republics. In May 1991 an explosion damaged the Moscow headquarters of Democratic Russia,★ without causing casualties, and oil pipelines were blown up by 'autonomists' at sixty points in Tataria.

**ASSOCIATION OF RUSSIAN ARISTOCRATS.** Body formed in 1990 to preserve pre-revolutionary connections. Its sixty or so members meet regularly in Moscow but are split on whether or not to take a more political line. A few dream of restoring a constitutional monarchy. (The pretender to the throne is Kiril Vladimirovich Romanov, a distant relative of Tsar Nicholas II now living abroad.) See also 'Monarchist'.

**ASTAFIEV,** Viktor Petrovich (1924–   ). Popular Siberian 'country'★ writer. His books include *Pechalnyi Detektiv* ('The Sad Detective', 1986), describing the contamination of Siberian village life by the values of the city.

**ATOM.** Divisible particle long portrayed as the key to a plentiful Soviet future (while forever threatening to destroy mankind in the hands of the West). Revelations of the Soviet arms stocks and the Chernobyl★ disaster confused this morally reassuring distinction, causing poets who had lauded the 'peaceful atom' to turn against its manipulators. For a while popular protests put the whole nuclear power programme in doubt. Reactors of the Chernobyl type were quickly modified, and no more built. Work stopped on nuclear stations near major cities (Odessa, Minsk, Krasnodar and Ulyanovsk). A station ready to go into operation at Voronezh was never started up, and the Yerevan station closed down. At the same time, ironically, the Estonian government, while protesting at pollution by Soviet factories, began a study of a nuclear plant that would make the republic energy-sufficient. Campaigns were also launched against the dumping of nuclear waste, following official admission of the 1957 Kyshtym (Urals) disaster, when an explosion of carelessly buried waste scattered radioactive material over thousands of square miles.

**ATOMIC BOMB.** Explosive device first detonated by the Soviet Union in 1949, four years after Hiroshima and America's 'Manhattan project'. According to new material from Khrushchev's* memoirs in 1990, production of the Soviet bomb was 'substantially helped' by information given by the Americans, Julius and Ethel Rosenberg. Khrushchev also revealed that the Soviet device exploded in 1953 was not a real hydrogen bomb, but an 'enhanced' A-bomb.

**AUCTION.** New trick for coaxing hard currency from foreigners (see 'Sotheby's'), later adapted for distributing scarce consumer goods among Soviets. In 1990 auctions began to be used for the official sale of foreign exchange to importers, paving the way to the setting up of a real money market.

**AUTOBIOGRAPHY.** Sudden gold-mine of Soviet leaders and Western literary agents. 1991 saw Gorbachev's account of the *putsch*,* Raisa's self-portrait as a President's wife, bids for memoirs by Yeltsin and Silayev,* and an offer of memoirs from Ligachev.* Anatoli Lukyanov* was writing love poems in prison. History was not made much richer.

**AUTONOMOUS KRAI** (area). Territorial division occupied by a small people,* with privileges similar to those of an Autonomous Oblast, (see below).

**AUTONOMOUS OBLAST** (region). Territorial unit smaller than an autonomous republic,* formerly having the right to elect deputies to the Soviet of Nationalities* (in which it differed from an autonomous *krai*). Officially non-sovereign until in 1990 a succession of autonomous republics and regions proclaimed sovereignty unilaterally. In 1991 there were eight autonomous regions, of which five were in the Russian republic.

**AUTONOMOUS REPUBLIC.** Territorial unit occupied by one or more ethnic minorities within a former Union republic.* Officially dependent until 1990, when successive ones unilaterally declared themselves sovereign. It differed from an autonomous *oblast* (see above) in having a structure similar to a full republic, with its own parliament, commissions etc. At the time of the Soviet break-up in 1991 there were twenty autonomous republics (sixteen in Russia, two in Georgia, one in Azerbaijan and one in Uzbekistan).

**AUTONOMY.** Formal status accorded to minorities integrated in a larger administrative entity. The idea was to safeguard minority cultures, but in practice 'autonomy' was often insufficient to prevent swamping by the dominant regional culture. Its protective value was rendered doubtful in

1990 when the country's fifteen Union republics successively proclaimed sovereignty* or 'independence'. Fearing domination by 'big brothers', small peoples* reacted by making one of three possible kinds of claim: to autonomy in the case of hitherto non-autonomous minorities (Poles in Lithuania, Gagauz* in Moldavia, Adzhars in Georgia, etc); to sovereignty in the case of autonomous groups (Yakuts, Bashkirs, etc.); to Union status in the case of the Tatars of the Tatarstan republic.

**AZERBAIJAN** (pop. 7 million). Transcaucasian republic on the Caspian sea, populated by Azeris (78 per cent), Russians (8 per cent), Armenians (8 per cent, until the 1988–90 riots) and smaller minorities (6 per cent). Present-day nationalism was touched off by Armenian claims to Nagorno-Karabakh.* Other causes were nostalgia for a 'greater Azeri community' embracing parts of the USSR, Iran and Turkey; refusal to be 'colonized' by Russians and Armenians; memory of the unpopular war in Afghanistan; the effect of the Islamic revival on a nation of Shi'as; and the depletion of the Caspian oil-field, once the source of prosperity for the capital, Baku. The Nagorno-Karabakh* dispute and the Sumgait* massacre put Azeris and Armenians in a state of war wherever the two lived face to face. In 1990 the formation of an Azerbaijan Popular Front was followed by murderous attacks on Armenians still remaining in Baku, then on Russian military families in the area. The growth of the Front alarmed the Communist Party, which was forced to yield to nationalist demands. Moscow sent troops to evacuate civilians, and the shooting following their entry into Baku caused 209 civilian deaths. The event became the Azeri counterpart of the Tbilisi* massacre for Georgians. Surprisingly, the 1990 elections produced a win for the communists – 320 seats out of 350. (Weakened by internal divisions, the Front alleged fraud.) The election brought the return to parliament of ex-Politburo member Geidar Aliyev,* but the republic's First Secretary, A. Mutalibov, was elected president. In December 1990, the parliament dropped 'Soviet' and 'Socialist' from the republic's title. In 1991 Mutalibov provoked riots by acclaiming the August *putsch** (the only republic leader to do so). Two weeks later he was re-elected President – the sole candidate in a poll from which the Popular Front withdrew in order to deny him legitimacy.

# B

**BACKFIRE** bomber (NATO code name). Tupolev-22M strategic bomber, coupled with SS-20 missile* in arms reduction talks preceding the INF treaty.* The missile was marked down for destruction, the bomber not.

**BAIKAL.** Siberian lake containing one fifth of the world's fresh water reserves. Since the 1960s it has been the object of an ecological rescue campaign by scientists and writers, especially Mikhail Sholokov and Valentin Rasputin,* as well as the subject of innumerable decrees and resolutions. Throughout, it has been under surveillance by the Institute of Fresh Water Sciences headed by Professor Grigori Galazi. Although the lake was declared an ecological 'crisis zone', the main source of pollution, the giant Baikalsk cellulose plant, continues to poison it with waste. Other factories dump chemicals into the Selenga river, which provides half the influx of water. A new threat is tourism. Baikal is more than 5,700 feet (1,740 metres) deep and 25 million years old. It contains 2,000 unique plant and animal species, including the fresh-water seal, the nerpa.

**BAKATIN,** VADIM VIKTOROVICH (1937–    ). Former Interior Minister (1988–90) appointed head of the KGB following the overthrow of the August 1991 *putsch*.* In December 1990 he was dismissed by Gorbachev under pressure from right-wingers, and replaced by Boris Pugo.* An unsuccessful candidate for election to the Russian presidency in 1991, he was accused by the Soyuz* group of having split the USSR Ministry of the Interior in such a way that the Ministries of Georgia, Estonia, Lithuania, Latvia and Moldavia received a status independent of Moscow. His stand against the *putsch*, and bitterness against Gorbachev for his earlier dismissal, made him a natural ally of Yeltsin, who named him to succeed Pugo* as head of the KGB. Although as Interior Minister he worked with the KGB against crime, he was never a KGB member. On taking over, he proceeded to root out politically tainted elements, dismantle the interior security apparatus and hand over foreign intelligence to the military. The organization remaining was later renamed the Inter-Republic Security Service.

**BAKU** (pop. 1.75 million). Once thriving capital of Azerbaijan,* its face changed by the exodus of minorities. The Armenians left in two waves, in 1988 after Sumgait* and in 1990 during riots in Baku itself, when Russians also left. The exodus robbed the city of many merchants and professional people, as well as key figures in industry and local government. Their place has been taken by other refugees, mostly rural, arriving from the opposite direction (Azeris from Armenia,* Meskhetian Turks* from Uzbekistan*). Without work or homes, and poorly received by the local community, the new arrivals played a leading part in the 1990 riots and a general rise in crime. In September 1990 the situation was so tense that the military closed the city to non-residents during elections.

**BALLISTIC** missiles. Missiles following a natural trajectory, unlike electronically guided cruise missiles.

**BALTIC REPUBLICS.** Estonia,* Latvia* and Lithuania.* Triad of states restored to independence after fifty years' rule by Moscow. They were annexed in 1940, after a brief inter-war existence, under a secret clause of the 1939 German-Soviet pact.* Although sharply differentiated by language and culture, they shared the struggle for freedom, meeting as from 1990 in a 'Baltic Council'. In December 1990 they launched their first joint call for international recognition and the withdrawal of 'foreign' troops. But a Lithuanian call for armed resistance was not taken up by Estonia and Latvia, which favoured a more supple approach in dealings with Moscow. In the winter of 1990–91 tension grew over moves by the Soviet army to round up young Balts evading call-up. On January 13, 1991 troops of the Ministry of the Interior shot their way into the Lithuanian television station in Vilnius, killing fourteen unarmed defenders; a week later OMON* troops killed five civilians in the Latvian capital, Riga. For the first time, the Baltic situation threatened Soviet-Western relations. The West made 'respect for Baltic rights' a condition of economic aid, and Moscow drew the lesson. The worst excesses of Soviet behaviour in the region were caused by circles connected with the August 1991 *putsch*,* whose failure led to the states' liberation.

**BAM** (*Baikal-Amurskyi Magistral*). Transcontinental rail-link designed to complement the militarily exposed Trans-Siberian line and open southern Siberia to economic development. The BAM became the last great adventure romantically offered to Soviet youth. Thousands of young people volunteered for work, which began in the late 1970s. A decade and a half later it was all admitted to have been a huge economic error. Billions were spent on building the poorly laid track across a zone that showed every reluctance to develop.

**BANKRUPTCY.** Major concern of foreign investors, despite a bill with Western-type provisions put before the Soviet parliament in 1991. Except where subjects are guaranteed by a bank (not necessarily a cast-iron arrangement), lenders are at risk so long as the usual forms of collateral (premises, land) remain in state or municipal ownership.

**BANKS.** Novel institutions mysteriously multiplying in parallel with increasing economic problems. Until 1989 the only Soviet banks that mattered were the State Bank,* in overall control of the economy, and five subsidiaries, responsible respectively for industrial construction, agriculture, housing, savings, and foreign trade. In 1990 economic reforms created three new kinds of bank: 'sector' banks (soon financially autonomous), regional banks, and co-operative (or private) banks. By mid-1991 co-operative banks numbered 1,400. In addition there were the state banks and banking systems of the fifteen republics. But the Soviet banking system, since taken over by Russia, still has little in common with that in most Western countries. Loans by the sector banks still need to be guaranteed by the State Bank, while most co-operative banks remain little more than clearing houses, taking their profits from a percentage on transactions.

**BAPTISTS.** Evangelical sect of half a million, grouped in five thousand congregations, according to the All-Union Baptist Council. In 1989 there were 2,531 local prayer houses (often private apartments). During the time of repression the Baptists suffered grievously under Article 142 of the penal code for insisting on instructing their children and refusing to work in collectives. Things were made worse by the fact that their spiritual headquarters were in America. In 1988 the Soviets sought to make amends by decorating the Baptist leader, Aleksei Bychkov, with the Order of Friendship among Peoples.

**BARANNIKOV,** Viktor Pavlovich (1940–). Police Academy General nominated by Yeltsin to head the Soviet Interior Ministry after the August 1991 *putsch,** and in December to be Russian Minister of Security and Internal Affairs (later simply Security Minister). He said his priority was the fight against crime. Closeness to Yeltsin did not prevent his refusal, in early December, to transfer Soviet MVD troops to Russian jurisdiction without the approval of Gorbachev.

**BARTER.** Anti-market practice rehabilitated in September 1991 when East European countries had factories at a standstill and the Soviet market was stalled for lack of foreign exchange. Later adopted internally.

**BEAR** bomber (NATO code name). Strategic bomber carrying air-launched cruise missiles, involved in START* negotiations.

**BEARDS.** Facial hair cultivated to suggest a Tolstoyan philosophy, if not due to a razor blade shortage. A variant is the Nicholas II look, implying scorn for proletarian society and a claim to an aristocratic past.

**BERIOZKA.** 'Luxury' shop originally accessible only to foreigners or, in some cases, Soviet contract-workers returning from abroad with foreign currency vouchers. In 1989 the 'Soviet' *beriozkas* were closed after envious fellow-citizens complained that the returnees were selling their purchases on the black market. In 1990 the remaining *beriozkas* (by far the greater number) were opened to any customer with hard currency, only to be closed a year later, except in some hotels. By then their monopoly had been decisively broken by foreign joint ventures (Swiss, Finnish, Italian, German, Irish) with ample stocks and professional marketing experience.

**BESSMERTNYKH,** ALEKSANDR ALEKSANDROVICH (1933–  ). Foreign Minister appointed in December 1990 to succeed Shevardnadze.* Soviet diplomats insisted that under Bessmertnykh the Ministry's new professionalism would continue unchanged. In subsequent East-West contacts – over a Middle East settlement, disarmament and economic aid – he appeared to justify the expectation, but was sacked for 'passivity' during the 1991 *putsch.**

**BITSA.** South Moscow suburb with the first permitted 'unofficial' art fair. In 1986–87, 70,000 visitors made their way to the local forest at weekends, causing protests from residents and ecologists. In May 1987 the sale of junk art was moved to Izmailovo.

**BIZINESMEN.** Word taken from English, at first used derisively, when legal private business was a novelty. From being synonymous with 'profiteer' it came to be adopted by budding Soviet Yuppies.

**'BLACK BERETS'.** See 'OMON'.

**BLACKJACK** bomber (NATO code name). Tu-160 strategic bomber capable of carrying short-range or cruise missiles (SRAMs or ALCMs). Involved in START* negotiations.

**BLACK MARKET.** For years the only free market that anyone knew, since legal transactions were confined to the state. In 1988 economist Tatiana Koriagina estimated turnover at $145 billion annually, of which $22.4 billion was for services (a quarter of the total in the country). Dealing in everything from cars to computers, it later became so professional as to be called a 'second generation' market in contrast to the 1970s when dealers bought jeans off tourists in the street.

**BLACKS.** Visiting world citizens, once brothers and equals but now resented as a drain on the budget. Hostility is mutual. Students at Patrice Lumumba university* would rather be in Bonn or Paris, and, to enliven their existence, turn neighbouring streets into souks. Terms of abuse are on a level with those exchanged in the West. The situation is aggravated by the 'girl' problem, especially in Central Asia and the Caucasus, where incidents have obliged universities to send blacks elsewhere. Wittingly or otherwise, official propaganda depicts blacks as possible AIDS carriers. Defying the trend, in 1990 a Nigerian joint venture opened Moscow's first Afro-style hairdressers.

**BLOC.** Group of political forces temporarily sharing the same broad idea, e.g. 'Democratic Russia'.* Numerous blocs were formed when cities escaped from Party control in the 1990 elections.

**BLOCKADE.** New method of political negotiation – the cutting off of supplies, including energy – adopted by Moscow in response to Lithuania's* declaration of independence, in March 1990. The blockade was lifted when Vilnius agreed to 'freeze' the declaration three months later. Other blockades have been those of Nakhichevan* by Armenia (1988, 1990), of Nagorno-Karabakh* and Armenia by Azerbaijan (in the same period), of North Ossetia* by Georgia (1989–91), and of the self-proclaimed republics of Dniestr and the Gagauz by Moldavia (1990, 1991).

**BOLSHEVIK PLATFORM.** Movement to crush the 'counter-revolution' and 'frustrate the restoration of capitalism', according to co-founder Nina Andreeva.* Launched at an all-Union conference in Minsk, in July 1991.

**BOLSHOI THEATRE** (founded 1776). Diminished glory of the Moscow artistic scene. Under the long dictatorship (1966–90) of Yuri Grigorovich, the ballet suffered a hardening of the arteries. Grigorovich directed his dancers like puppets and proved incapable of taking his repertoire beyond well-worn classics and 'socialist-realist' productions like 'Spartacus' and 'The Golden Age'. With the freeing of criticism in 1986, critics fell on the Bolshoi for resting on its former reputation. Two years later, when artists were freed to seek engagements elsewhere, both ballet and opera suffered a haemorrhage of talent. In 1990 Grigorovich caused a storm by signing a ten-year contract putting foreign tours into the hands of a British impresario, with the right to choose programmes and soloists.

**BONNER,** YELENA GEORGYEVNA (1923– ). Wife and fellow-campaigner of Andrei Sakharov,* lauded by admirers as a determined partner, giving an international dimension to the struggle of her brave but unassuming husband; declared by others to be a headstrong and ambitious woman who used him to satisfy her thirst for power and fame. Under Sakharov's will she became co-manager, with her American-domiciled son from an earlier marriage, of the foundation set up from the scientist's prizes and royalties. Sakharov's children, who remained at a distance after his re-marriage, showed bitterness at the arrangement.

**BOURSE.** One-time symbol of bourgeois-capitalist cupidity, now of economic sophistication. The Russian bourse was formally opened in November

1990, with a capital of R62 million and dealers limited to 324 places, i.e. one for each of the 124 founders who paid R500,000, and 200 for future partners, who would pay double. Organization was helped by Austrian, German and American firms. Trading is done in commodities, 'non-commodities' (mostly manufactured goods), and securities. The exchange is housed in the same building as the pre-revolutionary Bourse. A 1991-92 explosion of other "bourses" led to questions about the legality and financial background of many operations.

**BOVIN,** ALEKSANDR YEVGENYEVICH (1930–    ). Leading *Izvestia*★ political columnist in November 1991 appointed ambassador to Israel. His heavy appearance conceals a fineness of style and spirit. Against the fashion, he has boldly said that yesterday's heresies are not necessarily today's truths. In a finely nuanced portrait of Brezhnev (written when others were proclaiming their purity by totally denigrating him) Bovin once ventured to say that he had been on friendly terms with the former First Secretary and that, while he had nothing but condemnation for the corruption surrounding him, he rejected the picture of Brezhnev as a monster; in private life Brezhnev had been a 'jolly man, warm-hearted and open'. With the coming of *perestroika*, Bovin showed himself a staunch but discriminating ally to Gorbachev. He was one of the first to compare his reform programme with the hopes raised by Khrushchev's 1956 denunciation of Stalin (which had led Bovin to join the Party). In 1987 he was ahead of other reformists in breaking silence about the weight of resistance faced by Gorbachev inside the Party.

**BOY SCOUTS.** Unacknowledged model for the Soviet 'Pioneers'★ youth organization. A Scout group existed in Moscow before the revolution but was banned in 1917. The movement was allowed back with a founding congress of the Soviet scout organization in November 1990. Gorbachev's 'good deed' followed a holiday offered to 1,325 Chernobyl children by Scouts in fifteen European countries. In a subsequent development that Baden-Powell could hardly have foreseen, in the Western Ukraine the movement was taken over by Catholics for use against the Orthodox, and by nationalists for use against the Komsomol.★

**BREAD.** Sacred symbol of socialist sufficiency. For thirty years subsidies kept it at an unchanged price, causing farmers to feed it to livestock. When, in 1990, the Ryzhkov government proposed a threefold price increase, it was forced to back down and drop its economic reform programme. The increase was eventually imposed by the Pavlov government in April 1991. Another followed in 1992.

**BREZHNEV,** LEONID ILICH (1906–1982). Father of 'stagnation' (*zastoi*) and convenient scapegoat for every inherited or subsequent ill. Among other follies, he outlived his credibility. After a climb to power that began in the

Ukraine in 1946 and continued through Moldavia and Uzbekistan (soon to become bywords for corruption), Brezhnev became a full member of the Politburo in 1957. He participated in the dismissal of Khrushchev, taking over as First Secretary in 1966. His reign was marked by the people's first access to consumer goods simultaneously with the repression of dissent, in which he was aided by Suslov.* In foreign policy, his assertion of the right, and duty, of the Soviet Union to intervene in the affairs of fraternal countries to defend socialism became the basis of the 'Brezhnev doctrine', used to justify military intervention in Czechoslovakia (1968) and Afghanistan (1979). Vis-à-vis the West, he combined detente with a continuation of the arms race. He ended his days in Byzantine luxury, surrounded by greedy relatives and sharing the country's leadership with a coterie of ridiculous but dangerous septuagenarians. His love of honours led him to become a Lenin Prize-winner (1973), Marshal of the Soviet Union (1976), a recipient of the Order of Victory (the country's highest military honour, 1978), and winner of the Lenin Prize for Literature (for his memoirs, 1979). He had a passion for reckless driving and by his death owned fifty cars, including a wrecked Rolls-Royce.

**BREZHNEV** city. Depressing new industrial town in the Tatar autonomous republic. In 1987, under de-Brezhnevization, it reverted to its old name, Naberezhniye Chelny. It remains important as the home of Kamaz trucks.

**BREZHNEVA,** GALINA LEONIDOVNA. Tearaway daughter of the late First Secretary; epitome of the depravity of the Brezhnevian 'elite'. In 1990, seemingly indifferent to the fate of her former husband Churbanov,* she obtained restitution of a large part of her personal property that had been confiscated together with his. Judges ruled that she had acquired the goods with her own or her parents' money, or as gifts from friends, and not through corruption. The list included a Mercedes, a dacha, furs and jewellery, and shocked millions of people unable to buy anything in the shops.

**BRIGADE.** Unit consisting typically of several dozen workers; focus of attempts, accelerated under Brezhnev, to raise productivity without encouraging capitalistic competition between individuals. Brigades were allowed to contract with enterprises for above-normal pay for work completed in a fixed period of time. Success varied.

**BRODSKY,** IOSIF ALEKSANDROVICH (1940– ). Exiled poet and 1987 Nobel prize-winner. In 1965 he was sentenced for 'parasitism' to five years' administrative exile, working on a farm in the Arkhangelsk region. After eighteen months, following international protests and the first appearance of his work in the West, he was allowed home to Leningrad, where he lived by making translations from English. In 1972 he was stripped of his citizenship and expelled from the Soviet Union for allowing his poems to be published abroad without official permission. (Brodsky himself blamed anti-semitism.) He has since lived in the United States. A selection of his poetry appeared for the first time in the Soviet Union in 1987, in *Novy Mir*. It is non-political and critically associated with that of Akhamatova* and Mandelstam.* Millions of Soviets regard him as their greatest poet.

**BUDDHISM.** Popular religion of the Buryat, Tuva and Kalmyk autonomous republics and the Chita and Irkutsk regions near the Chinese border. The area contains several functioning monasteries (*datsans*) under a Board of Soviet Buddhists composed of abbots and other dignitaries. In 1990 Gorbachev used a visit to Moscow by Daisaku Ikeda, honorary president of the Japanese Buddhist sect, Gakkai, to announce the date of his 1991 visit to Japan.

**BUDGET.** Fiscal quagmire, resulting from weeks of parliamentary debate without precise data. Confusion reached a climax in 1991. Under a law passed the previous year, the budget should have been based on federal taxation, mainly on ,incomes and profits. But in December 1990 the situation was radically changed by the granting of more autonomy to republics. Instead of the central budget allocating funds to the republics in line with options in the annual Plan,* it was now up to the republics to levy taxes and make contributions to the central budget. A subsequent 'budget war' led to a shortfall of R123.1 billion in contributions towards a total expenditure of R276.8 billion.

**BUDGET DEFICIT.** Unplumbed chasm. In December 1990 Aganbegyan* told parliament that there were only 'political figures'; no one knew the real ones. The planned deficit for 1991 of R26.8 billion (compared with R58 billion in 1990, and R79 billion in 1989) had already been exceeded by April, when the actual deficit stood at R31.1 billion. By the time the Union broke up at the end of the year it was expected to reach R200 billion, equivalent to 20 per cent of the gross national product.

**BUKHARIN,** Nikolai Ivanovich (1888–1938). Bolshevik revolutionary and opponent of Stalin. He was shot in 1938, but rehabilitated with others in 1988, at which point his works were released from the *spetsfond*.* The memoirs of his widow, still living in Moscow, were published in 1990.

**BULGAKOV,** Mikhail Afanasyevich (1891–1940). Author and playwright 'rediscovered' in the Khrushchev period, only to be buried again until 1987. As a young man, Bulgakov (a doctor) saw the events of 1918 in the Ukraine, which he made the setting of his Civil War novel *The White Guard*, reportedly a favourite with Stalin. In the late 1920s, after a time of fruitful collaboration with the Moscow Arts Theatre, he was cut down by critics, who failed to appreciate his black humour. His gift for fantasy reached a peak in the novel *The Master and Margarita*, written during his last years. Another short satirical novel, *The Heart of a Dog*, was produced as a play in 1987. In the 1980s he became a cult with the young, who came so often to see his old Moscow apartment that the tenants of the block put a lock on the entrance. It has now been made a museum, after years of resistance by the municipality.

**BULGARIA.** Closest Russian ally, linguistically and historically. In 1990 the fall of the Zhikov government was accepted calmly, as was the country's vote to end the Warsaw Pact.

**BUNIN,** IVAN ALEKSEEVICH (1870–1953). Emigré writer and first Russian Nobel laureate (1933); rediscovered in 1987. As an aristocrat and author of mildly erotic novels, Bunin had everything to exclude him from official recognition. He died in Paris.

**BURBULIS,** GENNADI EDVARDOVICH (1945–    ). First Deputy Chairman of the Russian government, confidant of Yeltsin and his agent in the 1991 Russian presidential election. In September 1991, appointed Secretary of the (consultative) State Council of Russia, he was called Yeltsin's 'James Baker'. He comes, like Yeltsin, from Sverdlovsk, where he held a key instructional post in the Metallurgical Ministry.

*BURDA.* West German fashion magazine given a Russian edition in 1987, reportedly at the suggestion of Raisa Gorbachev.\* The deal nearly foundered when it was discovered that the Soviet Union had no means of making *Burda*'s famous dress-making patterns. Issues had to be produced in Germany and sold in *beriozkas*\* for hard currency. In 1992, street market copies sold for R200.

**BUREAUCRACY** (*byurokratiya*). Caste hard to fight, thanks to vague contours. Nevertheless, it has been forced to relinquish some of its all-pervading power, particularly since the dissolution of the Communist Party. In his celebrated Murmansk speech (1987), Gorbachev disclosed that 'administration' employed 18 million people. Of these, 2.5 million were in central government and 15 million in enterprises and organizations – about 15 per cent of the nation's manpower, costing R40 billion a year. Subsequently, a blind 'war' on bureaucrats in ministries and enterprises threatened to dispense with the only people able to keep the economy going while the country waited for the arrival of competent managers. The same problem faced city councils, as Moscow's reformist mayor, Gavril Popov,\* discovered when he found himself obliged to keep on the 'bureaucrats' responsible for day-to-day administration. In 1991 the problem was complicated by the purge of officials accused of having sympathized with the *putsch*.\* Independent republics have created their own bureaucracies.

**BURLATSKY,** FYODOR MIKHAILOVICH (1927– ). Chairman (1987–90) of the official commission set up to monitor the observance of human rights. Though handicapped by lack of essentials, such as access to state archives, the Burlatsky Commission was instrumental in obtaining the 1988 amnesty* for political and religious prisoners. Formerly a senior writer of *Literaturnaya Gazeta*,* Burlatsky returned to the newspaper in 1990 to take over as editor from the discredited Chakhovsky. A year later he was dismissed by a staff vote for not returning from holiday to stand against the August *putsch*.* In fact, staff were upset at the paper's move from literary to general coverage, and a loss of privileges through cutting links with the Union of Writers.*

**BYELORUSSIA/BELARUS** (pop. 10.2 million). Slavic republic forming part of the Russian heartland; formal possessor of one of three Soviet seats in the UN general assembly, and co-founder in 1991 of the Commonwealth of Independent States.* It suffered severely in the 1941 German invasion and again from the 1986 Chernobyl* disaster in neighbouring Ukraine. The disaster gave rise to a slow-starting nationalist movement, and in 1990 Byelorussia followed other republics in declaring its sovereignty* in advance of a new Union treaty. In 1990 one of the first acts of the newly elected parliament was to pass a bill of rights for victims of Chernobyl, while declaring the republic 'nuclear-free' and an ecological disaster zone. Unanimity ended soon afterwards when parliament split between 160 Party members supporting Gorbachev, and thirty non-communist deputies in a coalition of three parties (the Popular Front, the Democratic Club and the Agrarian Party) under the Front's leader Zenon Pozniak. The population consists 79 per cent of Byelorussians, 12 per cent Russians, 4 per cent Poles, 4 per cent other nationalities and (diminished by emigration) 1 per cent Jews. In December 1991 the breakdown of prospects for a new Union treaty caused it to join Russia and the Ukraine in the Minsk* summit. The chairman of the Supreme Council (president), Stanislav Shushkevich, immediately called for the removal to Russia of all nuclear weapons on its territory.

# C

**CADRES.** Principal members of Party or other organizations formerly constituting the leadership at different levels. In military terminology, 'cadre' means the skeleton organization of reserve units.

**CAMBODIA.** Long-time focus of Sino-Soviet power rivalry accentuated in the mid-1980s by the overthrow of the Peking-backed Pol Pot government by the forces of Moscow-backed Vietnam. At the 1990 five-nation Paris conference, Moscow agreed that the Cambodians should be left to 'choose their own system' – which they did.

**CAMPS** (1). System of incarceration based on the notion of 'rehabilitation through work', where the criminal pays his debt to society. Camps may be 'normal' or 'hard' regime. Prison is used mainly for preventive detention or for prisoners in transit. Minors are sent to 'colonies' where they are supposed to receive a 'severe but fair' education. In fact the latter are schools for delinquency, where minor offenders and violent criminals become indiscriminately mixed. After the amnesty* of 1987 and the 'humanization of judicial practices' the number of convicts was cut by half and 200 camps closed.

**CAMPS** (2). System of political repression better known by the name 'Gulag',* set up during the Civil War (see 'Solovetskiye Islands') to re-educate the enemies of the revolution, then those of bolshevism. Political prisoners lived side-by-side with criminal elements, since for the authorities they were all the same. Khrushchev closed the huge camps symbolizing Stalin's repression (Vorkuta, Kolyma), while simultaneously launching a violent campaign against religion. Under Brezhnev, camps (and psychiatric abuse) were a standard means of repressing dissent.

**CAPITAL INVESTMENT.** Long-term hope for boosting production, particularly of consumer goods, rudely deferred by the growth of the budget deficit.* Investment problems began towards the end of the Brezhnev era with a sharp fall in growth rates. Until 1981 capital stock increased by at least 50 per cent every five years. In 1981–85 the planned increase fell to 37 per cent, and in 1986–90 to only 30 per cent. In 1990 emergency measures for cutting the budget deficit included a halt to all investment except for housing and urgent social needs.

**CAPITAL PUNISHMENT.** Penalty under Soviet law for treason, terrorism, first degree murder, war crimes and genocide. (Until 1986 it could still be ordered for serious thefts of state property.) In 1990 the President granted clemency to eighteen people under sentence, and in 1991 considered 226 appeals. Sentences could be commuted to fifteen years. Despite calls for abolition, polls suggest that a majority of the population, alarmed by the rise in crime, want the death sentence kept. In 1990 a state executioner told the newspaper *Trud* that the condemned man was led to the execution room without being told what was about to happen. He was killed with a pistol shot, but not, as commonly supposed, in the back of the neck, which would be 'too uncertain'. The executioner gave no other details, except to say that the method was 'painless'.

**CAPITALISM.** Economic system long described as the enemy of socialism. 'The most frightening and dangerous monster' of the twentieth century, according to Gorbachev at the 1986 Party Congress. (Reagan's 'Evil Empire' speech belonged to the same period.) Five years later nearly all the main features of capitalism − profit-taking, private property, competitive buying and selling − had been taken into Soviet law, even the early figment of a 'socialist market' being abandoned.

**CARS.** Lethal weapons serving the Russian fondness for fantasy and anarchy. Poor maintenance, terrible roads and drunkenness at the wheel help to swell the number of casualties: in 1986, 19,000 dead and 143,000 injured; in 1990, 60,000 and 319,000 respectively. Fatalities − increased by poor emergency and medical services − are three times more numerous than in the United States, despite there being 13 times fewer vehicles in relation to the population.

**CASINO.** Fashionable place in which to lose money, in hard currency. The first post-revolutionary casino opened in 1989, in Moscow's Savoy Hotel.★ In 1990 plans were unveiled for a multi-storey gaming complex at the Moscow race-course (hippodrome). The shareholders include Professor Fyodorov's eye surgery foundation. Casinos are a convenient means of laundering black-market profits as much as a way of relieving the tedium of free-spending foreigners.

**CATHOLICS.** Principal religious community in Lithuania and western Ukraine, also in parts of Byelorussia and 'colonized' Kazakhstan, with a total of 1,150 churches. In Lithuania, contacts between the Kremlin and the Vatican led in 1988 to the release from house arrest of Archbishop Steponavicius.★ In return, the episcopate calmed the later vociferous nationalist movement. In western Ukraine, Catholicism was closely bound to the campaign for independence and openly hostile to Orthodoxy, popularly identified with rule from Moscow. In 1988 rapprochement between Moscow and the Vatican was sealed when the Pope received a visit from Gorbachev on his way to the Malta summit. But plans for a papal visit received a setback when, at the time of the 1991 ecumenical synod in Rome, Orthodox church leaders complained bitterly of Catholic moves to evangelize in traditionally Orthodox lands.

**CAUCASUS.** Explosive hot-bed of national rivalry. The agriculturally rich North Caucasus is divided among autonomous republics* and regions* of the Russian Federation (see 'Russian Federation'). Flash-points include rivalry between Ossetes* and Ingush,* Ingush and Chechens, and Chechens* and Avars; Islamic fundamentalism in Dagestan; and claims to former territory by Cossacks.* Some autonomous republics and regions would like to set up a Republic of the North Caucasus. The South Caucasus contains even graver tensions: between Georgia* and South Ossetia,* and between Armenia* and Azerbaijan,* which in 1988–91 came near to all-out war.

**CEMETERY.** Last stop of the lifelong queue-jumper. In 1988 cemetery workers, officially paid to fulfil an annual 'plan', were found to be making fortunes from bribes – for finding burial plots, digging graves in winter (R100 a time plus a bottle of vodka), engaging musicians for funeral music, securing buses for use as hearses, and rustling up coffins, often second-hand.

**CENSORSHIP.** Practice supposed never to have existed, since the censors' office (*Glavlit*) merely 'co-ordinated' the work of editors and publishers. Glavlit had an office in every newspaper and publishing house. Not even visiting cards could go to the printers without its stamp. 'Co-ordination' was ended for books in 1986, but continued for newspapers until killed by the Law on the Press* on August 1, 1990, a day hailed by *Izvestia** with the front-page headline 'Goodbye to Censorship'. In fact most newspapers had ignored the censor for some time, as when *Komsomolskaya Pravda** published an interview with the 'rebel' KGB officer, Major-General Oleg Kalugin.* But although censorship officially ended, the censors kept their jobs. Glavlit remained responsible for ensuring observance of a ban on pornography and the disclosure of state secrets, and the best way for editors to stay within the law was to engage former censors as consultants. The spectre of a more vicious form of censorship reappeared in December 1990 when Gostelradio* disconnected the wires of the Interfax* news agency and suppressed the popular television programme *Vzgliad* ('Look') because of its coverage of Shevardnadze's resignation. The same happened again after the programme's reports of the January crisis in Lithuania.* In 1991 there were threats from the opposite direction, as republics sought to 'protect national interests' by the allocation of paper supplies, the setting up of official news agencies, and the expulsion of visiting journalists.

**CENSUS.** Periodical audit supposed to help in drawing up five-year plans. The last, in 1989, dismayed researchers. The Ministry of Statistics, a state within the state, refused to include new questions, including one on linguistic affinity, needed for analysing current demographic problems.

**CENTRAL ASIA.** Conglomeration of five republics* with five common elements: Islamic traditions, a clan-based social structure, a young population owing to a high birth-rate, high unemployment caused by wilful immobility, and a peasant society of forcibly settled nomads. All of which helps to explain why the gulf between town and country is wider than elsewhere, why the national awakening was slow in coming, and why the intellectuals who lead it wanted to stay part of the Union. Especially after the collapse of communism, these intellectual leaders fear that under cover of grass-roots democracy and regional autonomy, the old clans will again seize power, helped by religious fanaticism. But they also want a rewriting of history to rectify the 'humiliating' version of relations between Asians and Europeans. With a cotton monoculture and a pattern of large families, the Central Asian republics were badly hit by 1991 – 1992 price increases. In December 1991, economic necessity led them to join the Commonwealth* founded by Russia, Byelorussia and Ukraine.

**CENTRAL COMMITTEE.** Supreme organ of the former Communist Party between congresses.* Up to 1988 the most important body in the country. Until dissolved after the 1991 *putsch** the committee met in plenary session as circumstances required, for an average of fifteen days a year. Day-to-day work was left in the hands of the political committee (Politburo*) and Secretariat,* whose members might be changed by plenums. Most members of the Central Committee elected in 1986 were also members of the previous one, elected under Brezhnev; and Gorbachev had to wait for the plenum of April 1989 to remodel the Committee in the way he wanted. (The collective letter of members 'retiring voluntarily' inappropriately mixed those who had done nothing dishonourable with rogues like Aliyev.*) In September 1989, Gorbachev got rid of the last Brezhnevite Politburo member, Shcherbitsky.* In 1990 the Twenty-eighth Congress* approved reforms intended to adapt the Committee to the conditions of a multi-party system. But in popular estimation, if not in reality, too many members of the Party were involved with the *putsch*ists for it to survive the events of August 1991.

**CENTRE BLOC.** 'Moderately radical' political alliance formed in June 1990 to oppose the extreme right and the extreme left, refusing also to be drawn into ethnic and religious rivalries. Among its founders were the Liberal Democratic Party of Vladimir Zhirinovsky,* the Popular Front of Moscow, a dissenting faction of the Russian Democratic Party led by Gari Kasparov,* and the 'Andrei Sakharov Alliance of Democratic Forces'. Not to be confused with the so-called 'Centrist Bloc' of Vladimir Voronin, formed at the same time to 'improve the health of the Soviet economy', and later blaming the Baltic authorities for the events of January 1991.

**CFE (CONVENTIONAL FORCES IN EUROPE) TREATY.** Twenty-nation treaty on conventional arms cuts. Its achievement resulted from a breakthrough in 1990, when Moscow agreed to asymmetrical force reductions – the issue which for twelve years (1973–85) had blocked MBFR (mutual and balanced force reduction) negotiations in Vienna. Signed by NATO and Warsaw Pact members in Paris in November 1990, the treaty was hailed as 'the end of the Cold War'. Its provisions included a 50 per cent cut in the 31,580 Soviet tanks in Europe. But a dispute arose over Western allegations that the Soviet Union had simply moved tanks beyond the Urals. Moscow denied this, saying that 4,000 tanks had been turned over to training, and 8,000 used to replace obsolete material in Asia; the rest were being scrapped. In February 1991 ratification was again held up when Moscow announced the transfer of three motorized infantry divisions to coastal defence under the navy (which was not covered by the treaty). The move would have given the Soviet navy more tanks than many European armies. In May 1991 the chief of the Soviet General Staff, Gen. Moiseyev, went to Washington to resolve the disagreement, which threatened to delay START.* In 1992 the treaty was endorsed by Commonwealth states, subject to agreed shares.

**CHAIKA.** Car of senior officials. Its status is below Zils (for Presidents and top ministers) but above Volgas (for lesser functionaries).

**CHAOS.** Favourite Gorby-word as in 'Chaos or me'. First used at the 1985 plenum; then in every confrontation with allies or opponents. Dropped when chaos materialized.

**CHARITY** (*miloserdiye*). Christian virtue rehabilitated as a way of extracting donations from expatriates to help the Soviet 'new poor'. Also to rediscover national solidarity. In 1987 *Moscow News* defined socialist charity as different from other forms of charity: 'Aware of their country's problems, people give freely of their aid, warmth and money.' Charitable activities could be undertaken by funds* or (after 1988) religious congregations. Approval of charities as an example of 'freedom of association' coincided with the discovery that the state budget could not cover all the needs of the most disadvantaged. It was soon expected that any successful firm would make donations to charity; if it forgot, it would be reminded of the fact by press or television – until, with new taxation laws, charity emerged as an easy means of tax evasion (not to mention fraud).

**CHAZOV,** YEVGENI IVANOVICH (1929– ). World-renowned heart specialist, formerly head of the Kremlin clinic, made Minister of Health in February 1987. His goal was to create a modern health service by the year

2000. Finding he was getting nowhere against the lethargy of ministries responsible for pharmaceuticals, building and equipment, and against budgetary and foreign exchange difficulties, he resigned in 1990 to resume medical practice.

**CHEBRIKOV,** VIKTOR MIKHAILOVICH (1923– ). Former Politburo member and KGB chief. A professional since 1967, he was chosen by Andropov to lead the crackdown on corruption in the Brezhnev clan. In 1985 he gave his support to Gorbachev and reforms, but otherwise stayed stolidly conservative. Under his direction, the KGB continued to harass dissidents* and refuseniks* up to 1987. He resigned in 1989, together with other 'old guard' figures.

**CHECHEN-INGUSHIA** (pop. 1.2 million). Autonomous republic of Russia, artificially created in 1934 by an amalgamation of two peoples. In 1991 Chechen outnumbered Ingush five-to-one, and friction between them verged on civil war. Both want to divide the republic, an idea resisted by the republic parliament and by the neighbouring autonomous republic of North Ossetia since the restoration of an Ingush state 'on its historical borders' would include a part of Ossetia. In November 1991 the proclamation of a 'Chechen Republic' by the retired officer Dzhokhar Dudayev resulted in a fiasco for Yeltsin when he tried to send in Russian MVD troops. Their landing was blocked by Dudayev's armed bands, and Yeltsin's emergency decree was cancelled by the Russian parliament. Three months later Dudayev was still in control. See also 'Ingush', 'North Ossetia'.

**CHEMICAL WEAPONS.** In June 1990, after long negotiation, the USSR and the United States concluded a treaty requiring each side to reduce its stock of chemical warfare agents to 5,000 tonnes by 2003. The treaty, whose obligations have since been assumed by Russia, provides for on-site inspection of production and storage facilities. Further cuts to 500 tonnes must be made within eight years of a global chemical warfare treaty coming into force. Soviet production stopped in 1987, when Soviet stock totalled 40,000 tonnes, and America's 38,000 tonnes. Anticipating the agreement, the Soviet Defence Ministry opened a R50 million plant capable of destroying 350 tonnes annually at Chapayevsk, in Kuybyshev *oblast*. But in late 1990 the plant was still only training personnel. Part of the Soviet stock dates from World War II and is in a dangerous condition. It includes nerve gases and Lewisite (a variant of mustard gas).

**CHEQUE.** Strange piece of paper legally usable by Soviet citizens since January 1988, but, like credit cards,* slow to win acceptance and replace the time-honoured suitcase full of banknotes.

**CHERNOBYL.** Modern world's worst accident, and watershed of Soviet policy on public information and technology. The disaster occurred at 1.23 a.m. (local time) on Saturday, April 26, 1986, when No. 4 reactor at the Chernobyl nuclear power station exploded during an unauthorized test in which the emergency cooling equipment had been switched off. The other three reactors were immediately shut down, but had to be kept running at low power to prevent overheating. The burning reactor sent a plume of radioactive particles hundreds of metres into the air, causing lethal contamination of the immediate area and soon spreading over half of Europe. There were no contingency plans, and it was thirty-six hours before 49,000 people were evacuated from the nearby town of Pripyat and two smaller settlements. A week later 50,000 more were evacuated, together with livestock, from a 30-kilometre radius zone, including Chernobyl (population 30,000) 15 km to the south. By then, Western experts calculate, the explosion had released 50 million curies of radioactive iodine and 6 million curies of radioactive caesium, much of it over neighbouring areas of Byelorussia and Russia. The emission of particles was eventually stopped by helicopters dropping tons of sand on the burning reactor, which was then encased in a concrete 'sarcophagus'.*

Thirty-one people, chiefly firemen and emergency workers, died almost immediately. Hundreds more were treated for serious radiation sickness. The longer-term effects, in the form of cancer among the tens of thousands exposed to radioactivity, are unlikely to be known for twenty to thirty years. In 1991 estimates by Soviet and Western scientists put the ultimate total of deaths from this cause at perhaps 4,000; but this was contradicted by an assessment made, at Moscow's behest, for the UN Atomic Agency Commission. The study, by 200 scientists from twenty-five countries, said the USSR had overestimated the amount of radioactivity released, and that the many cases of illness so far attributed to Chernobyl were actually due to anxiety and stress. (Earlier, the American doctor Robert Gale, who treated immediate victims with bone-marrow transplants, said much subsequent illness was simply due to the deplorable state of Soviet health services.) The UN report was called 'whitewash' by environmentalists, who pointed out that it excluded examination of the 116,000 people who had been living within 30 kilometres of the accident and of tens of thousands of decontamination workers, all now dispersed across the Soviet Union. The head of the so-called Soviet Chernobyl Assistance Group, chess master Anatoli Karpov, claimed that a thousand of the latter had died — a figure without official confirmation.

The material consequences of the disaster were catastrophic. The Chernobyl station was to have been fitted with two further reactors of the same RBMK design, and one was partly constructed. By 1990 the completed station would have been the main source of power for Ukrainian industry, with an output of 6,000 megawatts. Although the three surviving reactors continued in operation (they have been condemned by the Ukrainian parliament to close down in 1993), the loss of the others aggravated an already serious energy shortage (see 'Nuclear energy'). The evacuation of the 30-kilometre zone meant the loss of 300,000 hectares of farmland, raised to 1 million hectares when serious contamination was discovered elsewhere. Eventually 140,000 people had to be rehoused. In 1987 three senior officials at the station – the director, V. Brukhanov, the deputy director, R. Solovyov, and the chief engineer, N. Fomin – received prison sentences for negligence. The Ukrainian premier, Aleksandr Lyashko, was earlier dismissed for incompetence during the emergency operations.

**CHESS.** Game with a cultural status unique in the world. Soviet supremacy appeared after World War II, helped by Party insistence on the value of chess in developing intellectual discipline (both Marx and Lenin were players). In the late 1980s championship matches acquired a political dimension with the rivalry between Anatoli Karpov and Gari Kasparov.* Karpov stayed faithful to the Party while Kasparov joined the 'democratic' opposition. There are 3 million registered ex-Soviet chess-players, including some fifty grand-masters.

**CHILDREN.** First care of the state, but not always of parents. Newspapers regularly print stories of violence in cases of poverty, remarriage and drunkenness. In 1987 a novel, *Detskyi Dom* ('Children's Home') by Larissa Mironova, highlighted the plight of children abandoned by single mothers or taken from alcoholic parents and put into orphanages. Its appearance in the magazine *Ural* caused a national outcry.

**CHILE.** Dictatorship subject to a pragmatic reassessment, even before the departure of Pinochet. In February 1991 Chile's speedy economic recovery was retrospectively hailed as a model for the Soviet Union.

**CHINA.** Estranged partner invited to resume contact – albeit less warmly after the 1991 *putsch*,* which Peking ill-advisedly saluted. Moscow's first overture was in Gorbachev's 1986 Vladivostok speech. Other invitations were the Soviet military pull-back from Mongolia, the opening of talks on border issues, and the withdrawal of SS-20s from Asia. But, except for the restoration of inter-Party relations in May 1989, there were no immediate results. Gorbachev's visit the following month ended disastrously with the massacre of Tiananmen Square. A border agreement was eventually signed in May 1991. At Ashkhabad* participants recalled that China had not relinquished a territorial interest in Central Asia and that Alma-Ata had once been a Chinese city.

**CHINOVNIKI.** Derogatory term originally used in Tsarist times to denote petty functionaries; later used to describe 'villains, social parasites and natural enemies of reform' who sat at their desks and imposed 'command administrative* methods'. The *chinovniki* 'sabotaged efforts to introduce a

market economy', while their wives and children 'travelled in Chaikas*
and devoured the country's delicacies obtained in special shops'. Not to be
confused with members of the *nomenklatura*,* who were flamboyant
whereas *chinovniki* were grey.

**CHOLERA.** Endemic disease reappearing in Central Asia. In 1990 Aralsk,
on the Aral sea, had to be quarantined after hospitalization of 237 cases.

**CHORNOVIL**, Vyacheslav Maksimovich (1938– ). Popular runner-up
in the November 1991 vote for the Ukrainian presidency (23 per cent of
the vote). A former prisoner of conscience, he spent ten years in camps for
fomenting nationalism. After the 1990 regional elections, he became
leader of the council in the Lvov *oblast*,* soon a hotbed of Ukrainian
ultra-nationalism. He was also a member of the co-ordinating council of
the Galician assembly, an organization regarded by Kiev as harbouring
tendencies dangerous to Ukrainian unity. He has consistently presented
himself as a born anti-communist and during the election opposed
Kravchuk,* the former *apparatchik*, with a programme for economic
ultra-liberalism.

**CHRISTIAN DEMOCRATIC MOVEMENT OF RUSSIA.** Orthodox
Christian political movement founded in 1990 by Russian deputy Viktor
Aksiutich and others.

**CHRISTIAN DEMOCRATIC UNION OF RUSSIA.** Party founded in
1989 by the heads of eighty independent Christian organizations and
groups under the presidency of Ogorodnikov.* It claims membership of
the international Christian Democratic movement. In 1991 a group split
off to form the Christian Democratic Union of the Russian Federation.

**CHRISTIAN DEMOCRATIC UNION OF THE RUSSIAN FEDERA-
TION.** See 'Christian Democratic Union of Russia'.

**CHURBANOV**, Yuri Mikhailovich (1937– ). Former first deputy
Minister of the Interior and Brezhnev's son-in-law. Arrested in February
1987 for corruption, embezzlement and abuse of power, he was not
brought to trial until 1989, when he was sentenced to eleven years.
Although his case was aimed directly at the image of Brezhnev, it also
helped to expose the Rashidov,* Grishin* and (particularly) Kunayev*
clans. See also 'Brezhneva, Galina'.

**CHURCH.** See 'Religion'.

**CIGARETTES.** The first shortage to cause riots. In July 1990 a 24 per cent
fall in production, coinciding with a reduction in Bulgarian tobacco
imports, brought industrial cities to explosion point, with violent demon-

strations and work-stoppages. But the chance was missed to revive an anti-smoking campaign launched in 1988. In 1991, 70 million Soviet smokers spent 6.8 billion roubles annually on cigarettes, whose consumption had risen 23 per cent in twenty years. Smoking is forbidden in public places, in public transport and on Moscow's Red Square. Since 1986 packets have carried health warnings. Hoping to prevent a repetition of the 1990 fiasco, the Russian republic signed a mammoth contract with Philip Morris for delivery of 20 billion cigarettes before the end of 1991.

**CINEMA.** Pioneer of *glasnost* that lost its way with the ending of subsidies and orders to go commercial. In 1990, thirty-nine studios were listed as making 150 feature films and 1,000 documentaries annually – on antiquated equipment. There was only one Dolby sound-recording system, and the most up-to-date cameras were twelve bought by Mosfilm for the 1980 Olympics. In 1991 film stock still came from two antiquated plants, one using parts installed by Pathé in 1920. (Cameramen joke that Soviet film was the only kind in the world not affected by light.) Technical shortages explain a vogue for co-productions, where the foreign partner is expected to supply the equipment. In 1986, a revolt in the Film-Makers Union* led to the release of films that had often been shelved for years, beginning with Abuladze's* *Repentance*. There was also a wave of new films telling the story of the camps, repression and (seen from a less Manichaean viewpoint) the Civil War. A second wave addressed contemporary social problems such as alcoholism, prostitution and delinquency. But at the end of the 1980s, inspiration faltered. With commercialization came a drop in artistic standards and an urge to be 'modern' by breaking old taboos on sex and gratuitous violence. At the same time the country's 4,800 cinemas (136 in Moscow) were invaded by (mainly American) imports, seldom above the level of *The Return of King Kong*, *Rambo* and *The Terminator*. Collapse seemed terminal when in 1990 the reformist directors Klimov* and Smirnov resigned from leading the union they had helped to rejuvenate.

**CITIZENSHIP.** Former right of anyone born of Soviet parents. In August 1990, twenty-five people deprived of it under Brezhnev had it restored by presidential decree. Among them were the cellist Rostropovich,* the scientist Zhores Medvedev,* and the Russian writers Aksyonov* and Aleksandr Zinoviev. In addition to citizenship, all Soviet citizens had an official nationality (Russian, Georgian, Jewish, etc.) entered in their internal passports* (see 'Law on Citizenship'). In December 1991 republics rejected the idea of a common citizenship of the new Commonwealth* but agreed that nationals of any republic living on the territory of another republic should be entitled to dual citizenship.

**CLOSED CITIES/DISTRICTS.** Locations prohibited to foreigners, and sometimes Soviets, generally on grounds of national security. Real reasons could be ambiguous. Sebastopol remained closed to outsiders to prevent their buying goods intended for Navy families. In 1991 the list was greatly relaxed.

**CMEA.** See 'Council for Mutual Economic Assistance'.

**COAL.** White hope for energy supplies but, with notorious labour conditions, a black one for miners.* After years of decline, coal received high priority in the 1986–1991 Five-Year Plan. By 1995, new technologies were supposed to raise output to 795 million tons (from 772 million in 1988). Half today's production is from open-cast mines in Siberia, Kazakhstan and the Far East, which now contain the country's main coalfields. In 1990, deep pits in the Donbass* and Kuzbass* regions were promised accelerated modernization after miners there struck for improved pay and conditions, including safety. In the first six months of 1991 the extraction of coal was down 11 per cent against the same period the year before.

**COCA-COLA.** Magic potion giving drinkers the brief illusion of being in America. A franchise for 'Coke' was signed at the time of the 1988 summit, eight years behind 'Pepsi'. In 1991 the makers paid for a cosmonaut to drink from a can of Coca-Cola in space,* before television cameras.

**COCOM** (Co-ordinating Committee for Multilateral Export Controls). US-dominated body consisting of NATO countries plus Japan and Australia, set up to police technology exports to the Soviet Union and Eastern Europe. In the 1980s it was often accused by West Europeans of manipulating its criteria so as to limit their export chances. In May 1991 COCOM agreed to a major relaxation of barriers, but kept its ban on sales of the most advanced computers and fibre-optics telecommunications systems until after the *putsch*.*

**COLD WAR** (1946–88). East-West confrontation long sustaining a huge industry – military and academic – on both sides of what used to be called the Iron Curtain. Victory was finally claimed by the West, with the collapse of communism in Eastern Europe. But the real beneficiaries were Germany and Japan, which had contrived to exploit the civilian market, while the United States and the USSR put their costliest resources into increasingly bizarre military programmes. The Cold War's formal end, with the CFE Treaty,* left thousands facing unemployment. Sorely missed by protagonists on both sides, it was finally put beyond hope of revival by the failure of the 1991 *putsch*.*

**COLLECTIVE FARM(S).** See 'Kolkhoz'.

**COLLECTIVIZATION.** Forced integration of peasants and their goods in huge agricultural collectives, mostly in 1929–32 but in places up to 1936. The cruel operation, carried out at gunpoint, included the deportation of ten million *kulaks* (so-called 'rich' peasants), of whom between two and three million died from starvation or exposure in the wastes of Siberia. Others were shot. A famine in 1933 carried off another six million people. By turning agriculture into a grossly wasteful state-run industry, the campaign struck a blow from which the economy has never recovered. It also left wounds on the peasant mentality. At the start of *perestroika* collectivization was described as a basically enlightened policy that went wrong through excesses. But by 1987 doubts were being expressed about the whole principle of collective farms, and by 1990 reformers everywhere demanded their dissolution. However, when offered leases for 'family' or private farms, few collective farmers showed interest (see 'Agriculture').

**COMECON.** See 'Council for Mutual Economic Assistance'.

**COMMAND ADMINISTRATIVE SYSTEM** (*Komandno-administrativnaya sistema*). Method of fulfilling the state plan* by orders handed down through the bureaucratic pyramid. Later blamed for every failure of the economy, including those of reform. In 1988–90 'command administrative system' had to be mentioned in every speech or article if the author was not to be taken for a neo-Stalinist.*

**COMMERSANT.** Successful copy of a Western financial newspaper, with market-oriented political and cultural pages. Started in 1991 by the private bank Menatep, it then co-founded, with Fakt-Cooperative, the Post-factum news agency.

**COMMISSION** (*Komisya*). Usually an elected, not an appointed, body. In parliament, deputies elect 'commissions' with functions similar to those of 'committees' in the West. Not to be confused with *komitet*, which has usually meant a body equivalent to a ministry, e.g. the KGB* or the State Committee for the Environment.*

**COMMITTEE FOR RELIGIOUS AFFAIRS.** Body for controlling (and infiltrating) Christian, Muslim, Jewish and Buddhist religious institutions. It effectively ceased operating in 1988 and was abolished in 1991.

**COMMITTEE FOR THE OPERATIONAL ADMINISTRATION OF THE USSR ECONOMY.** Interim committee formed in August 1991 consisting of industrial heads and representatives of ten republics under premier Silayev.* Responsibilities were divided among three co-chairmen as follows: Volsky* (industry, including defence, construction, communications and transport); Yu. M. Luzhov (trade, foreign economic relations, the agro-industrial complex and social questions); Yavlinsky* (organization of an economic reform programme and its integration in the world economy).

**COMMON EUROPEAN HOME.** Soviet vision of an all-Europe security system, successor to NATO and the defunct Warsaw Pact, hopefully based on the CSCE.* Put forward by Gorbachev in 1987, echoing a notion of Brezhnev at the time of detente.

**COMMONWEALTH OF INDEPENDENT STATES (CIS).** Organization to replace the USSR, agreed by eleven republics – Armenia, Azerbaijan, Byelorussia, Moldavia, Kazakhstan, Kirghizia, Russia, Tajikistan, Turkmenia, Ukraine and Uzbekistan – at Alma-Ata* in December 1991. Founder-members agreed on the creation of a common trading area ('transparent frontiers'), a single command for strategic forces, and central control of nuclear weapons. There would be a 'Council of Heads of States' and a 'Council of Heads of Government', but no central structure as such. Minsk was named as the administrative centre. Despite remarks by Yeltsin, and counsellors Burbulis* and Shakhrai,* about the Commonwealth being 'the last chance to avoid the Yugoslav option', the haste of its invention, and its generally vague purpose, exposed it as being primarily a device with which to torpedo the Union and Gorbachev. It began with the December 8 meeting of the three Slav presidents – Yeltsin (Russia), Kravchuk (Ukraine) and Shushkevich (Byelorussia) – at Minsk,* where they first agreed on a Slavic commonwealth. Gorbachev, who had for months been trying to bring nine republics to sign a new union treaty,* only to see it finally killed by the Ukrainian independence referendum, at first welcomed Ukraine's participation in the Minsk agreement as a retreat from isolation. But the next few days saw a race by Yeltsin, abetted by Kravchuk, to deprive Gorbachev of any initiative, including even a chance to endorse the agreement, as well as to pre-empt any meeting of the Soviet parliament. When a week later the eleven presidents met under Yeltsin's patronage to sign the Alma-Ata agreement, Gorbachev's adviser Shakhnazarov* spoke of a 'pure *coup d'état*' and Shevardnadze* of a possible return to dictatorship. Others quick to protest were St Petersburg's Sobchak* and Yeltsin's own Vice-President, Rutskoy.* By declaring that the Union no longer existed, the Alma-Ata* declaration, without any constitutional basis, simply removed the entity over which the Soviet president presided. Gorbachev was left with no choice but to resign, and the Soviet parliament had to disband itself. But within days the Commonwealth showed serious strains. Although an agreement was reached on the creation of a central command for strategic forces, and joint control of nuclear weapons* stationed in Russia, Ukraine, Byelorussia and Kazakhstan, prospects for military co-operation were rocked by Ukrainian plans for a 400,000-strong army and, more dramatically, claims to the powerful Soviet Black Sea fleet. On the economic side, plans for a single rouble market were undermined when Russia unilaterally liberalized prices* and Ukraine introduced wages coupons (see 'Talon') in advance of a separate national currency. Other republics followed suit. Although Russo-Ukrainian rivalry was the most obvious cause of tension, it was far from being the only one in a body whose members had narrow ideas of national interest, disagreed on nearly every important point, and elected their presidents on predominantly nationalist and populist platforms.

**COMMUNIST PARTY OF THE SOVIET UNION (CPSU).** Self-appointed elite obliged to relinquish its monopoly of power, and later dissolved, having failed to change the world. In 1990 the dropping of Article 6 of the Soviet constitution* (enshrining its special position), and the adoption of the Law on Association, made the CPSU a party like any other. In many places it became the opposition – and the target of moves to uproot communists from education, the media, administration, the judiciary and the police. In western Ukraine, Moldavia and the Baltic states, legislators demanded the Party's proscription and seizure of its property. In Moscow some deputies put it on 'unofficial trial' for abuse of power (forgetting that some had been members themselves until recently). From within its ranks the Party faced desertion by key intellectuals* (despite a bid by Gorbachev to hold them back by raising salaries), while the Twenty-eighth Congress* saw divisions and ruptures and a subsequent haemorrhage of the rank-and-file. By the beginning of 1991 membership had dropped from over 21 million to 17 million, and a poll showed 12 per cent planning to leave. In February 1991, a Secretary of the Central Committee, Valentin Kuptsov, was appointed to head a new department 'for work with other political organizations'; and a more liberal attitude appeared towards the formation of different tendencies within the Party. In July 1991, a plenum of the Central Committee voted for its reform on a non-Marxist social-democratic basis, against surprisingly little resistance from conservatives. A month later, the involvement of hard-liners in the August *putsch* * caused Gorbachev to order the suspension of all its activities, the Central Committee to dissolve itself, and Party files and property to be seized. The *apparat* ceased to exist, and with it the privileges, such as special apartments, of *apparatchiks*. Members could still meet legally to discuss the formation of a successor – except in republics, including the newly independent Baltics, where the party was entirely banned. In Russia by early 1992 there were seven registered parties claiming to be heirs.

**COMPUTERS.** Top of the 1980s black market until ousted by Western and Japanese cars. A personal computer could buy a furnished *dacha*. Imports of mainframe and even some personal computers were supposed to be blocked by COCOM.*

**CONCERN** (*kontsern*). New model of industrial organization, much feted on its introduction in 1988 as a means of regrouping enterprises freed from 'dictatorial' ministerial control. Examples included 'Energomash', formed by fifteen enterprises in the energy equipment industry, and 'Technochem' which comprised eighteen chemical equipment makers.

**CONDOM.** Contraceptive device popularly called a '*galosh*' if of Soviet origin, in reference to its robust manufacture. In 1988 *Krokodil*★ described the nationwide shortage of condoms as a challenge to co-operatives. In 1990 it was planned to boost Soviet output of 2.5 million condoms per year with help from the British firm Virgin. Spurred by AIDS, the Health Ministry asked the Ministry for the Petrochemical Industry for a tenfold increase by 1995.

**CONFERENCE** (of the Communist Party). Assembly of delegates representing all parts, which could be summoned by the Central Committee at any time. The rule permitted discussion of questions that would otherwise have had to wait for a Congress.★ In fact, conferences were rare. The nineteenth, in June–July 1988, was the first since 1941. It concerned the future direction of *perestroika* and was preceded by a feverish campaign to elect delegates. This resulted in a victory for Gorbachev, who managed to assemble a not too conservative majority. At the time he still thought the Party reformable and united, destined to remain the country's driving force for a long time to come. The public evidently thought so too; thousands turned up to put suggestions into a box made available for the purpose. The Conference adopted seven resolutions: to reform the political system, to intensify *perestroika*, to democratize society, to curb bureaucracy, to promote inter-ethnic relations, to increase openness, and to reform the system of justice. It was the Party's last 'high mass' before surrendering its unique power to parliament.

**CONGRESS** (of the Party). Supreme source of Party authority. Rules required it to be summoned at least once in every four years, when it brought together some 5,000 delegates elected by organizations and cells. Congress alone had authority to change the membership of the Party's top organs (most importantly the Central Committee★ and the commission responsible for revising Party statutes). In plenary and commission sessions, usually lasting up to two weeks, it was required to debate and approve plans and reports and set guidelines for policy. From the 1930s until 1986, delegates rubber-stamped the decisions of the Politburo. But the Twenty-seventh Congress, in February 1986, set the foundation for reforms and marked a return to debate and democracy. The Twenty-eighth Congress, in 1990, was held in the aftermath of the Party's surrender to a system of parliamentary control and multi-party politics, and was marked by violent divisions. See separately 'Twenty-seventh Congress', 'Twenty-eighth Congress'.

**CONGRESS OF JOURNALISTS' UNIONS.** See 'Journalist'.

**CONGRESS OF PEOPLE'S DEPUTIES.** Highest body of state authority, established as part of short-lived constitutional reform; dissolved after only five meetings, its last act being to approve arrangements for an interim government after the August 1991 *putsch*.* One third of the 2,250 deputies were elected from territorial districts of roughly equal population, regardless of nationality. One third were from national-territorial districts (32 from each Union republic, 11 from each autonomous republic, 5 from each autonomous region, and one from each autonomous area). And one third were from 'all-Union social organizations', meaning the Party, the Komsomol,* trade unions, creative unions,* the Soviet Women's Committee and other Party-controlled bodies. The Congress met at least once a year, or in an emergency, with sole authority to amend the Soviet constitution. Its other functions included the election, from among its own members, of the Supreme Soviet;* the election of the USSR President and Vice-President; the appointment of a constitutional supervisory committee; and endorsement of Supreme Soviet ministerial appointments.

**CONSCIENTIOUS OBJECTION.** Ethical or political stand traditionally equated with desertion* and punishable by imprisonment. Now a right in some republics. Until 1989–90, most objectors were religious believers (notably Jehovah's Witnesses). After 1990 they were mainly political, refusing to serve in an 'occupation army' (as in the Baltic republics) or claiming the right to join their own republic's 'national guard'.*

**CONSCRIPTION.** Once the last step to Soviet manhood, via twice-yearly call-ups, in spring and autumn. In 1990 the military machine was sabotaged by nationalists. Several republics openly encouraged boycotts. In August 1990 the regional council of Lvov, in western Ukraine, promised young men immunity if they deserted from posts outside the republic and came home because of maltreatment. The Baltic republics already did the same. In October 1990 the army newspaper *Krasnaya Zvezda* ('Red Star') said that because of some republics' 'illegal' laws the army was 400,000 short of its required number. With the ending of the Union, military call-up became a matter for republics. See also 'Military Service'.

**CONSTITUTION.** Supreme legal text, put in abeyance after the August 1991 *putsch*\* pending signature of a new union treaty, which never materialized. The Soviet constitution was last revised in 1988–90, when changes were made to the 1977 'Brezhnev constitution', inherited by Gorbachev in 1985. These provided for a new model presidency and parliament (the Congress of People's Deputies* and a 'permanent' Supreme Soviet*) but were criticized by the Baltic republics. A commission was set up to draft a new constitution. Meanwhile, in December 1990, the Congress of People's Deputies* approved further amendments, providing for greater presidential powers, the appointment of a vice-president, changes in the character of the Presidential* and Federal Councils,* and the replacement of 'government' by a Presidential cabinet. In its post-

*putsch* emergency session the Congress voted for a new constitution to be drawn up, once it was established which republics wished to remain in the Union, and on what terms. With the break-up of the Union, republics set about revising their own constitutions.

**CONVERSION.** Problematic programme for switching defence production to the civil economy. Long before it started, defence factories used surplus capacity to turn out goods such as refrigerators and television sets. In 1988 moves were made to involve them more deeply, for example by switching some tank factories to the production of diesel engines and railway rolling stock. But with inadequate warning the plants had difficulty in finding new suppliers and outlets. In 1989 the government set up an advisory 'conversion commission' under Academician Vsevolod Avdnesky. Among its members are officials of the Military Procurement Committee (VPK),★ Gosplan,★ and the Ministry of Finance, as well as a variety of military and economic specialists ranging from Abel Aganbegyan★ to Marshal Kulikov.★ A five-year plan for 1991–95 covered 422 factories (of which fifty-six were to be totally converted within three years). In the same period the share of defence factories' output devoted to non-military goods was to rise from 46 per cent to 60 per cent. In October 1990, a visit to America by Marshal Moiseyev★ was followed by the setting up of a non-governmental conversion fund by Soviet and Western business partners interested in joint projects. The Americans reportedly identified twenty Soviet defence factories as 'excellent long-term investments'. Later, Soviet analysts gave a less optimistic picture: conversion would be a loss-maker for up to ten years, and billions of roubles of investment would be needed before returns were seen. In 1991 problems arose with the demotion of thousands of highly specialized technicians to humdrum and poorly paid jobs. Pockets of unemployment appeared in areas of high concentration by the arms industry (82 per cent in Russia). And in 1992 there was pressure to revert to arms manufacture for export.

**CONVERTIBLE ROUBLE.** Loch Ness monster of *perestroika*, promised the day-after-tomorrow since 1986. Attempts were made to overcome its absence (the biggest bar to Soviet participation in the world trade system) through a variety of artificial exchange rates (the 'tourist' rouble, the 'commercial' rouble, etc.) less remote from reality than the posted exchange rate. It appeared once again in proposals put before the Group of Seven in 1991–92.

**CO-OPERATIVE.** Form of commercial association once blessed with Lenin's approval (under NEP★); essentially a private enterprise under a collectivist flag. With *perestroika*, co-operatives were 'sold' to the public as a way to stimulate the economy and recycle people made jobless by reforms. Their path was prepared by the Law on Individual Economic Activity★ (1986). This allowed people to work for private ends either singly or in a group, but was very restrictive: only pensioners, students, and after-hours workers were covered, and any materials had to be surplus to the needs of state enterprises.

Only twenty-nine kinds of activity were permitted, many of them already common practice, like giving paid lifts ('taxi-driving') and dress-making. In such cases no one saw much point in paying for a licence and having to pay taxes. When the law came into force in May 1987 it was immediately sabotaged by municipal bureaucrats, simply by withholding licences. In March 1988 most of the restrictions were lifted: co-operatives were now allowed to pay staff and do business with foreigners. Then, in January 1989, came a retreat, when the government reissued a list of 'permitted activities', excluding, among other things, medicine, pub-lishing and film-making. August 1990 saw another about-turn, with the granting of near-total freedom in all fields. The only problem remaining was taxes, judged excessively high by co-operators but absurdly low by competing state enterprises. These were eventually modified. As a result, by the end of 1990 there were 260,000 co-operatives employing 6.2 million people, including people with more than one job (an increase of 40 per cent over 1989). Their output of goods and services amounted to R70 billion (in 1989, R40 billion), of which R10 billion was directly for the population. However, three-fifths of this total were not small co-operatives as originally conceived, but co-operatives created at former state enterprises to take over their production and, using production capital, supply state enterprises and organizations.

The impact of co-operatives on the consumer market (in garages, home decoration, household repairs, garment-making, catering, small-scale manufacturing, retailing, etc.) was statistically much smaller – in 1990 only 2 per cent of retail commodity turnover, according to officials. The same year co-operatives became the formula chosen for the creation of new banks and credit houses. They were also enabled to turn into capitalist 'firms' in all but name by a law allowing members to take out profits based on their investment as opposed to their work-share. While co-operatives have lent energy to the otherwise moribund economy, they have also caused deep resentment in the consumer sector, where they are accused of charging high prices, causing the disappearance of cheap goods from state shops, and charging for services in short supply but formerly free, such as medicine and schooling. Their members' display of personal wealth has frequently contributed to friction, seized on by conservatives.

**CORRUPTION.** Running sore of 'stagnation', first attacked in 1982–84 by Andropov.* In 1986 a new drive under Gorbachev caused a wave of arrests (by March 1988 seven of Uzbekistan's twelve regional first secretaries were in gaol). Other spectacular events were the Moscow stores trial (1986) and the trial of Brezhnev's son-in-law, Churbanov* (1989). Wide-spread corruption reappeared at lower levels of state employment in the 1980s with the disappearance from shops of essential goods (even drugs for the desperately sick vanished into the black market). The breakdown of morality disgusted decent citizens, who were drawn willy-nilly into the system of shady transactions. It also created a climate of almost universal cynicism, especially among the young. The continuation of anti-corruption operations caused ethnic disturbances in Central Asia, where inquiries by 'foreign' officials were portrayed as an insult to national honour. Figures given in 1990 showed that in 1985–89 14,000 people had been found guilty of large-scale thefts of state property, 19,000 of taking bribes, and 16,000 of abuse of their office. Losses to the state totalled R900 million. Investigators turned up gems of ingenuity. For example, officials in Tajikistan had used the effect of temperature changes on liquids to pocket the profit on the specific mass of oil loaded in Ufa at minus-20 degrees (centigrade) and registered on arrival in Dushanbe at plus-20. In 1988 obsession with corruption caused Soviet leaders to mistake the significance of Central Asia's first ethnic riots, which they blamed on 'corrupt elements' and thought to end by sacking First Secretaries.

**COSMONAUT**. Favourite hero of Soviet small boys, until Yuri Gagarin was ousted by Crocodile Dundee. Also of their mothers, judging by the number of 'Yuris' one still meets, from Leningrad to the tents of Central Asia, more than thirty years after the hero's first space flight.

**COSSACK**. Historic foe of the Revolution, now reinstated in folklore. In 1990, Cossacks elected a new *ataman* amid lavish celebrations of 500 years of history up and down the Dnepr. As well as in Ukraine there are large Cossack communities in Russia, Moldavia and Kazakhstan, where their traditions as farmer-soldiers can make them problematic neighbours. Following a declaration by the *ataman* in favour of the 'revival' of Russia, President Kravchuck offered to create a special Cossack regiment in the Ukrainian army.

**COST-ACCOUNTING**. See 'Khozraschet'.

**COTTON**. Central Asian monoculture, abiding memorial to the absurdity of central planning. The systematic extension of cotton at the expense of food crops brought malnutrition to millions. The industry's demand for water, sharply increased in the 1960s and 1970s, gave rise to an ecologically disastrous irrigation system involving the near-disappearance of the Aral Sea.* In 1990 Central Asian nationalists, whose rank and file supporters saw little or nothing of the profits registered by state budgets, gained a start to the restoration of cotton fields to food production. The Russian population saw little benefit either; today more than 90 per cent of its garments are synthetic.

**COUNCIL FOR MUTUAL ECONOMIC ASSISTANCE (CMEA)**, otherwise 'Comecon'. Organization for trade and technological co-operation, established in 1949 by the USSR and six East European countries – Bulgaria, Hungary, Poland, Romania, Czechoslovakia and East Germany. It was later joined by Cuba, Mongolia and Vietnam. In the ten years before *perestroika*, Moscow reduced its exports of technology within Comecon and replaced them with raw materials and energy which benefited from rising world prices. As a result some CMEA countries, especially East Germany, developed their own more advanced technology, which the Soviet Union was soon glad to import. In 1985, when oil revenues were hit by a price fall, Moscow arranged to supply CMEA partners with nuclear plants. The deal, like earlier ones, was undisguisedly to the Soviet advantage, and the East Europeans were reportedly delighted when the programme suffered a setback with Chernobyl.* In 1989–90 CMEA was shaken by the collapse of communism in Eastern Europe and the switch of half its members to some form of market economy. At the end of 1990 each Eastern country came to Moscow to ask for additional oil supplies, which, following the old system, the USSR granted against deliveries of consumer goods or machinery. From 1991 it was agreed that exchanges between members should be made in hard currency at world market prices – an evolution that signed the organization's death warrant. It was formally buried in February 1991 in Budapest.

**COUNTRY WRITERS.** School of writers who emerged with the Khrushchev 'thaw', concerned with the values of rural life as opposed to the dehumanizing life of the cities. Coming from the peasantry, they claim not to idealize a world now existing only in memory yet are ready to defend it to the extent of becoming anti-occidental. Thrust into the contemporary world, and favoured by *perestroika*, they still prefer to live in their rural fastnesses: Fyodor Abramov and Vasili Belov in the empty Russian north, Valentin Rasputin* and Viktor Astafiev* in Siberia.

**CREATIVE UNIONS.** Essentially social insurance organizations designed to provide artists and others with access to 'social consumption funds'* similar to those in industry; also with facilities for studios, galleries, visits abroad, etc. With the coming of *glasnost*, many members perceived union membership to be a form of artistic and political dictatorship yet remained members for the sake of the social benefits. 'Dictatorship' lost its terror when artists were allowed to make private contracts and exclusion from a union no longer deprived writers of publishers, musicians of a performance, painters of exhibitions. With a few exceptions (the 1986 revolt of the Film-Makers* and the 1989 formation of a new Theatre Workers' Union*) unions have remained conservative. During the Brezhnev period they did nothing to fight censorship, and *perestroika* found the Union of Composers still headed by Tikhon Khrennikov, appointed by Stalin to carry out a

1938 purge of its membership. Artists who have since been 'unanimously' rehabilitated were often unanimously expelled from their unions by the very same membership. At the time of the Soviet break-up in 1991, leading unions were the Writers' Union* (9,960 members), the Film-Makers' Union* (6,700 members), the Union of Composers (2,550), the Union of Architects (20,000), the Union of Artists (20,700), the Union of Theatre Workers* (56,000) and the Confederation of Journalists' Unions (86,600).

**CREDIT (1).** System of finance reformed in 1990 to accelerate transition to the market. Replacing inexhaustible ministerial subsidies, credits were henceforth made from state or commercial banks, on an assessment of the borrower's profitability.

**CREDIT (2).** Western handout with which to crank up the economy. Credits started with Bonn's promise of DM5 billion ($3.3 billion) on German reunification, plus DM15 billion for the withdrawal of Soviet troops from the former GDR. In May 1991 Moscow asked the Group of Seven for credits of $100 billion spread over three years. It was given $7.2 billion of credits with which to buy food and medicines (see 'Humanitarian aid') for the 1991–92 winter.

**CREDIT CARD.** Piece of plastic of which foreign newspapers were given pictures long before Soviets knew what it was all about. Soviet athletes were chosen as guinea-pigs to use the first Soviet cards at the 1988 Seoul Olympics – to the recipients' distress, since it enabled the authorities to track their purchases. Developed in co-operation with Visa, in 1991 the card stayed limited to a handful of users with hard currency accounts.

**CRIME.** Malady aggravated by greater access to consumer goods (mostly black market), breakdown of social restraints, drug abuse and family break-up. An alarming feature is the increase of gratuitous violence, especially in cases of robbery (murders are regularly committed for the theft of a video* or computer*) and rape. According to the Interior Ministry, in 1990 crime reached an all-time high with 2,786,605 registered cases, a 13.5 per cent increase over the previous year. The statistics include a steady growth of organized crime, officially divided into crime by local mafias* (store robberies, protection rackets) and crime requiring international connections (narcotics, art thefts). In 1991 the police noted 7,029 different gangs. In an ostensible crackdown, in March 1991 the central government ordered mixed patrols of troops and police in 184 cities (but the police questioned their value). In 1992 scarcity and the break-up of central authority led to more deterioration. See also 'Interpol'.

**CRIMEA.** Black Sea peninsula transferred from Russia to Ukraine in 1954. In January 1992 it became a focus of dispute when the Russian parliament recommended annulment of the transfer as unconstitutional. The peninsula contains the base, at Sebastopol, of the contested Black Sea fleet. In an attempt to win foreign support, President Kravchuk* offered to Bonn to open the Crimea to settlement by Germans,* of whom 400,000 had lived in the Ukraine before wartime expulsion. The offer was viewed poorly, by the existing inhabitants, as well as by Crimean Tatars.*

**CRIMEAN TATARS.** People deported, mostly to Kazakhstan, in 1944 for alleged collaboration with the Germans. In 1987–88 their demand to be allowed to return home, including a demonstration in Red Square, caused the setting up of a commission under President Gromyko.* The committee ruled in their favour. But the Crimea is now part of Ukraine: an *oblast* of 2.3 million people resolutely opposed to giving back Tatar lands or restoring the former Crimean Tatar autonomous republic. In 1991, to the Tatars' chagrin, a referendum called for the setting up of a Ukrainian autonomous republic of the Crimea. According to the Crimean Tatar National Movement, 600,000 Tatars were waiting to be reinstalled. Other figures ranged between 270,000 and 1.5 million. In 1991, 160,000 were reported to have returned to the peninsula illegally.

**CRUISE** missiles. Ground-, air- or sea-launched missiles guided to their targets by sensors and an electronic 'map'. US nuclear cruise missiles in Europe were traded for destruction with Soviet SS-20s* under the INF Treaty.*

**CSCE (CONFERENCE ON SECURITY AND CO-OPERATION IN EUROPE).** Forum of thirty-four nations perceived under Gorbachev as the basis of an all-European security organization replacing NATO and the Warsaw Treaty Organization – a 'Common European Home'.* The quest began under Brezhnev, whose foreign policy combined steps towards detente with an acceleration of the arms race. In 1975 a conference in Helsinki agreed on various confidence-building measures (including prenotification of troop movements) and to the further pursuit of detente and disarmament. NATO then concentrated on more confidence-building, emphasizing the need for on-site inspections, while Moscow, which rejected on-site inspection, talked only of disarmament. But with Gorbachev's arrival, Moscow changed its line; and when CSCE members (then including the GDR) came together in another forum – the Conference on Disarmament in Europe (CDE) – Moscow agreed to the extension of limited on-site inspections and a regular exchange of military data. The agreement was written into the 1986 Stockholm Accord. In February 1991, the CSCE established permanent headquarters in Prague. But differences arose over the right of the body to concern itself with what Moscow called members' internal affairs – an allusion to contemporary events in the Baltic region and Yugoslavia.

**CUBA.** Internationalist 'good deed' that turned sour. In September 1991, desperately short of resources for itself, and impatient of Castro's inflexible political line, Moscow announced the termination of its aid programme and the withdrawal of the Soviet military presence, always described as a 'training brigade'. Gorbachev said 11,000 men would come back − 5,000 more than the US had thought present. Later Shaposhnikov★ gave a figure of 2,800 soldiers, 2,800 military advisers and 2,100 members of the KGB and military intelligence. In 1990 a fuller edition of Khrushchev's★ memoirs disclosed that at the time of the 1962 Cuban missile crisis, Castro had wanted to involve Moscow in a nuclear strike against America. Three months later one of the first acts of the Russian foreign minister, Kozyrev,★ was to receive representatives of the anti-Castro opposition and promise to meet them again in Miami.

**CULTURAL FUND.** Artistic trust chaired by Academician Likhachev,★ with Raisa Gorbachev★ a member of its first board. Since its foundation in March 1986 it has been authorized to receive works of art for displaying in museums or at special exhibitions, and gifts of money towards restoring the decayed national heritage. In December 1991 it became 'Russian'.

**CUSTOMS.** Brake on foreign business investment belatedly reformed in 1990, with procedures 'better adapted to evolving trade patterns'. Within the Union 'customs wars' developed when separatist republics set up their own customs posts to collect dues and control the movement of goods. In May 1991 Soviet forces destroyed ten posts set up by Lithuania at a cost of R300,000. Warnings by Soviet and foreign experts that the erection of inter-republic barriers would be economic suicide were disregarded by leaders who saw customs controls as a symbol of independence and political maturity. In January 1992 their future awaited discussion within the new Commonwealth of Independent States.★

**CZECHOSLOVAKIA.** 'Land of the blighted spring' that took its revenge when, in 1990, 75,000 Soviet troops and 1,220 tanks were ignominiously sent packing. Talks begun with the new Czech government in February 1990 were concluded by April. Under the settlement half the force had to be out by June 1990, the rest by July 1991. The Soviet side, which had pleaded for a further six months for 'technical reasons', was even required to remove chemically damaged topsoil. Three-quarters of those leaving had no housing in the Soviet Union to return to. The evacuation left behind schools, hospitals, cinemas and ammunition dumps. Several dumps were simply blown up. The Czechs refused to pay for thousands of abandoned officers' apartments. Salting the psychological wound, Prague's Red Army Square was renamed Jan Palach Square, after the student who burned himself to death in protest at the 1968 Soviet occupation.

# D

**DACHA** (1). State-funded retreat of Party or national figures. In 1989–90 a proportion were put to public use, including Stalin's on the Black Sea, available to tourists for $330 per night.

**DACHA** (2). Wooden shack of weekend vegetable gardeners.

**DAGESTAN** (pop. 1.7 million). North Caucasian republic having a mosaic of peoples – Avars, Kumiks, Dargwa, Lezghi and thirty-nine more – cultivating old rivalries. The capital, Makhachkala on the Caspian, was the wider region's Islamic centre, a status contested in 1991 after long protests by other Caucasian Muslims who resented the appointment of officials by rotation among ethnic local divisions, as offensive to religious criteria. In June 1991 fanatics attacked government headquarters, demanding compensation for the increased price of air tickets for the pilgrimage to Mecca and a more generous quota of places. The following September saw a state of emergency declared when thousands of Avars and Chechens came on to the streets to protest over the distribution of building plots.

**DANIEL**, YULI. See 'Sinyavsky'.

**DANILOFF**, NICHOLAS. Correspondent of *US News and World Report* arrested in 1986 on a fabricated charge of obtaining military secrets. His release, in exchange for a Soviet agent, helped save the Reykjavik summit.

**DECREE** (*ukaze*). Presidential order with immediate effect, but requiring later endorsement by parliament to have the status of a law. The principal method of government, both Soviet and republican, in the transitional period after the 1991 *putsch*.\* Widely criticized for its disregard of democratic processes.

**DEDOVSHCHINA**. Bullying of army conscripts, in 1987 the subject of a scandal which gravely embarrassed the military. Newspapers published eye-witness reports and letters from parents about the unexplained deaths of young soldiers 'in training'. Confirmation came with publication of court-martial verdicts and articles by officers about deaths, suicides and desertions. Two novels appeared on the subject, *100 Days to Demob* by Yuri Poliakov (1987) and *Construction Battalion (Stroibat)* by Sergei

Kaledin (1989). In August 1990 the Judge-General, General Muranov, said that since 1985 there had been 4,000 disciplinary cases. Of 1,990 soldiers charged under Article 8 of the military code, 1,393 had been sent to punishment battalions and 334 to 'hard regime' correctional camps. There might have been other cases, because in 1989 some 3,800 soldiers had been listed as injured 'without explanation'. Muranov attributed a fall in the number of cases in 1990 to the effect of publicity. He said *dedovshchina* reflected behaviour in civil life. Ten per cent of conscripts had already come to the notice of the police for hooliganism; one in four punished for *dedovshchina* had already served sentences; and 18.9 per cent of military offenders had not completed their basic education. In about a quarter of the cases there might have been an ethnic element, generally involving friction between different Caucasian or Central Asian nationalities. In October 1990 the Soviet parliament appointed a commission of inquiry under Veniamin Yarin, a member of the Presidential Council.

**DEFECTION** (East to West). Way out of the system, sometimes at high cost, notably in the case of Oleg Penkovsky, defector-in-place, who was executed after his trial (recorded on camera) in 1963. According to another 'Oleg', General Kalugin,* three KGB officers defected to the West in 1960–80, and twenty people 'betrayed their country' in 1980–90. Some East-West defectors, like Tumanov and Yurchenko,* came back.

**DEFECTION** (West to East). Resort of Western misfits 'seeking freedom', like American Arnold Lokchine, alleging persecution for anti-Vietnam war activity (1986) and US Private Wade Roberts, with his German girlfriend (1987). Roberts thought better and returned, after spending five months as a snake-handler in Ashkhabad. Others crossing the line included tourists Ted and Cheryl Branch, 'fleeing US injustice', and Michael Souter, 'persecuted by the FBI'. Soviet officials suspected most fugitives of mental imbalance.

**DEFENCE BUDGET.** Bill long incapable of realistic valuation due to arbitrary exchange rates. Another difficulty is that even if given in good faith, as was probable in the later 1980s, Soviet figures excluded the military share of nuclear and space spending. In 1991 parliament passed a military budget of R96.56 billion – nearly R20 billion more than spending the previous year (a 'paper' increase officially explained by inflation). The 1990 figure had shown an 8 per cent decrease. At the time of the 1991 dissolution of the Union the government was pledged to cut military spending from 11 per cent to 5.5 per cent of the total budget over five years.

**DEFENCE COUNCIL** (*Soviet Oborony*). Top level political-military body set up in the mid-1960s as a means of establishing Party control over the military; once described as 'essentially a sub-committee of the Politburo'.

Membership consisted of the Party General Secretary, the head of the KGB, the chairman of the Council of Ministers, the Central Committee Secretaries for Ideology and for Cadres, and the Chief of the General Staff. Suppressed after the 1991 *putsch*.*

**DEFENCE DOCTRINE.** See 'Defensive Defence'.

**DEFENCE INDUSTRY.** Once voracious consumer of industrial and scientific resources. For years it was under the control of nine separate ministries, subordinate to the Council of Ministers through the VPK* and supervised by the Central Committee department for defence production. In the late 1980s it was subjected to organizational changes aimed at increasing its technical efficiency and integrating civil and military output. (See 'Conversion'.) Conversion appeared in nearly every Soviet request for economic aid and technical advice addressed to the West in 1991, partly because it looked good, and partly as the quickest way of getting foreign help in managerial organization.

**DEFENSIVE DEFENCE.** New strategic concept advanced by Soviet theorists from 1988 onwards and variously interpreted as meaning: (1) continuation of existing military doctrine, (2) limiting plans for any counter-offensive to the recovery of Soviet territory, (3) total abandonment of the counter-offensive and concentration on pure defence. In fact, in 1991 East German exercise plans made public by the Bonn government showed that as late as 1990, Warsaw Pact forces were still preparing for a 'counter-offensive' extending to the North Sea. This suggests that although 'Defensive Defence' may have been seriously embraced at the political level, military staffs required several more years in which to adapt training and equipment to the new doctrine.

**DEFICIT.** Catchword for shortages, of 'moral values' as well as tea and soap. According to the State Committee on Statistics, in 1990 — the fifth year of *perestroika* — the unsatisfied demand for goods and services increased by a colossal R55 billion. There were falls in the production of footwear, fabrics and many kinds of clothing, especially for young people. Dresses and knitted items fell by 7–18 per cent; suits, coats, jackets and shoes by 21–25 per cent. There were also falls in goods 'in mass demand', such as razor blades, school notebooks and pencils, rubber boots, soap and cigarettes. Nearly all kinds of food were down, some — like sugar and tea — severely. Statistics showed an increase in some household goods like television sets and vacuum cleaners, but there was no sign of them in the shops. See also 'Budget Deficit'.

**DELINQUENCY.** See 'Crime'.

**DEMOCRACY**. Sauce with which to spice every political proposition, with increasing confusion as to where democracy lies — in parliament or in the streets (where demonstrations always express 'the will of the people'). Gorbachev first spoke of 'democratizing' Soviet society in his September 1986 Krasnodar speech. In fact, there was only partial progress with the introduction of a working democracy in the Soviet Union. Most of the new deputies elected to parliament in 1989 were quite unprepared for the tasks suddenly thrust on them. To make the job harder, they lacked the most basic facilities — secretaries, committee rooms, assistants, libraries, reference materials. The effects were conspicuous during the next two years' economic debates, when they had nowhere to go for disinterested advice, and scarcely any reliable figures. Another 'deficit' has been in ability to compromise or reach consensuses. Hence the constant splitting of movements and political parties. An official list in mid-1991 gave the names of fifty-five — only a fraction of the total.

**DEMOCRATIC FORUM OF RUSSIA**. Radical organization with a prog-ramme, 'Action 1990', so confused in direction as to be simultaneously labelled both 'nihilist' and 'neo-bolshevist' by opponents. It proposed delegating government to 'micro-parliaments' and transferring state prop-erty to producers. Meanwhile, to combat young people's inertia, it advocated civil disobedience, strikes and the seizure of Party premises. Its appearance coincided with anti-parliamentary tendencies among groups disappointed by the slowness of reform and wanting to put power in the hands of mass organizations. To charges that it looked like a provocation to discredit democrats at a moment when the country was living on rumours of a coup (1990), conservative newspapers answered that the Forum's propositions could be found almost verbatim in the speeches of Yuri Afanasiev* and the *Moscow News* journalist Len Karpinski. Refor-mers dissociated themselves from the programme, which had been drawn up by a few dozen ultra-radicals.

**DEMOCRATIC PARTY OF RUSSIA**. Party founded in May 1990 by the radical wing of the Democratic Platform* to campaign for 'equal opportu-nities' and liberalization of the economy. In 1991 the chairman, Nikolai Travkin,* claimed a membership of 26,000 in a hundred cities.

**DEMOCRATIC PARTY OF RUSSIAN COMMUNISTS**. Party founded in October 1991 on the basis of the 'Communists for Democracy' faction of the Russian Vice-President Rutskoy.* It was headed by Vasili Lipsky, previously coordinator of a 'democratic movement' founded by young communists close to the Marxist Platform.*

**DEMOCRATIC PARTY OF THE SOVIET UNION**. Party founded in August 1989 by 'entrepreneurs, co-operators and supporters of the new economy', mainly in Siberia, the Urals and the Ukraine.

**DEMOCRATIC PLATFORM.** Name given to a programme for radical reform put forward by Yeltsin,* Shostakhovsky* and other 'democrats' at the Twenty-eighth Congress* of the Party in 1990. Conservatives put forward a rival 'Marxist Platform', supported by a majority in the newly created Russian Communist Party. Both 'platforms' challenged the line of Gorbachev and the Politburo. The defeat of the Democratic Platform caused many reformists to leave the Party.

**DEMOCRATIC REFORM PARTY.** Party operating within the Movement for Democratic Reforms* and describing itself as 'a centre-right party serving the political interests of the middle class'.

**DEMOCRATIC RUSSIA.** Largest Russian-based parliamentary opposition movement, founded 1990. Founders included Yuri Afanasiev,* Nikolai Travkin,* Arkadi Murashev* and Gari Kasparov.* Its first congress, attended by 2,000 delegates from nine smaller parties and eighteen organizations, voted to 'fight totalitarianism, create a free market by privatization, end the Communist Party's monopoly of activity in the armed forces, and suppress the KGB.' At its third congress, in April 1991, there was a split between supporters of Travkin and those of Murashev and Kasparov, who accused Travkin of 'abandoning the anti-communist drive'. In September the same year it reacted badly to the formation of the Movement for Democratic Reforms,* which it saw as its chief rival. Murashev proposed co-operation but excluded merging. Another leading member, the economist Pavel Bunich, insisted that there was a political difference – while the Movement for Democratic Reform called itself a 'middle-class party', Democratic Russia put more emphasis on social justice.

**DEMOCRATIC UNION.** Party formed in May 1988 round Igor Tsarkov and Valeria Novodvorskaya,* preaching civil disobedience as 'a means of awakening the individual'. It supports private property and claims to have a roughly equal membership of students, intellectuals and workers, mainly in Moscow, Leningrad and Novosibirsk.

**DEMOGRAPHY.** See 'Population'.

**DEMONSTRATION.** Spontaneous event requiring official permission in order to qualify as an expression of popular will. (All other demonstrations being acts of political adventurism or base provocation.) In July 1988, the tendency of crowds to demonstrate their enthusiasm for reform caused a decree to be published, laying down the rules. Local authorities had to be told the names of the organizers, the expected number of participants, the general theme, and the intended route and duration of any procession. After demonstrations by Crimean Tatars,* Moscow city council prohibited demonstrations in Red Square and fourteen other places. A subsequent order made a distinction between 'sanctioned' and 'non-sanctioned' meetings (whose organizers risked five days' gaol and fines of up to R300). In 1990 the government recycled several hundred police into riot squads, with flak jackets, black berets and truncheons.

**DE-POLITICIZATION.** Word coined by radicals to suggest the un-making of the Soviet Union (cf. others in the same sense — 'denationalization', 'demonopolization', 'demilitarization', 'decentralization', 'de-Sovietization'). It included the exclusion of communists from the teaching profession, public administration, the magistrature, etc; and abolition of the Armed Forces Political Directorate.

**DEPUTY.** Member of the former federal parliament, a republic parliament, or any lower elected assembly (all called 'soviets' in Russian). Under the revised system of 1989–90, one third of those elected to the supreme national assembly, the Congress of People's Deputies,★ were chosen by the Party or its subservient organizations. Others were chosen by universal suffrage, as were members of republic and regional parliaments.

**'DEPUTY'** (Minister etc.). Usually one of several, not necessarily the Number Two, who is always designated 'First Deputy'.

**DESERTION.** Occurrence barely acknowledged before 1990, when several republics took to encouraging their nationals to walk out of barracks with impunity. The same year saw scores of desertions by Soviet soldiers in East Germany (in the three days before unification, 200 in the Potsdam region alone). Most asked for political asylum, putting the Germans in a quandary, especially when deserters were reported to be selling weapons taken from armouries. See also 'Conscription'.

**DIAMONDS.** Russian, not Soviet, gems, according to Boris Yeltsin, when he took over Russia's natural resources as republic property. In 1990 he declared invalid a contract signed by the Soviet government with De Beers. The $5 billion deal gave De Beers the exclusive right to trade in Soviet diamonds over a period of five years. Foreign specialists estimate Soviet diamond production at 10–14 million carats annually, making it second only to South African production.

**DIPHTHERIA.** Endemic infection reappearing in Moscow in 1990 (nine deaths in a day). The outbreak was traced to a breakdown in children's vaccination, because parents feared the use of badly sterilized needles.

**DIPLOMACY.** See 'Foreign Policy', 'Parallel Diplomacy'.

**DISINFORMATION.** Favourite weapon of the Cold War, reluctantly abandoned. In 1986, the KGB spread a story that the AIDS virus came from a US military laboratory. Next year the CIA spread a so-called defector's 'admission' that he had been buying up small Western publishing houses to spread the 'lie' that *glasnost* was serious.

**DISSIDENTS.** For years, with refuseniks,★ the focus of Western interest in Soviet affairs. Their mantle was often borrowed. Artists, in particular, had only to call themselves 'dissidents' in order to get noticed. When repression ended, nostalgia for 'dissidence' gripped a new generation of intellectuals too young to have known it, causing protests to be hurled against conditions that no longer existed. For real dissidents, like Andrei Sakharov★ and Roy Medvedev,★ the path of disagreement with authority was beset with sharp turns. Their movement began in the late 1960s, flourished under persecution throughout the 1970s, but was decapitated by arrest, deportation and exile in the early 1980s. In 1986–87 it was triumphantly rewarded by the moral burial of Stalin and Brezhnev; but it lost its *raison d'être* with the coming of parliamentary opposition and freedom of association. The end was sounded in June 1987 with a presidential decree freeing 150 political dissidents from camps or prison. Most signed an undertaking (later often broken) not to resume political activity. Religious dissidents, sentenced under article 70, had to wait a few more weeks for the amnesty★ on the 70th anniversary of the October Revolution. Though there were subsequent cases of arbitrary arrest, dissent was no longer repressed in the historic sense of the word.

**DOBRYNIN,** ANATOLI FYODOROVICH (1919– ). Long-serving Soviet ambassador in Washington brought into the Central Committee *apparat* in 1986, as a Secretary and head of the International Department. His intended role as a liberal reformer of foreign policy was stolen by the unexpectedly energetic Shevardnadze.★ Officially retired in 1988, he remained an informal presidential adviser.

**DONBASS.** Basin of the river Don in Ukraine; a vast industrial and agricultural region, scene of the first major strike for twenty-eight years — by coal-miners in July 1989. In October 1991 a Donbass coal-pit became the first in the industry to declare bankruptcy, dismissing 1,000 miners. Twelve others were reported near the same state, with work halted at scores of coal-faces for lack of modern or serviceable equipment.

**DOSAAF.** Armed forces and Party organization to prepare 14–17 year-olds for military service. Suspended after the 1991 *putsch*★ for 'having kept a low profile'. It was replaced in September 1991 by OSTO (Organization for Defence, Sport and Technics). Most DOSAAF activities involved sports and hobbies, like radio 'hamming', rather than military training. OSTO's do the same. DOSAAF stood in Russian for 'Voluntary Society for Aid to the Army, Air Force and Navy'.

**DRUGS.** Social problem long supposed to exist only in the West, with occasional bland references to 'old traditions' in Central Asia. According to the fiction, poppies were grown only for the pharmaceutical industry, on collective farms under the eye of incorruptible guards (or in Ukrainian and Byelorussian backyards for poppy-seed cake). In January 1987, the country was told that there were 175,000 users, of whom 48,000 were on hard drugs – nearly double the total three years before. By 1990 the official figure had risen to half a million, and by 1991 to 1.5 million. Police started raiding growing areas in Central Asia but were hampered by a shortage of men and equipment. In 1989, alarmed by the size of customs seizures and evidence of the involvement of an international network, the Soviet Union finally decided to join Interpol.★ According to sociologists, whereas drugs were formerly a 'southern' problem, and alcohol a 'northern' one, each latitude has now infected the other.

**DRUZHINIKI.** Civilian police auxiliaries. Their red armbands are now less in evidence, except during crowd-control at official parades. In 1989 it was proposed to replace them with a new force, composed of volunteers recruited from workplaces. Members were to carry rubber truncheons and, unlike *druzhiniki*, have powers of arrest. The idea was dropped after protests from radical deputies and warnings by the militia that the 'amateurs' were liable to get into situations beyond their control.

**DUSHANBE** (pop. 552,000). Capital of Tajikistan.★ Scene of 1990 riots leading to the killing of twenty-two people, mostly Russians. In September and October 1991 the state of emergency had to be reimposed after disturbances in support of new presidential elections. The organizers were the Democratic Party of Tajikistan, the Rastakhez ('Rebirth') Popular Movement and supporters of the Islamic Movement, which demanded registration.

# E

**EASTERN EUROPE.** Soviet post-war hunting preserve, until in 1990 the 'empire' collapsed in a space of months. Moscow took the debacle philosophically, with the line that East Europeans must decide their own future and that what had happened was all due to Stalin and stagnation. The fact was that the Kremlin had problems enough of its own. The Soviet media reported the change openly, showing pictures of crowds celebrating in Prague and Berlin. The East European countries soon found that to part from the Soviet Union was tougher economically than it was politically. In 1991 Moscow retained only 30 per cent of its barter deals, marketing oil in foreign currency. And Eastern Europe had difficulty finding markets for its finished goods, only 25 per cent of which met international standards.

**ECOLOGY.** Science brought to prominence by *glasnost* and Chernobyl.* But it was not until 1988, when rules were eased, that accurate assessments became possible, since nearly all the data remained a military secret – even the identity of the substances used or produced in most factories. Yet it was the destruction of the environment that gave rise to the first big public demonstrations, in Siberia and the Urals. The first the country heard about some of its biggest disasters was in 1986. Among them were changes of climate due to the massive diversion of water from the Kara-Bogaz-Gol lake in South Turkmenia to the Caspian, the slow disappearance of the Aral Sea,* the biological death of Lake Ladoga,* the poisoning of Lakes Sevan in Armenia and Baikal* in Siberia, and the disturbance of the eco-system of the North Caucasus springs. In 1991, 16 per cent of Soviet territory was classed as an ecological 'crisis zone'; 50–70 million people lived in regions 'dangerous for health' (in addition to areas affected by Chernobyl); the pollution in sixteen major cities was fifty times above internationally recognized norms; 75 per cent of the Union's fresh water reserves were dead or dying; 20 per cent of the water in some rivers consisted of effluent; the concentration of pesticides made 30 per cent of all food products a health risk; and only 8 per cent of milk was safe for children. See also 'Environment'.

**EC/EEC.** See 'European Community'.

**ECONOMIC PERFORMANCE.** In 1990, according to the USSR State Committee for Statistics (report in *Ekonomika i Zhizn*, January 5, 1991):
- GNP fell by 2 per cent, produced national income by 4 per cent and productivity of labour by 3 per cent;
- the state foreign debt rose by R150 billion to more than R550 billion;
- the state budget deficit was R58.1 billion;
- industrial output fell by 1.2 per cent;
- of the 505 capital construction projects covered by state order only 155 (31 per cent) had been completed;
- there remained a backlog of 103 state order projects still not completed from 1989;
- 200,000 people were absent from work daily, causing a year's total of ten million lost man-days;
- inflation, taking account of suppressed inflation (unsatisfied demand for goods) and higher prices, was more than 19 per cent.

In 1991, GNP fell by a further 17 per cent and industrial production by 17 per cent 'or more'. See also 'Foreign Trade'.

**ECONOMIC UNION.** Association provisionally agreed by leaders of twelve republics in October 1991. Uncertainty remained over essential details, such as a central banking system, a common currency, and payment of tax contributions to the centre, when two months later the project was overtaken by the formation of a Commonwealth.★

**EDUCATION.** See 'Teaching'.

**ELDERS' COUNCIL.** Traditional body with which political authorities are still obliged to exist in some towns and villages after vainly attempting to hold it up to ridicule. In whole areas of the Caucasus and Central Asia former *kolkhoz* directors were often unable to put the collective to work properly until their nominations had been officially approved by the 'elders'. After the 1990 Osh riots (see 'Kirghizia'), 400 elders drawn from the warring Uzbek and Kirghiz communities assembled to find a solution to the question of building land allocations, which had caused so much bloodshed.

**ELECTIONS.** Empty exercise until the first 'free' elections to the new Soviet parliament in March 1989. Even then these were prepared in confusion. Election commissions, used to registering the name of one candidate chosen between Party organizations, were overwhelmed by the number of entries. Inside the Party, every organization wanted its own candidate. Otherwise, anyone could stand with the backing of a collective★ or 500 signatures. So, as well as checking credentials, the commission had to settle disputes. In many places a second round was needed because no one had thought to change a rule that a winner must have at least 51 per cent of the votes. Of the 1,500 electoral districts, 384 had lists with only one candidate, and 953 lists with only two. The remainder had up to a dozen. Although 85 per cent of candidates were Party members, the results included a huge victory for Baltic nationalists, the rejection of Party first secretaries in five major cities (including Moscow and Leningrad), and the defeat of five regional First Secretaries, including four in Central Asia. A marked feature was the drop, compared with earlier polls, in the number of worker candidates (only 23 per cent compared with 35.2 per cent in 1984) and of collective farmers (11.3 per cent compared to 16.1 per cent). Both figures were well below the two groups' share in society (38 per cent and 19 per cent respectively). The following year (1990) local and regional elections took place in even greater confusion, and in some places in violence. The defeat of the Party in several republics and cities led to clashes between the central and local authorities. Nationalist and reformist groups proved unable to form stable majorities, and democracy began to look like disorder and a blind struggle for power. In 1990 opinion polls, only 17 per cent of those questioned expressed confidence in their legislators.

**ELECTRICITY.** Energy supply in constant shortage only partly explained by Chernobyl.* In the first six months of 1986 there were record losses (500 million kilowatt-hours) in the distribution system. Between October 1986 and April 1987 production fell sharply due to breakdowns of old equipment and local resistance to the building of new installations (sixty projects abandoned in 1986–90). By 1991 the shortfall in output was 80 million kilowatts, and officials spoke of a 160 million kilowatt deficit – about half the existing capacity – 'in the near future'. In 1991, 12.5 per cent of Soviet electricity came from nuclear power stations, 70 per cent from thermal stations, and 18 per cent from hydro-electric plants. A generating capacity reserve of only 4–6 per cent (compared to 20–30 per cent in most Western countries) meant that any accident was liable to deprive large areas of power.

**EMIGRATION.** One-time trickle that quickly became a flood. Restrictions were eased grudgingly in 1987, after demonstrations and international pressure; then, in 1988, with a rush. In 1990, 400,000 left, double the 1989 figure. A law passed in May 1991 granted anyone freedom to emigrate as from 1993. The first wave of emigration permitted by *perestroika* involved whole communities – Jews, Germans, Pontine Greeks, Armenians – rather than individuals. But its volume raised problems abroad. In July 1988, the US cut the granting of immigration visas for budgetary reasons, then ceased to treat Soviet emigrants automatically as refugees. Jews who left with an Israeli visa, then switched destinations in Vienna, were exempt; but not Armenians, whose rate of departure had risen to 1,625 in June 1988. With 233,680 departures of all kinds – a third of them under 18 and a quarter retired people – 1988 became a watershed between group emigration and a new emigration, essentially of individuals wanting to escape from economic conditions. Western governments became increasingly selective, as applicants stormed the embassies of traditional host countries – Australia, New Zealand, Canada, the US. By August 1990 the US embassy in Moscow had 400,000 applications on its books, for only 60,000 places, of which 90 per cent were reserved for applicants with family connections. Up to 3 million people were expected to leave when the new law of 1991 became effective, according to Western estimates. But in the Soviet parliament, opponents of the measure gave an estimate of 7 million, saying the exodus of young skilled workers would impoverish society. Eastern as well as Western countries expressed alarm at the prospect of a Soviet invasion of their labour markets, and considered steps to tighten immigration laws. Ironically, free emigration had first been demanded by the West as a condition of helping the Soviet economy. For Jewish emigration, see separately 'Jews', 'Refuseniks'.

**EMPLOYMENT.** Up to 1991, still everyone's right under the Soviet constitution despite blatant contradiction by moves to the market. In 1988 Abel Aganbegyan* predicted that 16 million people, including 30–50 per cent of Soviet white-collar workers, would have to change their jobs by the year 2000. But he ruled out mass unemployment because, he said, millions of new jobs would be waiting to be taken over. Something like this happened when tens of thousands were made redundant in the Russian Federation by the closure or amalgamation of ministries and government offices; 56 per cent received different jobs in the same enterprise, and 26 per cent jobs in other fields. Eighteen per cent were given retirement. But in 1990 the state Labour Commission forecast that eventually one Soviet in four (40 million people) would lose his or her job through the closure of uneconomic enterprises. The forecast began to take on reality with the deepening economic crisis and, from January 1992, the closure of thousands of enterprises in republics as a result of the ending of Soviet state orders. See also 'Work'.

**ENERGIA.** Giant booster for space shuttles. First launched from Baikonur in 1986, it has eight liquid-hydrogen motors developing 170 million horsepower and is claimed to be the most powerful in the world. With a launch weight of 2,000 tonnes it can orbit vehicles of more than 100 tonnes. The rocket took nine years to develop and was central to plans for a permanently manned space* station until the 1991 economic crisis, when production ceased and it became the focus of attempts to sell off technology to the West.

**ENERGY.** Missing key to industrial renewal. Soviet plans for the period to the year 2000 were based on balancing a levelling-off of oil production by big increases in the output of natural gas, coal and nuclear energy. But in 1990, oil output fell by 6 per cent (to the 1978 level) because of delays in developing new fields and accidents, stoppages and spillages caused by an inability to carry out repairs. Officials said development of new fields in the Caspian Depression and the Yamal Peninsula was going 'slowly'. Gas production rose, but only by 2 per cent, while coal production declined by 9 per cent because of strikes, a wagon shortage and technical problems. Soviet power generation continues to be affected by a revision of plans since Chernobyl,★ a cut in the building of new stations, and the need to keep old equipment going. With supplies only 0.3 per cent above the 1989 level, in 1990 there were serious drops (up to 14 per cent) in Armenia, Georgia and Moldavia. Nine per cent of all Soviet energy production is wasted by old installations, double the international average. Yet the industry employs a tenth of the total labour force and in 1991 received 40 per cent of all industrial investment.

**ENTERPRISE.** General word for unit producing goods or services, most often a factory. Invariably state-owned until 1990, when the 1987 Law on Individual Economic Activity★ was amended to permit 'family enterprises' employing up to 200 people. In 1987 the Law on State Enterprises★ ended control of the latter by ministries and gave enterprises managerial and financial autonomy★ (one third in 1988, the rest in 1989). The Law was followed by a brief but spectacular wave of shop-floor elections, in which managers were chosen by employees. But the law's impact on the economy was limited by a system of 'state orders' that prevented enterprises from fixing prices, quotas or types of production; although 'autonomous', enterprises had little incentive to make profits since they themselves kept only 14.4 per cent, the rest going to feed the state budget or towards the running of the overseeing ministry. Above all, such enterprises lacked capable managers, accountants and decision-makers. Exclusively Soviet until the start of joint ventures,★ from the end of 1990 enterprises – now 'privatized'★ and often more simply called 'firms' – could be wholly or partly owned by foreign banks, companies or stockholders.

**ENVIRONMENT.** In 1991 officials gave measurements of toxic concentrations at 500 water points tested by the State Committee for Hydrometeorology. In seven rivers, including the Poltava in the Western Ukraine, the proportion of some highly dangerous compounds exceeded the safety limit a hundredfold. Each year industry sends 55 million tons of harmful substances into the atmosphere; and in nearly 130 towns the concentration of at least one harmful substance exceeds the safety level by a factor of ten or more on certain days. In one town, Bezmein, cement dust can surpass the limit 115-fold; in Volgograd and Kiev, hydrogen chloride can be over the limit by factors of sixty-eight and ten respectively; in Chimkent, in Kazakhstan, lead can be nineteen times over; in Omsk, acetaldehyde ninety-nine times; and in Ruzbezhny, nitrochlorobenzene two hundred times. Each year, according to the State Committee on Statistics, 250 million tons of dangerous industrial waste reaches dumps and slag heaps, where less than 40 million tons are decontaminated. See also 'Ecology', 'State Committee for the Environment'.

**EROFEEV,** Venedikt Vasilyevich (1938–1990). Idiosyncratic writer, famous for a single short novel, *Moskva-Petushki*, about an alcoholic tramp who stumbles about Moscow and sleeps in trains. Never part of the recognized 'dissident' movement but a defiant individualist, he lived for years in the sordid world of his anti-hero. He was discovered by *perestroika* shortly before his death.

**EROFEEV,** Viktor Vladimirovich (1932– ). Rare 'new' writer, like Vladimir Sorokhin, Dmitri Prigov and Tatiana Tolstoya, owing nothing to the vogue for books banned before 1986. In 1990 foreign translations introduced his novel *Russian Beauty* to Western readers. In 1979 he was persecuted by the Union of Writers for contributing to the illegal 'Metropol' collection published by Aksyonov,★ Vysotsky,★ Iskander★ and others. A full version of their 'Unofficial Almanac' was published in the Soviet Union in 1990.

**EROTICISM.** Notion alien to Russian, and subsequently to Soviet, culture. Confused with pornography by its defenders as well as its detractors, in the late 1980s it made a ponderous appearance in the arts – mainly literature, rarely in painting and sculpture, very occasionally in the cinema.

**ESPIONAGE.** Game altered, but not ended, by detente. Adapting slowly to foreign policy changes, in the late 1980s Soviet intelligence shifted its priority from military to commercial targets. Not in time to stop a row over the bugging of the new American embassy in Moscow (1987–88), and the same thing at the new Soviet embassy in Washington. (In the autumn of 1991 the new KGB chief, Bakatin,★ gave the US ambassador 'technical documentation' about the bugging, reportedly helping to save on the $220 million cost of a new building.) In September 1991 Soviet foreign intelligence activities were transferred from the KGB★ to a new organization under Primakov.★ By giving the KGB a purely security role, the move suggested a division similar to that between the CIA and the FBI in the United States, while the choice of Primakov, a Middle East expert, portended a shift from former Cold War targets to regional matters. In 1990–91 the KGB exploited propaganda and commercial potential by permitting four broadcasts by Kim Philby★ and selling film of the trial of Oleg Penkovsky.

**ESTONIA** (pop. 1.7 million). Republic★ restored to independent statehood in 1991 amid dreams of a prosperous economy, but having to reckon with a mixed population (65 per cent Estonian, 28 per cent Russian, 3 per cent Ukrainian and 2 per cent Byelorussian). Non-Estonians provide most of the unskilled labour. In 1987 Estonian experts produced a plan for 'financial autonomy', originally due to come into force in January 1990. On November 16, 1988, during a Union-wide debate on amending the constitution, the Estonian parliament declared the supremacy of Estonian over Soviet laws – a measure quickly declared unconstitutional by Moscow. A law was passed making Estonian the only official language and imposing a residence qualification on candidates in the 1990 republic and local elections. These 'harassments' caused Russian-speakers, mainly workers and technicians, to form so-called defence committees whose violent language alienated resident Russian intellectuals. Adding to the complexity, the Estonian Communist Party declared itself autonomous – the first in the Union to do so. In 1990 non-Estonians, under the banner of Inter-Front,* held strikes to demonstrate their importance to the Estonian economy. After the elections (which followed the Union-wide trend by returning a majority of nationalist candidates), the first wave of nationalism abated; the Estonian Communist Party suffered an eclipse (losing 57,000 of its 105,000 members); and a split appeared in Estonian political forces. In autumn 1990, the 'independent' government ran into trouble over a temporary milk and meat shortage caused by the abrupt ending of subsidies, and parliament was obliged to reintroduce partial price control. Generally higher price levels, and the efficiency of Estonian agriculture, saved the republic from the wave of hoarding and shortages that swept other parts of the Union in the winter of 1990–91. But an open conflict developed when the president of the Bank of Estonia, Rein Otsason, attacked President Savisaar's price policies for once again delaying the introduction of an Estonian currency, the 'crown', originally planned for December 1990. In March 1991 Estonians voted decisively for independence in a 'referendum' held simultaneously with a similar one in Latvia. In June 1991 the republic joined five others – Latvia, Lithuania, Georgia, Armenia and Moldavia – in boycotting discussion of a new draft Union treaty* (see 'Kishinev Forum'). But events moved faster than expected. On September 6, following the defeat of the 1991 *putsch*,* the new Union Security Council recognized Estonia's independence.

**ETHNIC CONFLICT.** Unforeseen consequence of relaxed central control, beginning cataclysmically with Sumgait* in February 1988. Over the next three years there were 4,648 officially listed pogroms,* leaving 946 dead, 18,652 injured, R10 million worth of material damage, and 800,000 people homeless. The exodus of 200,000 refugees (mainly Russian) from Central Asia threatened a serious shortage of scientists, engineers, doctors, nurses and skilled specialists.

**ETHNIC GROUPS.** Pieces of the ex-Soviet mosaic, numbering more than a hundred, of which twenty-four are more than a million strong. The roll includes 140 million Russians, 43 million Ukrainians, 11 million Byelorussians, 7 million Kazakhs, 7 million Tatars, 6 million Azeris, 4 million

Armenians, 3.5 million Georgians, 3 million Moldavians, 3 million Lithuanians, 3 million Tajiks, 2 million Turkmen, 2 million Chuvash, 1.4 million Latvians, 1.4 million Bashkirs, 1.2 million Mordvinians and 1 million Estonians. Until reduced by migration, there were 2 million Germans and 1.8 million Jews.

**EUROPEAN BANK FOR RECONSTRUCTION AND DEVELOP-MENT (EBRD).** London-based development bank of the European Community. First international financial organization of which the Soviet Union became a full member (April 1991). It gave the Soviet Union its first two loans – and in 1992 opened its doors to successor republics.

**EUROPEAN COMMUNITY (EC).** Body reviled as the economic arm of NATO, until the magic idea of a 'Common European Home'* made a possibly interesting financial partner. An early deal, in the 1980s, put 181,500 tons of EC surplus butter into Soviet shops. Moscow would have liked to see a formal relationship between the EC and Comecon,* but the EC refused to accept Moscow as Comecon's spokesman. After a period of coolness, contacts were re-established in 1986–87, and in June 1988 the Community and the Soviet Union signed a declaration of mutual recognition. In 1991, after a hiccup over Soviet actions in Lithuania, the EC agreed to give $1 billion in food aid; and permanent missions were exchanged between Moscow and Brussels. For further EC action, see 'Humanitarian aid'.

**EVA.** Association formed in 1990 'to bring a feminine face to business'. Chaired by a businesswoman, Natalia Bortchik, it started up seminars, lectures and commercial courses, mainly for women in service industries and shops.

**EX-.** New prefix in political life since expulsions ceased to lead automatically to extinction. Today ex-First Secretaries continue to live comfortably in most republics. Sergei Medunov, sacked for corruption in Krasnodar, has remained a Hero of Soviet Labour in Moscow; Vasoli Mzavanadze, fired for the same reason in Georgia, is at home enjoying retirement; Kunayev* in Kazakhstan is even back in parliament. No criminal proceedings have been taken against either Leningrad's Romanov* or Moscow's Grishin.* And Galina Brezhneva,* ex-wife of Churbanov,* continues to have her Mercedes and her luxurious dacha outside Moscow. In 1992 Gorbachev set a new style for ex-presidents.

**EXPORTS.** Dream of prosperity belied by the quality of Soviet manufactures. In 1990, 85 per cent of listed Soviet exports were still those of many under-developed countries: oil and gas, raw materials and semi-finished goods. In the first six months of 1991 exports were down 23 per cent (by value) compared with the same period the previous year. Oil exports were down 47 per cent and gas exports 6 per cent.

**EXTERNAL DEBT.** Nightmare of economic reformers. In September 1991 the Soviet Union owed an estimated $77 billion (including $17 billion in interest). The post-*putsch*\* authorities applied for rescheduling, saying they had a problem of liquidity, and that payment of interest would entail 'printing money' and dangerously increasing inflation. To reassure foreigners, eight independent republics (all except Ukraine, Uzbekistan, Georgia and the Baltic states) agreed to accept whatever was agreed as their share of the federal debt. In return, seventeen nations agreed to defer payment of principal on medium- and long-term debts contracted before January 1991, on condition that the republics kept up interest payments and pursued economic reforms. But by the end of February 1992, none of the others having transferred their share, 85 per cent of the down payments fell to Russia. Ukraine, by withdrawing all its assets from the Vnezekonombank,\* appeared to have indicated that it would not pay anything at all.

# F

**FALIN,** VALENTIN MIKHAILOVICH (1926–   ). Diplomat and journalist, in 1988 appointed successor to Anatoli Dobrynin* as head of the International Commission of the Central Committee, where he argued for pragmatism in foreign affairs. After unorthodox analyses while ambassador in Bonn (1971–78), he was sidelined to a secondary post in a department of the Central Committee. In 1983 he moved to the editorial board of *Izvestia*, and in 1986 was appointed head of the Novosti Press Agency.* His pragmatism once caused him to defend the Molotov-Ribbentrop Pact as a case of military expediency.

**FAMILY BENEFITS.** (1) 'Perks' provided by enterprises, such as vouchers for places in holiday camps, rest centres, creches etc.; (2) direct cash grants by the state. In 1990 the first kind was put in jeopardy by the 'privatization',* obliging managements to rationalize their budgets. The second was given greater importance, particularly in the case of low-income families, by price increases. Allowances in general were raised by 60–80 per cent. In addition there was special compensation in the form of increased children's allowances, depending on the circumstances of parents, with emphasis on the needs of single mothers. These included a R250 allowance on the birth of each child, plus a special supplement of R80–110 monthly for children up to 18 months. Republics were expected to add to these benefits. The average national wage at the time was R260 a month. In April 1991 there was a further revision, at the discretion of republics, following Union-wide price increases on most goods and services of about 250 per cent. But no amount of manipulation could keep up with inflation.* With the dissolution of the Union responsibility for providing state benefits fell entirely on the republics.

**FAMILY PLOTS.** See 'Private plots'.

**FAMILY REUNIFICATION.** Right denied to partners in marriages with foreigners and members of families separated by emigration until 1987, when concerted action, including a hunger strike by Soviet spouses, highlighted the enormity on the eve of the Soviet-American summit.

**FARM** (*Fyerm*). Term first used in 1987 to distinguish the newly proposed 'co-operative' and 'family' farms from collective farms (*kolkhozy**). The difference was that co-operative farms would be voluntary associations, whereas collective farms were the result of enforced collectivization. In the reformers' dream the 'farm' was either that of a hyper-mechanized American farmer or that of a small Dutch farmer with a house full of computers. The problem (see below) was to get volunteers. Of 24,000 farms in Russia in 1991, only 6,700 were started by workers coming from collective or state farms.

**FARMER.** Reformers' name for a new kind of being, hard-working and ambitious; everything the collective farmer is not. The reformers ignore facts of human nature and history: the lack of family farming tradition in vast areas that were still under serfdom only fifty years before the revolution; the peasant's inbred conservatism; the unwillingness of wives to become their husbands' unpaid assistants; a sense of equality in poverty dating from the old peasant commune (the *mir*); and deep suspicion of the law allowing leases. The economists see leases as giving security; most peasants see them as a way of nailing their children to the land. In May 1991 reformers claimed that there were 40–50,000 private farmers in the Soviet Union, including 24,000 in Russia. But with a stated average of only nine hectares, most such 'farms' were little more than private plots,* worked by collective farmers in their spare time. In December 1991 a Russian decree (copied in most other republics) gave collective and state farmers the right to leave their farms and start smallholdings. Farm managers were obliged to allocate them the necessary land within a month. In 1992 republics passed land laws allowing sales.

**FASHION.** Anarchy of styles beyond foreigners' comprehension. A penchant for Western models is made ridiculous by shortages. Designers fail to recognize their creations when they see them. Factories refuse a design unless the designer agrees to remove complicated features; then colours are changed in production. Moscow's first 'festival of fashion', staged in November 1987 with Zaitsev's* instant mannequins, picked off the street, highlighted the Soviet couturier's difficulties.

**FEDERAL COUNCIL.** Body created in 1990 to surround the President with representatives of the fifteen union republics (the mayors of Moscow and Leningrad could also be included on occasion). As well as strengthening the structure of federation the aim was to acquaint Gorbachev with each republic's views about what kind of federation should emerge from a new treaty of union. Separatist republics immediately saw it as a move to legitimize a central authority whose substance they rejected. They gave a similarly hostile reception to the creation in October 1990 of the Inter-Republic Economic Committee, a Federal Council task-force composed of scientists and officials. Despite improvements designed to make the Council a forum for decisions among republics, it died with other institutions in the aftermath of the 1991 *putsch*.*

**FEDERATION.** Structure created in 1922 to unite different peoples in a supra-national state. Seventy-five years later, after decades of intermittent agitation and repression, the argument over its future turned towards economics. The Estonian delegation used the 19th Party Conference* to demand wider economic and political powers for the republics, and greater independence for republic communist parties. The Conference resolved that these should be granted. But when, in October 1988, they failed to materialize in the draft for a new constitution, the Estonians proclaimed the supremacy of the Estonian constitution over the Soviet. Other republics were about to follow when, once again, economics came to the fore with the Soviet parliament's adoption of a plan for moving to the market.* This plan contained the principle of economic decentralization but was followed by a law confirming the pre-eminence of federal law in order to avoid a 'war of laws'. The choice had still to be made between federation, confederation or a Soviet 'Commonwealth'. In September 1990 Gorbachev proposed a new name for the structure: the 'Union of Sovereign Socialist States' (SSSG in Russian), while members of the Soviet of Nationalities* suggested 'Union of Sovereign Socialist Republics' or (to avoid arguments over the word 'socialist') 'Union of Euro-Asian Republics'. All except the Central Asian republics opposed the continuation of a single Soviet market, while Estonia and Lithuania took steps to create their own currencies and customs controls. The draft of the new union treaty* was approved by the Soviet parliament in December 1990 (keeping the name USSR) but rejected by so many republics that it had to be returned to the drawing-board. A successor was torpedoed by the 1991 *putsch*,* which gave the question of federation an entirely new dimension and led four months later to the agreement of eleven republics on the creation of a Commonwealth.*

**FILM-MAKERS' UNION.** Creative union* turned upside down at its fifth congress in 1986, through the ousting of its old bosses, Kulidzhanov and Bondarchuk, by the reformist directors Smirnov and Klimov.* Elem Klimov, especially, spoke for a group of liberal intellectuals devoted to *perestroika*. He immediately set up a committee to review films that had been shelved for political reasons for up to twenty-five years. He was supported by similar spirits in the new Theatre Workers Union* and (less politicized) the Union of Artists. In 1988 the Film-Makers' Union encouraged the setting up of separate professional associations (producers, actors, scriptwriters, critics) on the American pattern. In 1989 the Soviet cinema* was stopped in its tracks by orders to go commercial, and at the union's sixth congress in 1990 Klimov and Smirnov handed over to a more pragmatic leadership.

**FILSHIN,** GENNADI INNOKENTEVICH (1931– ). Economist and Russian deputy premier, co-author of the Russian Federation's 'Five Hundred Days' plan* for moving to a market economy. He resigned in February

1991 – the third minister to leave Yeltsin's* government in two months – following a financial scandal, exploited by Soviet Premier Pavlov.* (There was no evidence that Filshin himself had acted dishonourably.) He returned to the political scene in May 1991 as Russian Deputy Foreign Trade Minister.

**FINANCIAL AUTONOMY.** Status imposed by the 1987 Law on State Enterprises* (1988–89); not always welcomed when it killed off subsidized losers and saddled managers with a burden of responsibility that few wanted. Autonomy proved difficult to exercise in practice for a variety of reasons: absence of a real market, a shortage of competent decision-makers, the incoherence of successive economic measures, and lack of interest by workers. An unforeseen complication was the tendency of powerful sectors such as coal, oil and gold-mining to sit on their profits. Another was the authorities' inability to mobilize production workers for urgent but personally unrewarding tasks on behalf of the general economy – like helping to bring in the 1990 harvest.

**FINNS (1).** Unconscious visitors littering Russian and Baltic hotels on 'vodka tours' (over 400,000 annually).

**FINNS (2).** Ethnic community, 78,000-strong, in Soviet Karelia,* annexed after World War II.

**FIREARMS.** Weapons forever escaping from their legal possessors – soldiers, licensed sportsmen – into the hands of gangs and extremists. In July 1990, apropos of a peak of activity by 'private armies', the Minister of the Interior, Bakatin,* said there were 4.7 million registered guns in the country: 3.6 million privately owned and the rest with organizations. The police were still looking for 11,680 stolen weapons, after 164,000 – including 24,000 rifles – had been confiscated or handed in. The situation deteriorated gravely with the worsening conditions of army life, and by the winter of 1991–92 even tanks and artillery pieces were passing to armed groups in Georgia and elsewhere.

**FIVE HUNDRED DAYS PLAN.** Programme drawn up by radical economist Grigori Yavlinsky* and seen by partisans of Boris Yeltsin* as a formula for rapid transition to the 'market'. Advanced in the summer of 1990, it was far more radical than a plan prepared by advisers of Ryzhkov* two months before. A compromise worked out by a committee under Shatalin* was put before the Soviet parliament in the autumn. It involved 'soaking up' 200 million surplus roubles by the sale of apartments and state property, the closure or amalgamation of ministries, and a partial decollectivization of agriculture. But in deference to public feeling, price increases were put off until later – which lessened the plan's credibility. The compromise emerged from the Soviet parliament in tatters. The

Russian parliament, which had meanwhile adopted Yavlinsky's plan and voted for it to start in October 1990, postponed it to January 1991, then abandoned it altogether, saying part of the 500 days had already been lost and that in any case it had been sabotaged by the 'centre'. Yavlinsky returned to Harvard, where with American help he worked on another plan, geared to a programme of US aid.

**FIVE-YEAR PLANS.** Method of the past (see 'Plans'), retained for strategic planning. Plans were officially designated as follows: VIII, 1966–70; IX, 1971–75; X, 1976–80; XI, 1981–85; XII,1986–90; XIII,1991–95; XIV, 1995–2000. (They lapsed with the end of the Union in December 1991.)

**FOREIGN MINISTRY** (popularly the 'MID'). For years a Soviet professional backwater, the home of bureaucrats and freeloaders, owing to Brezhnev's and Gromyko's custom of conducting foreign policy through Party channels. Shevardnadze's* first act was to cut out dead wood and corruption, and an example was made of Tokyo ambassador Pyotr Abrasimov, dismissed for smuggling home Japanese videos. In 1987 Shevardnadze summoned senior staff and diplomats from abroad to lecture them on new rules of behaviour and flexibility. The reformed spirit appeared to survive Shevardnadze's departure (December 1990) and short-lived succession by a conscientious career diplomat, Aleksandr Bessmertnykh.* After the 1991 *putsch*\* a meeting of the MID and the foreign ministers of eleven republics decided to set up a Council of Foreign Ministers to act as the country's top diplomatic body. In November 1991 Gorbachev sought to renew his authority by bringing back Shevardnadze. Three weeks later the Soviet Ministry was physically taken over and suppressed as such by Yeltsin on the eve of the Alma-Ata* conference, which led to the creation of active MIDs in eleven republics. As a temporary measure it was agreed that the interests of the new Commonwealth* states would be represented abroad by Russian embassies.

**FOREIGN POLICY.** For the first three years of *glasnost* (1985–88), Soviet foreign policy remained almost wholly a professional matter, with none of the public debate taking place on domestic issues. In the words of a Western commentator, the 'New Thinking'* advanced in 1986–87 're- mained a rather slim body of principles accompanying diplomatic over- tures.' Gorbachev did not attack Brezhnev's foreign policy, as he did his domestic policy, until 1988 when the Geneva agreement to end the war in Afghanistan started a general debate on the use of force, the role of the military, the requirements of national security etc. Inside government, changes had started with Shevardnadze's house-clearing of the Foreign Ministry,* followed by moves to free foreign policy from imprisoning ideological restraints and to institute an element of pragmatism. Inside the Party (which up to 1988 continued to assume a role in foreign affairs) the argument was over East-West confrontation. At opposite poles were Ligachev's★ argument that one must 'proceed from the class nature of international relations' and Shevardnadze's★ assertion that 'the struggle between the two spheres is no longer the prevailing trend in the present era.' Gorbachev took a middle line: that although the foreign policies of states had a class nature, this did not mean that international relations could be reduced to a struggle between two systems. Later, with the ending of the Cold War, Soviet foreign policy took on new dimensions. Moscow began to work with the United Nations and the West for the settlement of regional problems, in the Middle East, South-East Asia, Africa★ and − closer to home − Afghanistan. A development complicated by the break-up of the Union, which led to the pursuit of separate policies, often in inexperienced hands.

**FOREIGN POLICY ASSOCIATION.** 'Independent' association devoted to 'developing new political thinking in international affairs'. Its thirty-four founders (February 1991) included the Diplomatic Academy, the Bank for Foreign Economic Activity, the Soviet Peace Fund, the Moscow and Leningrad City Councils, the Tass news agency, the Ministry for the Aviation Industry and the Ministry of Communication. Edvard Shevard-nadze★ was appointed first chairman.

**FOREIGN TRADE.** Exchange upset by the 1987 fall in oil prices and a sharp rise in import costs. Four years later the situation was in crisis due to the state of the domestic economy. In 1991 total foreign trade turnover fell at current prices by 38 per cent (to R81.5 billion compared with R135.5 billion in 1990). Exports fell by 28.4 per cent (to R43.5 billion) and imports by 46.2 per cent (to R38 billion). Internally, efforts were made to ease bureaucratic restrictions. In 1988 the ending of monopoly control by the lethargic Foreign Trade Ministry enabled twenty production minis-tries and seventy large enterprises to start trading without an intermedi-ary. The measure was gradually extended. But the creation of foreign exchange funds was slow to get going and the State Commission for Foreign Trade (watchdog of state interests) heavy-handed. In September 1991 the Ministry of Foreign Economic Relations was abolished and replaced by an inter-republican body responsible for co-ordinating trade and co-operation among the twelve republics remaining after the depar-ture of the Baltic states. From 1992 this became a disputed function of the Commonwealth.★

**FOREIGN TRADE ORGANIZATION (FTO).** Office formerly in each industrial ministry, in charge of all business between Soviet enterprises and foreign companies. In 1988 the sudden closure of FTOs caused a counter-productive 'feudalization' of foreign trade, due to managements' lack of experience and connections. By 1990 producers were virtually bankrupt. They had no foreign exchange with which to pay suppliers, since the Bank for Foreign Trade (*Vnezhekonombank**) refused to meet the bills of firms 'in the red', on the ground that they were now on their own. Later restrictions were eased slightly and firms could buy foreign currency at auctions.

**FOUNDATIONS.** See 'Funds'.

**FRIENDSHIP.** Sentiment given a political dimension with 'friendship among peoples'; since diminished by Moscow's inability to continue picking up friends' lunch tickets. A variant, 'internationalism', died in Afghanistan.

**FRONTIER.** Once precious hymen protected by 230,000 KGB border guards — till the duty and personnel were transferred to the army after the 1991 *putsch*.* In 1987 virginity was lost to Mathias Rust,* ironically on 'Border Guards' Day' when a hundred border guards were arrested in Moscow for drunkenness.

**FUNDS (FOUNDATIONS).** Public organizations, mostly created after 1986, to receive gifts for charitable purposes. The largest, the Soviet Cultural Fund,* collected and preserved works of art and historical relics. Other funds were the USSR Ecological Fund, the Soviet Fund for Health and Charity and the Lenin Soviet Children's Fund.

**FYODOROV,** SVIATOSLAV NIKOLAEVICH (1927– ). Rouble millionaire and eye surgeon. When private enterprise was still a dirty word he turned his micro-surgery clinic into a boundless foreign currency earner, later investing part of the profits in the Moscow racecourse casino. Academician turned pro-reform deputy, in 1991 he headed the Soviet Fund for Health and Charity while leading the life of a gentleman farmer.

# G

**G-7.** Group of Seven Most Industrialized Nations (USA, Britain, Canada, France, Germany, Italy and Japan); last address of Soviet appeals for massive economic aid. In 1991 Gorbachev addressed its July 'summit' in London. Members agreed to recommend Moscow for associate membership of the International Monetary Fund but delayed a collective decision on aid until they could be sure who would be in charge at the receiving end, and had evidence of a coherent reconstruction plan. After the Soviet break-up they planned to meet again on the question at the end of January 1992.

**GAGAUZ.** Bulgarian minority of 173,000, of whom 138,000 live in Moldavia.* In 1989, feeling threatened by Moldavian nationalism, Gagauz deputies declared an autonomous republic. In 1990 tension grew over attempts from Kishinev* to impose the Moldavian language. Defying the capital, the Gagauz held elections. The Moldavian government declared a state of emergency and called for volunteers to 'protect Moldavian territorial integrity'. After serious incidents, Gorbachev effected a precarious conciliation. New troubles arose when, following the August 1991 *putsch*,* Moldavia expressed the intention of joining Romania and accused minorities of having supported the putschists.

**GALICH,** ALEKSANDR ARKADYEVICH (real name, Ginzburg – 1919–1977). Satirical poet and guitarist, expelled from the Union of Writers in 1971 and forced to emigrate in 1974. His popularity survived his accidental death and gave him an immense come-back in the 1980s.

**GAMBLING.** Historic Russian passion supposed to have been relegated to the past by communism; now an approved source of revenue – from lotteries, racecourse betting, slot-machines and casinos.* But the big money is still behind closed doors, where hundreds of thousands of roubles change hands in a single game, most often backgammon. A 1988 law prescribes fines or a prison term. But compared with the sums involved, the fines (up to R1,000) are trivial.

**GAMSAKHURDIA,** ZVIAD KONSTANTINOVICH (1939– ). Human rights activist turned Georgian tyrant. Soon after being acclaimed the Soviet Union's first freely elected republican president, in 1990, he denounced all opponents as agents of Moscow and mounted a blockade against South Ossetia.* In September 1991 increasing resistance to his dictatorial rule (muzzling of the Press, arrest of critics) led to public demonstrations and the defection of his Foreign Minister and the commander of the national guard, Tengiz Kitovani. Three months later the latter moved to depose Gamsakhurdia, surrounding him in the parliament building. In two weeks' fighting some eighty people died (see 'Tbilisi') before, on January 6, 1992, Gamsakhurdia and his bodyguard escaped in an armoured convoy to Armenia. In Tbilisi, a government of national unity was proclaimed by the former premier, Tengiz Sigua. But the emergence of factions and the reappearance on the streets of Gamsakhurdia supporters showed that Georgia's troubles were far from over. No one could yet predict what might come of an offer by Shevardnadze* to return to Georgian politics.

**GAS.** Since 1986 the main source of Soviet energy* (meeting 32 per cent of needs) and an important hard currency earner through exports to Western Europe. Production has risen steadily: 407,000 million cubic metres in 1979, 770,000 million in 1988, 850,000 million (planned) in 1995. But there are geographical and technical limitations, and in 1991 exports were down 6 per cent against the same period in 1990. The chief gas centre, Yamburg, is 200 miles north of the Arctic Circle; and of the 197,000 miles of pipeline, 25,000 – plus most of the turbine pumping stations – must be replaced by the year 2000. Yamburg was developed under the twelfth Five-Year Plan (1986–90), which also included construction of a 4,600-kilometre pipeline to Eastern Europe and six new pipelines to the Soviet interior. These would complete a 36,000-kilometre network built in 1981–84. In 1991, 205 million Soviet users were supposed officially to have had access to natural gas. But plans to equip rural areas were far behind schedule. A shortage of sheet metal caused a deficit of one million household cookers. A serious problem is defective piping, the cause in June 1989 of the Bashkiria disaster (see 'Accidents').

**GATT** (General Agreement on Tariffs and Trade). UN-sponsored device for reducing world trade barriers; long decried, like the IMF,* as an economic tool of American imperialism. In 1986, having fourteen years earlier refused an invitation to join GATT's Tokyo Round, Moscow applied for admission. Its application was turned down on technical grounds (the US insisting on first seeing a 'real change' in US-Soviet relations), but in 1990 it received observer status.

**GAYDAR**, YEGOR TIMUROVICH (1956– ). Economist made Deputy Premier of Russia (November 1991). A graduate of Moscow State University, he replaced Yavlinsky* as wonder worker of radical economic reform. His previous career was outside politics: as a journalist with *Kommunist* and *Pravda*, then as director of the Institute of Economic Policy. In January 1992 he emerged as architect of prices liberalization, which caused him to be stigmatized as a privileged technocrat, forgetful of the human dimension of reforms.

**GDLYAN,** TELMAN KHORENOVICH (1940–   ) and **IVANOV,** NIKOLAI. Prosecutors charged with investigating corruption in Uzbekistan,\* later dismissed for using strong-arm methods. The affair became a political issue when Gdlyan and Ivanov became candidates in the 1989 parliamentary elections, claiming to have been victimized by 'people in high places'. When they directly accused Politburo members Solomentsev, Ligachev\* and Chebrikov,\* the presidium of the outgoing Supreme Soviet charged them with defamation. In fact, they were protected by parliamentary immunity. To clear the case up, the new parliament appointed a commission of investigation, chaired by Roy Medvedev.\* After a long and contentious inquiry the commission found that Gdlyan and Ivanov had indeed obtained results by the use of blackmail, improper arrests and intimidation of witnesses. In 1991, while Ivanov occupied himself with parliamentary duties, Gdlyan formed the People's Party of Russia.

**GEORGIA** (pop. 5.4 million). Former Union republic with a fierce history of nationalism – the only one, apart from the Baltic states, not to sign the Alma-Ata\* agreement. Situated between the Caucasus and the Black Sea, its population comprises 69 per cent Georgians, 9 per cent Armenians, 7 per cent Russians, 5 per cent Azeris, 2 per cent Ossetes and 8 per cent a mixture of smaller minorities. There are two autonomous republics (Abkhazia and Adzharia) and a former autonomous region, South Ossetia, arbitrarily suppressed in 1991. Georgian nationalism, driven underground in 1921 (when the independent republic set up by Mensheviks in 1917 was taken over by Bolsheviks), re-emerged in the freer conditions provided by *perestroika*. With it emerged divisions among Georgians themselves, as well as frictions with the Abkhaz and Ossetes. (Georgians also oppose the return of Meskhetian Turks.\*) From 1988 a series of bloody incidents was triggered by the revolt of non-Georgians against 'Georgian imperialism'. In April 1989 disturbances in Abkhazia\* caused Georgians to demonstrate in the streets of Tbilisi. When they refused to disperse, they were violently set on by troops of the MVD\* (see 'Tbilisi') and twenty were killed. Stunned, the already precariously balanced communist government severed all relations with Moscow. The following winter, riots in South Ossetia\* caused the republic authorities to impose a blockade, adding further to anarchy preceding the 1990 elections. (Rival factions engaged in shoot-outs, and a fire mysteriously consumed local KGB archives.) A month before voting, moderate intellectuals formed a coalition, the Round Table, temporarily reconciling the two main wings of the Georgian independence movement under the leadership of Zviad Gamsakhurdia.\* Foreign observers were invited to witness what was billed as the Soviet Union's first 'multi-party' election, contested by no less than thirty-five parties. With a 65 per cent turnout the Round Table won 54 per cent and the Communist Party 24.4 per cent. The new parliament immediately voted Gamsakhurdia chairman, put the republic under the protection of Saint George, and declared its refusal to sign a new Union Treaty with Moscow. Soon afterwards, a dissident Round Table faction joined extra-parliamentary opponents to form a 'Georgian National Congress', where-upon Gamsakhurdia suspended the Soviet-based constitution and the following year (1991), encouraged by a pro-independence referendum result and his own popular election as president, turned Georgia into a *de facto* dictatorship. In August, moves by Gamsakhurdia to suppress the opposition caused mass demonstrations in front of the Tbilisi parliament building, in which police opened fire and killed four people. When the opposition was joined by defecting deputies, the Foreign Minister and half the National Guard, the Western media prepared to bury the Georgian 'liberator' they had earlier espoused. For the events of winter 1991–92 see 'Gamsakhurdia', 'Tbilisi'.

**GERMAN,** ALEKSEI BORISOVICH (1938– ). Film-maker sidelined under Brezhnev. His works were among the first to be released by the Klimov* decensoring committee in 1986. Among them were *My Friend Ivan Lapshin* (a picture of small-town life in the 1930s) and a famous war film, *Proverka na Dorogakh* ('Control of the Streets'). In 1987, in a poll of twelve leading critics, the former narrowly beat Eisenstein's *Battleship Potemkin* as the best ever Soviet film.

**GERMANS.** Long-established dwellers on the Volga until deported to Central Asia after the Nazi invasion. In 1989 they woke up to their situation. Some of them elected to return to their roots in Germany (148,000 in 1990), the rest to return to the Volga despite opposition from the Russian inhabitants of Saratov and Volgograd. A proposal to avoid this by creating an autonomous region round Kaliningrad was dropped in 1990 under the impact of German reunification and in view of possible Lithuanian independence. Some of those deciding to remain then formed a movement called 'Revival' (*Vozrozhdeniye*), still with the idea of restoring an autonomous region on the Volga (the movement split in 1991 on tactical questions); others voted for an 'Association of Germans of the USSR' with a special status in the Russian Federation. In Kazakhstan the one million Germans remaining after mass emigration became preoccupied with the problems of existence in a land of deserted villages. The number arriving in the Federal Republic had meanwhile caused some Germans, like the Social Democrat Oskar Lafontaine, to think that it was time to 'help our compatriots in the Soviet Union to stay where they are and join in developing the region where they live'. In September 1991, Sobchak* invited Kazakhstan Germans to come and settle in deserted villages round Leningrad, and in 1992 Bonn put pressure on Yeltsin to set up an 'Autonomous Republic of the Volga' with German aid.

**GERMAN-SOVIET PACT.** Pact signed by Foreign Ministers Molotov★ and Ribbentrop on August 23, 1939. Secret clauses partitioned Poland and gave the Baltic states, Bessarabia and Transylvania to the USSR. The treaty is now admitted to have been immoral. Its anniversary is commemorated with bitterness in the Baltic states and Moldavia, and elsewhere with shame.

**GERMANY.** Historic enemy reunified in October 1990. Like real capitalists, the Soviets turned their agreement into cash: $10 billion just for withdrawing their troops, $29 billion of aid and credits. In the USSR, people followed what happened indifferently, more concerned with shopping than with geopolitics. The Soviet-German treaty of reunification was eventually ratified in March 1991 after stormy parliamentary debates.

**GINZBURG,** EVGENIA SEMYONOVNA (1904–1977). Early Party activist and survivor of Kolyma labour camp. She described her experiences in a classic of the Gulag, *Krutoy marshrut*, published in English in two volumes: *Journey into the Whirlwind* and *Within the Whirlwind*. Released after ten years, in 1947, she stayed in Magadan to be near the man who became her second husband. She was accompanied for a time by her son Vasily, the writer Aksyonov.★ Although she was rehabilitated in 1956, her book was not published in the Soviet Union until after her death. In 1988 the Sovremennik Theatre staged *The Hard Road*, based on the book. The packed audience was rent by arguments between a new generation of sceptics and those who, like Ginzburg, stayed faithful to communism, which had merely been 'betrayed' by Stalin.

**GIPSIES.** Nomadic community, an estimated half million strong, living mostly in European Russia, Byelorussia, Ukraine, Moldavia and the Baltic republics. In addition to Romany, nearly all speak a local language and (making a precise count difficult) may register their children as members of the local nationality. A separate group of 8,000, the 'Mugat', live in Central Asia. Attempts to settle them have only partly succeeded. Most gipsies continue to roam the countryside, entering cities to beg or sell small artefacts.

**GLASNOST.** Pillar of reforms defined by Gorbachev in his book *Perestroika* as 'openness in public affairs, in every sector of life'. Although *glasnost* was first dismissed abroad, and even at home, as 'cosmetic', its application in 1986 transformed Soviet existence. At first applied to cultural life and the press, it quickly came to mean everyone's right to information and discussion with a say at work and in day-to-day affairs. Later it invaded politics and history, enabling the Soviet people to know what was going on in the country and the world. In December 1991 Western governments made respect for *glasnost* and human rights a condition of recognizing the newly independent republics.

**GLAVKOSMOS.** Soviet space* agency, created in 1986 to exploit the success of Soviet launchers and the interruption to American commercial launchings by the 'Challenger' disaster. At the time the market was estimated at $3 billion a year, with forty-five satellites waiting to be orbited. When a Glavkosmos delegation visited Houston, the Americans were embarrassed to learn that a US satellite launch by a Soviet Proton rocket would cost $40 million, compared with $80 million for a launch by the European Space agency and $200 million for a launch by an American vehicle. In July 1990 the US government approved an agreement whereby America's United Technologies Corporation would use Glavkosmos *Zenit* rockets to launch commercial satellites from Australia in 1995. By the end of 1991 virtually everything in the Soviet space inventory was for sale.

**GLAVLIT.** See 'Censorship'.

**GLAZUNOV,** ILIA SERGEYEVICH (1930–   ). Popular painter of monumental canvases, an uninhibited self-publicist who explains the hostility of colleagues as envy of the millions attracted by his exhibitions. Enemies describe him as a mediocre artist who, when it suited, stooped to becoming a Brezhnevian court painter. His apartment is a museum of icons and antiques, his studio as vast as his pictures, which are largely devoted to literary subjects such as the Russia of Boris Godunov and the defeat of the Tatars. His gigantic canvas, 'Twentieth Century', depicts a host of public figures from Churchill to Gorbachev. Guests are left to contemplate his works with the help of recordings of Beethoven.

**GOLD.** Customary safety device for balancing deficits with hard-currency trading partners. Suddenly made to look shaky when in September 1991 Yavlinsky* told Moscow television viewers that Soviet gold reserves had dwindled to 240 metric tons, worth less than $3 billion at the time. Most Western experts had put the reserve at five to eight times that amount. Yavlinsky estimated that the country sold off two thirds of its gold in 1990 and that for some time gold sales had been running at more than 400 tons annually, well above the production rate. Some suspicion existed that Yavlinsky might have exaggerated the figure to prod Western governments into granting Moscow relief on external debt* payments. Gold production figures have not been officially published since 1928.

**GORBACHEV,** MIKHAIL SERGEYEVICH (1931–   ). Author of *perestroika*, catalyst of detente, liquidator of the Soviet empire, last head of the Union. The son of a tractor driver in Privolnoy village, Stravropol *krai*, Gorbachev at 15 became a combine operator's assistant while continuing school. At 18 he was awarded the Red Banner of Labour for agricultural and Komsomol work. In 1950 Gorbachev entered Moscow State University Law Department, where he met and married (1954) Raisa Maximovna Titorenko (see Gorbacheva, Raisa, below). In 1955 he graduated and returned to Stavropol, where he soon became head of the city, then the *krai*, Komsomol Committee. In 1962 he transferred to the *krai* party organization. At the same time he took a correspondence course with the Stavropol Agricultural Institute, graduating (in economics) in 1967. In 1966 he was elected first secretary of the Stavropol *gorkom*\* and in 1970 of the *kraikom*. He had meanwhile made his first known visit abroad, in 1969, to Czechoslovakia. (Subsequent journeys were to Belgium, 1972; West Germany, 1975; Canada, 1983; and Britain, 1985.)

At the Twenty-fourth Party Congress in 1971 Gorbachev was elected a member of the Central Committee, where his high-level friendships came to include Andropov,\* Suslov\* and Kosygin.\* In 1978 he took over as head of the Central Committee agricultural department following the success in Stavropol *krai* of the Ipatovsky\* agricultural experiment. He was also elected a Central Committee Secretary and candidate member of the Politburo (full membership, 1980). In 1979 he stood in Ipatovsky for election to the Supreme Soviet, and in 1980 in a Siberian *krai* for the Russian parliament. Partly due to weather, the harvests during his Secretaryship were disappointing, and but for Brezhnev's death (November 1982) his political rise could have ended. Caught in the succession struggle between Andropov and Chernenko, he supported Andropov, and, when Andropov sickened, became his *de facto* deputy, supervised by Ustinov\* and Gromyko.\* On Andropov's death (February 10, 1984), Chernenko's seniority and Gorbachev's relative inexperience caused the Politburo to name Chernenko his successor, with Gorbachev as second-in-command. On Chernenko's death within barely a year, a majority in the Politburo, intent on continuing Andropov's clean-up, gave Gorbachev the advantage over his chief rival, the former Leningrad Party boss, Grigori Romanov.\* He was elected General Secretary on March 10, 1985, and against opposition from Party hard-liners, proceeded to implement the programme of reforms denoted by the catchwords *perestroika*,\* *glasnost*\* and 'new thinking'.\* As part of the last he undertook the withdrawal from Afghanistan\* and the ending of the Cold War.

In 1988 Gorbachev took over from Gromyko as Chairman of the Presidium of the Supreme Soviet; on March 15, 1990 the Congress of People's Deputies\* elected him the country's first executive President with greatly increased power; and in July 1990 he was re-elected Secretary General by the Twenty-eighth Congress\* of the Party. But despite this seemingly strong position, he still faced hostility and obstruction from inside the bureaucracy. Simultaneously plagued by secession among republics, and attacked for the slowness of reforms by 'democrats' under Yeltsin,\* in the winter of 1990-91 he tilted towards the right, notably in his appointments. The move alienated allies such as Yakovlev\* and Shevardnadze\* and led to his personal isolation. Soon afterwards he 'corrected course' by presenting the Party's July plenum\* with a social-democratic programme and proposing acceptance of a liberal union treaty.\* This was too much for the small group of right-wing diehards who staged the August *putsch*.★ For three days Gorbachev and his family were held under house arrest in the Crimea. Liberated, thanks to the resistance of Yeltsin and others in Moscow, he returned to the capital in a politically weakened state. Confronted by critical deputies, he admitted having made serious misjudgements, 'suspended' the Communist Party, ordered high-level ministerial replacements, and called an emergency session of the Congress of People's Deputies, which approved an interim form of government pending agreement on a possible confederation. But Gorbachev failed to realize how much moral and actual authority he had lost by his appointment of the *putsch* leaders. Nor did he realize what power had been given to Yeltsin by the worsening economic situation, and near exhaustion of the federal treasury by republics' failure, often deliberate, to hand over their contributions. In November the last attempt at a union treaty was given a fatal blow by the overwhelming vote of the Ukrainian people for complete independence. Three weeks later Yeltsin took revenge for his four-year humiliation in the Central Committee★ by way of the Minsk★ and Alma-Ata★ agreements, setting up the Commonwealth★ and simultaneously destroying both the Union and the presidency. In his last days in office, Gorbachev regained a stature that had recently eluded him, finally accepting the inevitable and handing over with grace. His conduct contrasted with that of Yeltsin, whose haste to oust Gorbachev physically from the Kremlin even dismayed some supporters. In 1992 few people believed that he would long limit his energies to academic directorship of the newly created Gorbachev Foundation.

**GORBACHEVA**, RAISA MAXIMOVNA, *née* TITORENKO (1932– ). School-teacher, sociologist and candidate in philosophical sciences (Ph.D). She met and married Mikhail Gorbachev in 1954, when both were students at Moscow State University. Her candidate's thesis (1967) was presented to Moscow State Pedagogical Institute and concerned the daily life of collective farm workers in the Stavropol region. From 1985, as wife of the General Secretary, she became active in the arts and was sometimes seen as effectively the Minister of Culture. In 1987 she became a founder and board member of the Soviet Cultural Fund. A strong personality ill suited to secondary roles, she attempted, sometimes maladroitly, to create the role of 'first lady' in a country where husbands and wives keep out of each other's professional lives. After first winning marks for giving foreigners a sophisticated image of the Russian woman, she attracted criticism for seeming 'too forward'; and campaigns of defamation focused on her personal spending and her influence over appointments. The Gorbachevs have a daughter, Irina (born 1959), a doctor married to another doctor, and two grandchildren. In August 1991 Raisa Gorbacheva was severely unnerved by three days under arrest with her husband and their family in their Crimean holiday home. She returned to Moscow in time to launch an autobiography in which she referred to the strain of living under constant political threat from Party conservatives.

**GORBUNOVS,** ANATOLIJS; previously Anatoly Valeriyanovich Gorbunov (1942– ). Former Secretary of the Latvian Communist Party Central Committee, appointed Chairman of the Presidium of the Latvian Supreme Soviet, i.e. formal president, in October 1988. A rare popular communist who has maintained good relations with the Latvian Popular Front.

**GORDIEVSKY,** OLEG ANTONOVICH (1938– ). Double agent who defected to London in 1985. His importance may have been exaggerated by Western intelligence services, which claimed that he helped to neutralize Soviet contingency plans for a nuclear attack. When his revelations were published in the West, the KGB unexpectedly gave them publicity in order to 'put things into proportion'. He was sentenced to death *in absentia*. In 1991 he was cleared of all charges in the wake of the *putsch\** and reunited with his wife and children, till then held under surveillance in Russia.

**GORKOM.** Party committee in town or city.

**GORKY,** MAXIM (1868–1936), real name Aleksei Maksimovich Peshkov. Writer of diminished reputation. His image suffered fatally during the debate over Stalinism, when pictures showed him visiting 'work' camps and naively supporting the official picture of the Gulag. In 1990, Moscow's Gorky Street reverted to its old name, Tver Street. But Gorky Park stayed the same: a favourite haunt of families on Sunday, veterans on Victory Day, and lovers and tourists throughout the week.

**GORKY** (city). City and port on the Volga, 500 km from Moscow; home-in-exile (1980–87) of Andrei Sakharov.\* In 1990 it was reopened to foreigners and given back its old name, Nizhny-Novgorod.

**GORSHKOV,** ADMIRAL SERGEI GEORGYEVICH (1910–1988). Architect of the Soviet high seas fleet. Retired without ceremony, in December 1985, and replaced by Admiral Chernavin, a submariner. The creation of an enormous surface fleet, intended to rival that of the US Navy and carry the Soviet flag to all points of the globe, quickly became an anachronism. In the 1970s its 'threat' was rattled like a collecting box by western naval lobbies. A decade later Gorshkov was almost forgotten.

**GOSAGROPROM** (*Gosudarstvennyi Agropomyshlennyi Komitet* – State Agro-Industrial Committee). Super-ministry established in 1985, replacing five ministries and state committees with a single organization responsible for the whole agro-alimentary network. A symbol of the time when it was thought possible to improve the economic system without changing it radically. Its failure was one of Gorbachev's first disappointments. Agriculture continued to deteriorate, and Gosagroprom was no more than a cosmetic. After developing into a bureaucratic colossus staffed by officials of the previous ministries, it was ignominiously disbanded in March 1989. See also 'Agriculture'.

**GOSBANK.** See 'State Bank'.

**GOSKINO.** State Committee for the cinema. At the end of the 1980s its continuing monopoly of film distribution contributed to the artistic death of the Soviet cinema.*

**GOSKOMSTAT.** State Committee for Statistics, for years serving to sustain the illusions of rulers and public alike. As statistician-in-chief, Stalin had the bright idea of the so-called 'biological yield' (a glance at the density of growing crops) on which to base harvest statistics. Until 1986 many important statistics were simply kept secret. Hence public ignorance about anything from cotton production to life expectation. Military statistics were never published, with the result that the only figures came from NATO intelligence sources. Since 1986 Goskomstat has published figures on civil industry, agricultural production, health, social welfare, population etc. In 1987 the Ministry of the Interior began to publish criminal statistics, and the Foreign and Defence Ministries details of force deployments and military expenditure. But official figures, whether of the former Union or of independent republics, should be treated with caution. Figures for farm and industrial output take no account of quality; monetary figures are often made meaningless by the depleted value of the rouble; demographic statistics are confused by the tendency of some ethnic minorities to register as members of the regional majority; and defence statistics are complicated by differences of accounting methods vis-à-vis the West.

**GOSPLAN** (*Gosudarstvennyi Planovyi Komitet* – State Planning Committee). Former state within the state, shaken but not eliminated by the reforming Law on State Enterprise of 1987–88. The law removed Gosplan's political power but preserved its technical function: to draw up the State plan* for submission to the Party leadership and government, then oversee its fulfilment. Enterprises* were unable to profit from their new freedom until the reform was extended to all the organs of the Plan (Gossnab,* Goszakaz* etc.), a move not made until 1990.

**GOSPRYOMKA** (*Gosudarstvennaya Priyomka Gotovykh Izdelii* – State Inspection of Production). Name given to a system of quality control introduced at the beginning of 1987 but soon ineffective due to pressure on inspectors by the management of enterprises, and the protests of workers who lost their bonuses when their production quota was not fulfilled. Gospryomka replaced an earlier system of inspection by so-called technical control departments (OKT). These were subordinate to the enterprise management, whereas Gospryomka technicians and officials were employees of the State Committee on Standards (Gosstandard*). Gospryomka inspectors were well paid but subject to deductions in the event of complaints. In the first month of operation (January 1987), Gospryomka rejected 15–20 per cent of the output of the 1,500 enterprises subjected to control, causing a lowering of national production. In some factories it was necessary to hold back 80–100 per cent. After some months Gospryomka existed only on paper.

**GOSSNAB** (*Gosudarstvennyi Nablyudenye* – State Committee for Technical Supplies and Materials). A kind of civilian Ordnance Corps for putting suppliers in touch with clients. Suppressed in 1990.

**GOSSTANDARD** (*Gosudarstvennyi Standard* – State Committee for Control of Quality and Standardization). In October 1990 it signed an agreement with an American company, Globetech, covering use of Globetech laboratories, the training of specialists, and the setting up of Soviet control laboratories to meet international market requirements. In 1991 Globetech opened a Moscow office and a technical centre for the programme in the US.

**GOSTELRADIO** (All-Union State Television and Radio Company). After real innovation – live discussion programmes, international 'telebridges' – in the first years of *glasnost*, the former central broadcasting authority turned unreformable beyond a certain point. The grip of the Party was still powerful, and in the republics Gostelradio was seen as an instrument in Moscow's domination. In 1991 a take-over by conservatives, symbolized by the appointment in 1991 of Leonid Kravchenko, caused the departure of the best journalists and a boycott by some popular entertainers. Servility during the 1991 *putsch** caused Kravchenko's dismissal and replacement by Yakovlev.* At the same time Gostelradio's second channel, plus part of its establishment, was handed over to TV Russia and Radio Russia. With the ending of the Union, Gostelradio became the Russian State TV and Radio Company (Ostalkino) and its first channel, still broadcasting over former Union territory, was named the 'Inter-State' channel. See also 'Radio', 'Television'.

**GOSZAKAZ** (*Gosudarstvennyi Zakaz* – State Committee for Orders). Organization formerly handling all industrial production orders. Its continued existence nullified the law of January 1988 that gave enterprises autonomy over their output, since they had first to fulfil state orders, which often took all their production. In the end Goszakaz was reformed rather than suppressed, since in the transition to a market economy certain prices (for energy, raw materials, machine-tools) were to be fixed by state orders to prevent profiteering.

**GOVERNMENT.** Instrument for the application of policy decisions – till 1988 those of the Party, afterwards those of the President. Changes in December 1990, turning the Council of Ministers into a Presidential 'cabinet', diminished the authority of the prime minister (a move the new premier, Pavlov,* attempted to reverse). After the 1991 *putsch** the Presidential cabinet was replaced by a State Council* assisted by other 'interim' bodies. Non-Russian republics quickly complained at the number of Russians nominated to the latter by Yeltsin.*

**GRACHEV**, ANDREI SERAFIMOVICH (1941–  ). USSR presidential spokesman appointed September 1991, succeeding Ignatenko.* Formerly deputy head of the Central Committee international department, orientalist and graduate of the Moscow State Institute for International Relations.

**GRAECO-CATHOLIC.** See 'Uniate Church'.

**GRAIN.** Enigma turned scandal when in 1990 a record production (240 million tons in the field, 218 million harvested) ended in a record shortage. Only 68 million tons were delivered to state stocks, 18 million tons short of the state order. Part of the crop rotted for classic reasons (shortage of transport and silos). Growers withheld part of it for specific reasons, including postponement of a promised increase in payment. A simultaneous increase in meat and milk payments caused grain intended for human consumption to be fed to livestock. Another disaster was threatened in 1991 when, by the end of September only 151 million tons had been gathered, compared with 211 million tons the previous year. Of this, only 46 per cent had been purchased for state stocks, making large imports essential. Soviet history is punctuated with harvest disasters. But a vicious circle started with the import of American grain in the heyday of petro-dollars (a purchase of 24 million tons in 1973). The problem is quality. Even in the worst years, the country produces 70–75 million tons, well over the tonnage (latterly about 38 million) consumed directly by people. But high quality output, especially of wheat, is insufficient. The low quality goes to cattle. In 1989, 37 million tons were imported; in 1990, 32 million. Grain deals are a two-sided game on the international market. In 1988, after months of bargaining, President Reagan had to bow to pressure from the US farm lobby and offer wheat at prices subsidized by the US tax-payer. In 1991 the lobby again applied pressure when President Bush hesitated about extending a suspension of the Jackson-Vannik amendment.* In the end, the government guaranteed loans to the Soviet government for the purchase of grain worth $1.5 billion.

**GREAT PATRIOTIC WAR.** Soviet version of World War II. Since officials revealed more about its origins, including details of the 1939 German-Soviet Pact,* the theme of patriotic mobilization has lost some of its aura. There has even been a move in the opposite direction, with journalists using extracts from Western Cold War literature to diminish the Soviet role. Young people, too, are weary of hearing about military exploits that have been superseded by the experience of Afghanistan. Yet the war remains an unassailable part of the national consciousness, with the memory, close to everyone over sixty, of 20 million dead (7.5 million military). In the same war British and Commonwealth forces lost 398,000 dead and US forces 292,000.

**GREENPEACE.** Organization with a Soviet/Russian section formed in 1990 under marine biologist Professor Yablokov.* In October 1990 a Greenpeace boat, flying the Dutch flag and protesting against underground nuclear tests, was intercepted by maritime frontier guards near the Novaya Zemlia islands.

**GREENS.** Powerful early ingredient of national movements, particularly in Armenia and Moldavia. Armenian 'greens' gained a halt to the Yerevan nuclear power station; their Moldavian counterparts fought pesticides and agricultural pollution. Within the movement, scientists and writers have campaigned to save lakes and the Siberian *taiga*. In March 1990, twenty Green 'associations' proclaimed a confederation in Kuibyshev, but there was no Green Party until 1991. Parties then appeared in most republics, including a Russian one under Aleksandr Dronin.

**GRISHIN,** VIKTOR VASILYEVICH (1914–  ). One-time Moscow Party boss and in 1985 challenger to Gorbachev for leadership of the Soviet Communist Party. As Moscow's First Secretary, he was detested by Muscovites, who detected the 'Grishin mafia' behind a city housing racket. He was also responsible for bludgeoning the arts and was identified with Lubimov's* sacking from the Taganka* theatre. His resignation as Moscow chief in 1985 was the first sign of Gorbachev's determination to fight corruption at the top. In February 1986 he left the Politburo, in June the Supreme Soviet, and in September the Russian supreme soviet. Each step was dictated by Gorbachev, who gave him the choice of resigning or facing trial – a policy of discretion abandoned later in the case of Churbanov.*

**GROMOV,** COL.-GEN. BORIS VSEVOLODOVICH (1943–  ). Former commander of Soviet forces in Afghanistan, appointed First Deputy Minister of Internal Affairs in December 1990. In September 1990 a parliamentary deputy, Col. V. Martirosian, accused Gromov of being among a number of generals ready to carry out a military coup. Gromov brought an action for libel. In 1991 he was chosen by Ryzhkov* as running mate in an unsuccessful bid for the Russian presidency. Three months later, accused of neutrality towards the August *putsch*,* he was dismissed from the Ministry and returned to the Army. He claimed to have devoted all his efforts to preventing MVD troops from becoming involved in street fighting.

**GROMYKO,** ANDREI ANDREEVICH (1909–1989). Long-serving Foreign Minister (1957–85) and architect of Soviet 'Cold War' diplomacy, known abroad as 'Mr Nyet'. In March 1985 he nominated Gorbachev as candidate for Party General Secretary, but within four months was replaced by Shevardnadze, making way for what Gorbachev called 'new thinking'. He was given the honorific post of Chairman of the Presidium of the Supreme Soviet. Still a member of the Politburo, Gromyko tended to side with the conservatives Ligachev,* Chebrikov* and Solomentsev.* In September 1988 he was obliged to relinquish the so-called 'presidency' in order to give Gorbachev maximum authority (as head of state as well as of the Party) to carry out major constitutional changes – the creation of a new parliament and executive presidency. He also retired from the Politburo. In 1990 his memoirs betrayed no secrets. His son Aleksei is head of the African department of IMEMO.*

**GROSS NATIONAL PRODUCT (GNP).** Figure intended to indicate economic performance. According to Western (CIA) figures, in 1988 the Soviet GNP was $8.865 per head, compared with $19.770 per head in the US. In 1988–89 it rose marginally, before dropping in 1990 ('sharply' according to the CIA, by 2 per cent according to Goskomstat*). Officials reported that in the first quarter of 1991 it was down a further 10 per cent against the previous year's figure.

**GROSSMAN,** VASILI SEMYONOVICH (1905–1964). Writer best known for his monumental war novel *Life and Fate*. In 1941–45 he served as a war correspondent for *Krasnaya Zvezda*. His difficulties began in 1953 after his novel *In a Good Cause* was published in *Novy Mir.** The book was criticized for failing to create a single hero in its description of the battle of Stalingrad. He continued with a second volume, set in the period when the Soviets had taken the offensive, but this did not save it from being banned. He was called before Suslov,* who told him it could not be published for another two or three hundred years. The manuscript was confiscated but eventually found its way to the West on microfilm – according to one account, thanks to a sympathetic KGB agent. In 1980 it was published in Lausanne, and in October 1987 in *Ogonyek.**

**GROZNYI** (pop. 393,000). Capital of the Autonomous Republic of the Chechen and Ingush,* seen by a number of nationalities as that of a future autonomous republic of the North Caucasus. An informal 'parliament' began meetings in 1988.

**GRU** (*Glavnoye Razvedyvatelnoye Upravleniye*). Chief Intelligence Directorate of the armed forces, a division of the Soviet General Staff responsible for the collection of strategic, tactical and technical military intelligence. With the break-up of the Union it effectively passed under the control of Russia.

**GUBENKO,** Nikolai Nikolayevich (1941–   ). Theatrical producer and reformist, appointed Minister of Culture after the 1989 elections. As Minister he had the distinction of a creative rather than a bureaucratic background, having worked with the Taganka* Theatre since 1964 as well as making films. In 1987, within weeks of taking over the Taganka on the death of Lubimov's* successor, Anatoli Efros, he confirmed a reputation for controversy by putting on *Doctor Zhivago*, which had still not been passed for public performance. In 1988 he created a sensation by playing the title role in his own production of *Boris Godunov*, devised by Lubimov six years before, and banned. In 1991 he resigned in protest at the August *putsch*\* but was reinstated by Gorbachev; critics accused him of having waited a day 'for reflection'.

**GULAG** (*Glavnoye Upravlenye Lageri* – Chief Administration of Labour Camps). Internationally known symbol of Stalinist repression since publication of Solzhenitsyn's* *The Gulag Archipelago* (1974). According to files discovered in 1989 by the Institute of History, in March 1940 – a high point – the Gulag 'political' and 'criminal' population numbered 1,668,200. It was held in 53 camps, 425 'corrective labour colonies' and 50 camps for juvenile delinquents. There were 107,000 guards, including 'trusties', who at one time numbered one in four. The number of prisoners serving sentences under Article 58 (counter-revolutionary activities) rose from 12.6 per cent in 1936 to 59.5 per cent ten years later. In 1947, the last year covered, nearly 8 per cent (139,000) of Gulag prisoners were marked as agents or informers. Other official figures show that in the thirteen years up to 1947 registered deaths totalled 963,766. After the 1987 amnesty* the camp system ceased to be used for political prisoners and 'Gulag' became a dead word. A three-year campaign produced some improvements in the conditions of criminal prisoners. See also 'Camps', 'Repression'.

**GULF CRISIS.** First test of Soviet-US rapprochement. In 1990, Iraq's invasion of Kuwait coincided with a meeting, in Irkutsk, of Foreign Ministers Shevardnadze and Baker to prepare a second Bush-Gorbachev summit. Washington and Moscow immediately demanded Iraq's withdrawal. Over the next seven months Moscow supported, and meticulously observed, UN Security Council resolution 660 and eight others related to a withdrawal. As the deadline for Iraqi withdrawal approached in February 1991, Moscow made a series of last-minute initiatives, in collaboration with Iran, hoping to prevent a war within 300 kilometres of its border and liable to excite its Muslim population. After the fighting, in which it took no part, Moscow concentrated its efforts on obtaining a general Middle East settlement.

**GUM** (*Gosudarstvennyi Universalnyi Magazin*). Former state department store, built as a private emporium in 1888. It now accommodates co-operative retail shops and Western joint-ventures.

**GUMILEV,** Nikolai Stepanovich (1886–1921). Acmeist poet, essayist and critic, husband of Akhmatova,* executed in 1921 for alleged counter-revolutionary activity. Republication of his works in 1986 was taken by the intelligentsia as first proof of the liberation of culture from political control.

# H

**HAMMER,** ARMAND. (1900–1990). Genial Midas, friend of Lenin and the USSR. In the 1920s, already a millionaire, he helped to restore the Soviet economy with grain shipments and industrial investment. He backed off under Stalin but returned in the 1950s with his Occidental Petroleum Company to assist in the development of Soviet oilfields. His friendship for Russia again acquired a special warmth with Gorbachev. After Chernobyl he sent a medical team to treat radiation victims, and after the Spitak earthquake plane-loads of aid for Armenian relief. The American-born son of poor Russian immigrants (his father was an early American communist), Hammer also donated a valuable collection of twentieth-century Russian and Soviet art, acquired during his visits in the 1920s, to the Soviet Cultural Fund.*

**HARD CURRENCY** (*valuta*). For the state, a necessity forever in short supply because of the unfavourable foreign trade* balance. For private citizens, a ceaseless traffic. Until 1990 its possession was illegal for both firms and individuals. (For a long time, trafficking was the only charge available against prostitutes.) Then, to bolster state reserves, people were allowed to bank it freely, with no questions asked as to source. The change of rule sharply divided society, into those who had *valuta* and could use it in foreign currency shops and those who did not. In June 1991 the State Bank was authorized to refuse sales of *valuta* for buying personal cars, computers etc — a move to stop exploitation of their position by executives of enterprises. The allocation of reserves and the right to trade in hard currency became points of controversy in the debate over a new union.

**HARE KRISHNA.** Hindu sect finally registered as a religious community in 1988. Previously members were liable to two years' gaol for 'unauthorized propaganda'. The same year Indian communists protested to Moscow at the presence of the Soviet consul in Calcutta at a Hare Krishna festival attended by Soviet adherents.

**HEALTH TREATMENT.** One of many free services promised by the former Soviet constitution (article 42) but far from being generally available. Treatment is often a privilege dependent on a factory polyclinic. In European Russia, local polyclinics have one doctor per 1,700 inhabitants, a ratio calculated to permit twelve minutes' treatment per patient.

Oculists are supposed to treat ten patients per hour, ENT specialists eight patients. (Ministry civil servants are luckier, with one doctor per 800, and creative unions★ luckier still, with one per 430.) In April 1987, the new health minister, Chazov,★ gave a revealing picture. Planners, wanting to boost the number of hospital places, had installed beds in apartments and wooden huts. In twenty years the share of the budget devoted to health had steadily declined, with the result that an annual increase of 8 per cent was needed to restore an adequate level by the year 2000. In Central Asia most hospitals were without running water, central heating or main drainage. Only a fifth of the Union's rural polyclinics had proper buildings. There was a universal shortage of medicines – 15 per cent below need for general use, 50 per cent below in the case of antibiotics and cardiac medication. Doctors graduated without being able to read an electrocardiogram or X-ray, and there was a shortage of ambulances and of cars for visiting patients at home. Of 333 institutes working for public health, only fifty to sixty were doing real scientific work; eighty to a hundred 'could be closed without loss'. In 1990, three years after Chazov's strictures, doctors' salaries were doubled to an average R390 per month, nearly the wage of a Moscow bus-driver.

**HELSINKI FINAL ACT.** Final document of Helsinki Conference on Security and Cooperation (CSCE), 1975. Bible of activists monitoring Soviet human rights. The promise of the signatories, including the USSR, to respect freedom of speech and belief was seized on by the so-called Helsinki Monitoring Group founded shortly afterwards by Sakharov,★ Anatoli Shcharansky, Yuri Orlov and others. The group disbanded in 1982 when most of its members had been imprisoned or forced into exile. Dissidents freed by the 1987 amnesty★ set up a Moscow section of the new International Human Rights Association.★

**HIJACK.** Fastest way to a drink in Scandinavia, attracting six successful and seven unsuccessful attempts, mostly by young people, in the summer of 1990. In the ten years up to 1988 only four out of twenty attempts succeeded. In March 1988, eleven members of the Oveshkin family hijacked a plane carrying 76 passengers between Irkutsk and Leningrad. A clumsy rescue operation killed five members of the family, three passengers and a hostess. In December 1988, bandits hijacked a bus carrying schoolchildren and teachers in the Caucasus. The gang were given a plane in which to fly to Israel, from which they were promptly returned.

**HISTORY.** For seventy years a Marxist 'science' taught under Party instructions. When communism collapsed, the system was so short of real historians that 'blank spots' were left to be filled in by creative writers, whose emotions clouded the facts. Journalists were no better, as they rushed to be first with each new 'revelation'. Articles appeared that would have brought a blush to the faces of even the most anti-Soviet Western writers. Conservatives asked how the country could hope to hold together if it went on tearing up its past. In June 1988 the Ministry of Education suspended final-year history exams, and teachers were told to use newspaper articles for class discussion. In 1991, real historians were heartened by a promise to open up Party archives.*

**HOMELESSNESS.** Condition swollen by thousands fleeing from inter-ethnic violence. The homeless are called *BOMZH* in Russian, an acronym standing for 'persons of no fixed abode'. Otherwise homelessness comes of falling out of the bureaucratic chain that says 'no work = no *propiska** = no apartment'. Its victims, in 1990 numbering about 15,000 in Moscow, include children running away from home, alcoholic husbands ejected by their wives, ex-prisoners, fugitive criminals, and 'squatting' artists.

**HOSPITALS.** Source of unending scandal, since admission can depend on 'knowing the right person', nursing on bribes, and meals on food brought by relatives. Surgeons perform brilliant operations only to see patients die of infection; decrepit buildings (90 per cent in Moscow dating from before the revolution) are breeding-grounds for germs; and wages of staff are among the lowest in the country. A few 'private' hospitals, like Fyodorov's* eye clinic, are gold mines, with quasi-recreational features, including 'nurses' available for the needs of rich clients. There are also a few up-to-date state hospitals, generally specialized, for example for cardiology and cancer treatment. In 1991, to counter the drainage of staff to private consultancy work and medical co-operatives, doctors and nurses were awarded slightly better pay (see 'Health treatment').

**HOTEL.** Rest centre for staff, cruelly taxed with the duty of receiving guests. In scores of provincial cities even Intourist's tatty standards are unheard of. Telephones fail, restaurants refuse to serve meals, hot water and heating barely function. In 1991 an improvement was promised by the opening of hotels by co-operatives and joint ventures, and the 'privatization' of Party hotels and sanatoria. But even expense-account visitors blanched at daily room rates of up to $500 (for a suite at the Metropole), $100 more than at New York's super-luxury St Regis. See also 'Savoy'.

**HOUSEHOLD SHOPPING.** In 1991, even before price increases, consumer of over three-quarters of the average family's income. Pensioners, single parents and parents of large families were awarded partial compensation via social allowances.

**HOUSING.** National stock in short supply and shaky condition: still publicly owned nearly everywhere, despite ambitious projects for 'privatization'.* In 1990 Moscow voted to sell 2 million apartments to tenants; a year later it had sold only 75,000. Questions still needing to be settled include the method of valuation, the apportionment of maintenance charges, and the provision of credits. Evidence suggests that the vast majority of tenants would prefer to stay as they are, with rents for two- or three-room apartments equivalent to 5–10 per cent of average official wages. The all-Union construction target, set in 1987, was to give every family a dwelling of its own by the end of the century (programme 'Housing 2000'). In 1991 this would have meant constructing 24 million new dwellings in eight years. But returns indicated a previous year's total of only 1.8 million, 340,000 less than in 1989. According to Goskomstat,* at the start of 1991 there were 14 million urban families or individuals in need of improved housing, nearly a quarter of the overall number. 'In need' meant with less than 7 square metres of accommodation per person. Seventeen per cent had only 7–9 square metres, and 16 per cent lived in shared or communal flats. A serious problem is the decay of housing due to lack of maintenance and, in the case of many newer buildings, use of sub-standard construction materials.

**HUMAN RIGHTS.** Rare deficit made good by *perestroika*. The first move was to appoint the Burlatsky* commission. Partly for tactical reasons and partly from conviction, Gorbachev rejected both the narrow Western concept of individual rights and the rigid Soviet concept of collective rights. He advanced a compromise, in which individual and collective rights (to work, housing etc.) were presented as complementary. The Soviet 'return to civilization' was liable to heavy orchestration, as with the call, first made in 1986, to hold a meeting of the CSCE* entirely devoted to human rights, in Moscow. The meeting took place in 1991.

**HUMANITARIAN AID.** Western assistance called into being by the 1990 harvest and subsequent failures. By September 1991, gifts from fifty countries were valued by officials at $700 million, of which $500 million was in food and the rest in medicines. For the winter of 1991–92 Western countries allocated aid, mostly in food, worth $5.3 billion, of which $2.4 billion came from the US and Canada, $2.4 billion from the European Community and $500 million from Japan. The EC credits were half for purchases from Community countries and half for purchases from Eastern Europe, contingent on adequate Soviet distribution arrangements. Moscow had asked for $14.7 billion of aid, a request later cut to $10.2 billion. Deliveries were accelerated amid fears of social unrest following January 1992 price rises.

**HUNGARY.** Former ally unlikely ever to forget 1956. In 1990, the Budapest parliament called for an apology like that given to the Czechs for the Soviet invasion of 1968. It also demanded a faster Soviet withdrawal (the last soldier left in June 1991) and announced its intention to quit the Warsaw Pact (ended as a military entity in 1991). In the mid-1980s the liberalization of the Hungarian economy was taken as a model for *perestroika*; but with scant attention to mistakes. By 1991 Hungarians, though still having their own problems, were deeply scornful of the progress of Soviet reform. In 1990 Budapest warned the Ukraine of its concern for the welfare of the 150,000-strong Hungarian minority in Transylvania.

**HYGIENE.** Commonly a euphemism for its opposite. Also a pretext for outlandish practices, such as barring fathers from visiting maternity hospitals, and subjecting women to a degrading (and grossly unhygienic) examination before issuing swimming bath tickets or, even more strangely, taxi-driver's licences. See also 'Sanitary day'.

**HYPNOSIS.** Therapy popular in Soviet society, forever fascinated by the paranormal. Recommended for slimming, headaches, psychological disorders, period pains, rheumatism, drug addiction and drinking.

# I

**ICBM.** See 'Intercontinental ballistic missiles'.

**IGNATENKO**, VITALI ALEKSEYEVICH (1941– ). Journalist appointed in August 1990 as the President's press chief in place of Arkadi Maslenni-kov,* and in September 1991 director of TASS.*

**IMEMO.** See 'Institute of World Economy'.

**IMF.** See 'International Monetary Fund'.

**IMPORTS.** Acquisition progressively constricted by the breakdown of barter deals, shortage of exchange, and worsening terms of trade. The halt to imports of prime necessities has had serious repercussions on popular living standards, particularly since 1989 when the shortage of medicines affected hospitals and obliged the chronically sick to look for medication on the black market. In 1990, 36 per cent of Soviet imports consisted of consumer goods. In 1991 the bill was cut by nearly half in an attempt to stabilize the external debt.

**INCOME.** Term introduced in distinction to 'pay'. Until 1987 the only form of income was a state salary. The Law on Individual Economic Activity* changed this, reversing a campaign launched the year before against 'unearned income', i.e. anything earned privately. Income could now come from professional fees, co-operative profits, payments by foreign firms or joint ventures, or from 'family' farms. Hence a need for tax inspectors.* The change accompanied a sharp cleavage in income levels. In 1990, the average per capita monetary income among workers and employees was R172 per family member per month, and many pensioners were obliged to live on R70. But co-operators and *bizinesmen** could receive up to two hundred times as much. See also 'Pay'.

**INDEPENDENCE.** Under the Soviet constitution, a status requiring a two-thirds vote in a republic referendum, followed by a five-year wait. In 1991 five republics – Estonia,* Latvia,* Lithuania,* Georgia* and Moldavia* – declared independence (or their intention of taking it) before the August *putsch.** In the aftermath the State Council* recognized the independence of the Baltic republics, but not that of Georgia and

Moldavia. The remaining republics also declared their independence but adhered to an interim political and economic union while deciding their future.

**INDIA**. Non-aligned ally bound by a treaty of peace and friendship since 1971, counter-balancing China in Soviet plans for an Asian security system; hence Moscow's concern over any threat to India's internal stability, as during the 1991 elections.

**INDUSTRY**. National asset painfully accumulated, then wasted by addiction to gigantism, rigid planning and centralization. (In 1991 ten per cent of enterprises still accounted for three-quarters of industrial output, often with one giant plant serving the whole country.) Depreciation of material, technological conservatism and workers' indifference accelerated the process. In 1986, Abel Aganbegyan* recommended planners to renovate existing factories instead of building new ones (R200 billion having gone into developing unused sites) and to use up R500 billion worth of uninstalled machinery and equipment before acquiring more. In 1991 two-thirds of all industrial installations required renewing, but the previous five years' annual replacement rate never passed 4 per cent. Calls for greater productivity based on machine-tool production remained unanswered. In fact, productivity fell by 11 per cent in the first six months of 1991 after an overall fall of 0.9 per cent the previous year. The 'disastrous situation' (Gorbachev's description) was further worsened by the August *putsch** and the subsequent break-up of the Union.

**INF TREATY**. See 'Intermediate-range Nuclear Forces'.

**INFANT MORTALITY**. Figures for 1990 put the USSR fiftieth in the world table, below many developing countries. As with life expectancy and alcoholism, statistics were long kept secret. But in 1986 it was officially disclosed that twenty-six out of every thousand children were dying within one year of birth. Causes included lack of medication, absence of pre-natal examination (one in three women reaching confinement with illnesses not diagnosed during pregnancy), and in Central Asia pregnancies too close together, combined with the extreme youth of many mothers.

**INFLATION**. Condition once 'unknown' in Soviet history, raging out of control by 1991. The long concealed process began with a period of unproductive investment and surrender to wage demands in the last years of Brezhnev. By 1990 the Ryzhkov* government was caught in a vicious circle. The situation demanded a realistic prices policy; but this would have meant serious deprivation for millions. Another necessary step, the closure of uneconomic enterprises, entailed the risk of social disorder. In the end, the government shirked a decision; and in the economic anarchy caused by state shortages, especially of food, private producers (and speculators) had a seller's market. At the end of 1990 *Izvestia* put the inflation rate at 18 per cent per year. Twelve months later it was 300 per cent, and economists feared 1000 per cent in 1992. See also 'Rouble'.

**INFORMAL.** Non-Party social or political group, permitted as from 1987. A few 'informals' eventually developed into political parties, others addressed real social needs (defence of the environment, consumer protection). But most became mere talking shops for individuals obsessed with their own ideas.

**INGUSH.** North Caucasian people (186,000), of whom 135,000 live in the Chechen-Ingush* autonomous republic, the rest in North Ossetia.* Victims of mass deportation in 1944, they were allowed to return home from 1956, causing regional instability. Their co-existence with the Chechen was always precarious, though short of the kind of violence seen between Ingush and Ossetes in North Ossetia. They want restoration of the Ingush autonomy suppressed in 1934.

**INHERITANCE.** Entitlement limited to money and household effects until the Law on Property* (1990) sanctioned transference of leases. In a separate development, the creation of the Cultural Fund* caused the state to look abroad for émigrés willing to bequeath it collections. It was also made easier for people to receive bequests from relatives. Newspapers now regularly carry notices from executors in America seeking the kin of departed uncles. In 1991 it was still mandatory for legacies to go through a Soviet bank, which credited the recipient in roubles, and deducted an inheritance tax in hard currency.

**INSTITUTE OF THE UNITED STATES AND CANADA (ISKAN).** Prestigious 'think tank' of the Soviet Academy of Sciences, concerned with the analysis of international affairs, often going far beyond the description in its title. Under Georgi Arbatov* (still its head in 1992), ISKAN developed a reputation for independent thinking in the Brezhnev period, exploring ideas that later became part of Gorbachev's 'new thinking'.* Since 1986 it has engaged in active dialogue with similar organizations in North America and Europe.

**INSTITUTE OF THE WORLD ECONOMY (IMEMO).** Institute of the Academy of Sciences concerned with the study of world affairs. Like ISKAN,* it ranges far beyond the specialized field suggested by its title. Founded in 1956, IMEMO began as an attempt under Khrushchev to provide foreign policy-makers with a better understanding of what was going on outside the Soviet Union and the communist countries. By exploring the possibilities for East-West co-operation it contributed expertise to an important series of measures for detente which extended into the Brezhnev era – the 1963 Limited Test Ban Treaty, the 1968 Nuclear Non-Proliferation Treaty, the 1971 Strategic Arms Limitation Treaty (SALT 1), and other arms limitation agreements. By 1976, with a staff of nearly 600 researchers, it had given birth to four other institutes: ISKAN, the Institute of Africa, the Institute of Latin America, and the Institute of the International Workers' Movement.

**INSURANCE.** State monopoly broken for the first time in October 1990 by a joint venture of the Russian Republic and Germany's Colonia. The move followed a reorganization of the Soviet State Assurance Administration (Gosstrakh), which turned its various departments into autonomous joint-stock companies. Lack of an adequate system of insurance was seen by foreigners as a major obstacle to doing business in the Soviet Union. At the same time the huge market represented by 290 million people without insurance was seen as a golden opportunity for Western insurance companies.

**INTELLECTUALS.** Academically qualified members of the intelligentsia, a community (see below) which intellectuals, now more numerous because of the expansion of higher education, are tending to dominate and replace as a force in society. Gorbachev was the first leader to see intellectuals and the intelligentsia as potential allies. His predecessors, from Stalin to Brezhnev, were always suspicious of them and did everything possible to preserve the traditional gulf between the labouring masses and 'soft-handed parasites'.

**INTELLIGENTSIA.** Not quite the same as in the West. First so called by the nineteenth-century writer Boborikin to describe people of different social backgrounds but with a shared interest in culture. The absence of social identification remained characteristic of the Soviet intelligentsia (which was largely self-taught) until *perestroika*. Membership offered a form of social awareness to people denied the right of expression through the ballot box. It was the first sector of society to benefit from Gorbachev's reforms allowing freedom of creation and movement. Becoming his indispensable ally, it transmitted these benefits to the people at large, pointing them towards freedom. But thanks to the changes it helped to bring about, it ceased to have the special force it had had earlier as the conscience of a muzzled people. And as Soviet society emerged from its isolation, it became aware of the cruel difference between its own intellectual standards and those of the outside world. The shock was hardest for artists and scientists. At the same time, by taking part in the political system, the intelligentsia lost the freshness of rebellion – and with the advent of the market, its superb indifference to money.

**INTERCONTINENTAL BALLISTIC MISSILES (ICBM).** Land-based ballistic* missiles, the most important weapons covered by START.* The

Soviet Union early made them the principal basis of its nuclear strength, whereas the United States dispersed its resources liberally in a 'triad' consisting of ICBMs, submarine-launched missiles (SLBMs), and long-range bombers.

**INTEREST RATES**. Capitalist device rehabilitated by reformers looking for sources of finance and inspired by R200 billion of the people's money lying in the State savings bank.\* In 1990, interest on state bonds was set at 10 per cent, and in 1991 at up to 30 per cent, in an attempt to keep pace with inflation.

**INTERFAX**. Joint-venture news agency founded in 1990 by journalists of Gostelradio\* in conjunction with a Franco-Italian organization. It has a nationwide network of correspondents (often employees of Gostelradio) providing prompt and reliable news. In December 1991 it was the first with many 'inside' stories concerning the break-up of the Union and the formation of the Commonwealth.\*

**INTER-FRONT** (or **INTER-MOVEMENT**). Organization formed by Russophones to oppose Popular Fronts in secessionist republics. In Estonia and Latvia it received help from Soviet state enterprises.

**INTERNAL SECURITY**. Until August 1991 the concern of the Ministry of the Interior (MVD)\* and the KGB.\* Following the *putsch*,\* responsibility was transferred to the Army, which took over the KGB troops and part of the MVD forces. The KGB forces, 230,000 strong, consisted of 23,000 frontier guards, the Kremlin guard, and special units of 40,000 men with equipment including tanks, helicopters and patrol boats. The Ministry of the Interior had a force of thirty divisions (340,000 men), including several tank units. In 1992 internal security became the responsibility of the MVD of each republic.

**INTERNATIONAL HUMAN RIGHTS ASSOCIATION**. Frankfurt-based association founded in 1972 after appeals by Sakharov\* and Solzhenitsyn.\* It took over from the Helsinki Monitoring Group (see 'Helsinki Final Act'). Among its founders were the specialist on psychiatric abuse, Aleksandr Podrabinek, and the Christian militant, Aleksandr Ogorodnikov.\* Both later became parliamentary deputies.

**INTERNATIONAL MONETARY FUND (IMF)**. Institution dismissed at its creation as a Western plot for world economic domination; courted, with other international financial organizations, forty years later. Soundings about membership were first made unofficially in 1986. But it was not until 1990, after the G-7\* summit in Houston, that IMF director Michel Camdessus was invited to Moscow for talks about help in restructuring the economy, price reform and a convertible rouble. Moscow was allowed to send observers to the IMF's forty-fifth meeting later the same year, and in 1991 received special associate membership with the backing of the G-7 London summit. As from 1992 the place of the Soviet Union was taken by Russia. Other republics applied for equal status.

**INTERNATIONALIST**. Ancient hero convinced of the duty of different nationalities to help one another. The vision died in Afghanistan.

**INTERMEDIATE-RANGE NUCLEAR FORCES (INF) TREATY**. First bilateral disarmament agreement signed between the USSR and the United States. It differed from all previous agreements by imposing cuts, not just limitations; also in its detailed provision for verification. Another feature was the asymmetry involved. British and French nuclear forces — an earlier cause of contention — were not mentioned.

**INTERPOL**. International agency finally joined by the Soviet Union after some effective combined operations, including the smashing, with the help of the Royal Canadian Mounted Police, of a ring shipping drugs from Afghanistan. The development of links between Soviet and international gangs made adherence inevitable. The break-up of the Union has reinforced the need for an inter-republican 'Interpol' to combat criminal activity across borders.

**INTER-REGIONAL GROUP**. Informal alliance of radical parliamentary deputies formed in 1988 to press for devolution of power to republics. It was to have led the opposition to Gorbachev after the 1989 elections but lost cohesion with the election of new republic parliaments the next year.

**INTER-REPUBLICAN ECONOMIC COMMITTEE** (later Inter-State Economic Committee). Committee formed in September 1991 by the State Council★ to take over economic co-ordination after the *putsch*.★ Chaired by Silayev,★ it was suppressed after the Minsk★ meeting.

**INTERVIEW**. Coitus interruptus, in which the Russian interviewer invariably withdraws on seeing his questions approaching a climax. Interviewers have a choice of three concluding observations, always included in the printed account or transmission: (1) 'You have said some extremely interesting things, and I trust our readers/listeners think the same'; (2) 'Your opinion has greatly enriched the discussion, even if not all our readers/hearers will agree with you'; (3) 'Thank you Ivan Ivanovich; we wish you all success in your splendid career.' Soviet journalists conducting a 1988 interview with Margaret Thatcher (the first on television with a visiting premier) were later criticized, not for letting her wipe the floor with them, but for their 'bad manners' and 'lack of respect for a prime minister and a lady' in asking pointed questions.

**INTOURIST**. State organization for policing foreign tourists. In 1987 Intourist hotels were ordered to accept Soviet guests on the same basis as foreigners, making them, in many provincial cities, a rendezvous for young people observing what they took to be the Western way of life. Intourist's monopoly was broken, like others, in 1990.

**INVALIDS**. Collective term for the physically or mentally handicapped. In 1991, 7 million lived on pensions below the poverty line. Urban conditions (long flights of stairs, design of housing) make life difficult for physical invalids, while popular tolerance for the mentally retarded stops short of the truly mad. Handicapped children may enter special centres, often far from home. In 1990 parents in Khabarovsk, in the Soviet Far East, formed a self-help group.

**INVESTIGATIVE JOURNALISTS**. New species with a post-1986 heyday exposing scandals and public figures. They lost impact when officials were released from an obligation to answer them. The worst took to writing sensational reports, saying that secrecy prevented verification, while some of the best paid with their lives for investigating mafias.

**INVESTMENT**. Achilles' heel ever since the last years of Brezhnev. Until 1981, capital investment rose 50 per cent with every five-year plan period. But in 1981–85, it rose only 37 per cent; and in 1986–90, only 30 per cent. With *perestroika*, a decision was made to increase investment in consumer goods production; this was thwarted by the growing budget deficit. When joint enterprises* failed to attract the hoped-for amount of foreign investment, the government in 1991 introduced a draft law allowing wholly foreign-owned companies for the first time in Soviet history. Prime Minister Pavlov said R50 billion was needed to modernize industry. The draft promised freedom to repatriate profits, removal of import and export restrictions, and guarantees against arbitrary nationalization. Only defence-related industries were excluded from foreign participation. Western experts said they would wait to see what would happen in independent republics after the Soviet break-up.

**IPATOVSKY EXPERIMENT**. Agricultural experiment, involving the use of large mechanization units, in Gorbachev's Stavropol region (1977). Devised by his patron, Kulakov, its success was important to his Party career and earned him the Order of the October Revolution.

**IRAN**. Unsettling neighbour for ex-Soviet Asian republics, with a population of 50 million. Azerbaijan Shi'as (co-religionists of Azeris across the border) are deluged with Iranian religious broadcasts, and illegal frontier crossings are commonplace. Iranian emissaries tour Azerbaijan and Central Asia, setting up 'cultural centres' among rural communities. In February 1992, at a time of intense competition for influence in Central

Asia,* Iran hosted the Teheran 'economic summit' attended by all the Muslim ex-Soviet republics plus Turkey, Pakistan and the majority of Muslim states world-wide.

**IRAQ**. Political client from the 1960s, receiving advanced Soviet weapons, including the 'Scud' missile and the T-72 tank. In 1990 the Soviet Union voted with other UN Security Council members for resolutions condemning Iraq for its invasion of Kuwait, and applying a blockade until it withdrew. Some 7,000 Soviet technicians became *de facto* hostages, but were extricated before fighting started. In 1992 Iraq was accused of trying to buy Soviet materials and nuclear experts in the aftermath of the Union break-up.

**ISKAN**. See 'Institute of the United States and Canada'.

**ISKANDER**, FAZIL ABDULOVICH (1929– ). Abkhazian* short-story writer, novelist and poet, in 1991 living mostly in Moscow, caught between love of his people's culture and fear of becoming a hostage to their nationalism. His books include *The Goat-ibex Constellation* (a satire on the theories of the geneticist Lysenko), *Sandro from Chegem*, and *The Old House below the Cypresses*.

**ISLAM**. Religion of every fifth (ex-)Soviet citizen, fast uniting the populations of Central Asia and expanding, less militantly, in Kazakhstan, the Volga region, the Urals and Siberia (the most fanatical adherents are in the Caucasus). Muslims are administered by four regional boards, headed by muftis, at Ufa, Buinaksk, Baku and Tashkent. Clergy are trained at the Mir-i-Arab Madrasseh in Bukhara and the Ismail al-Bukhari Islamic Institute in Tashkent. Nine-tenths of believers in the region are Sunni, Shi'ism being mostly confined to Azerbaijan. With the ending of religious restrictions in 1987–88, Muslims (like Christians) began to take an increasingly active part in politics. In 1991 the all-Union Islamic party *Vozrozhdeniye* ('Rebirth'), claiming 20,000 members, was banned by communist governments in Uzbekistan and Tajikistan. But in the aftermath of the *putsch** Islam had a greater chance of taking power from the old communist leadership. In the years of repression, coexistence with communism was easier for Muslims than for Christians, since Islam does not demand a definitive choice. But Muslims were a target of atheist propaganda until the holding (1986) of an international Islamic conference in Baku under the aegis of the state Religious Affairs Committee.* Soon afterwards the government made it easier to make the *hadj* to Mecca, with special Aeroflot flights from Muslim-populated areas. Islamic sentiment was sharpened by the war in Afghanistan, when a number of conscripts refused to take oath, and by events in Nagorno-Karabakh* and Baku.*

**ISPOLKOM**. Local executive committee administering a city, district or region on behalf of the elected authority. Designed for a one-party system, in which the local Soviet and the *ispolkom* took orders from the same Party First Secretary, *ispolkoms* worked badly under multi-partyism. When the 1990 elections removed cities like Moscow, Leningrad and Lvov from Party control, the newly elected councils included many young novices impatient to take over matters formerly left to the *ispolkom*, which had now to be 'weeded out' in the name of fighting bureaucracy. Bitter battles ensued with *ispolkom* chairmen.

**ISRAEL**. Early recipient of Soviet approval before Moscow made friends with the Arabs. Relations were severed after the Suez invasion (1967) and stayed in suspense until 1988, when consular missions were exchanged on the pretext of Soviet concern for Orthodox church properties in Jerusalem. Later, Israeli diplomats took up residence in the Dutch embassy, then in due course opened their own consulate (in 1990 the target of demonstrations against the killing of Palestinians). In May 1991 the first visit to Israel of a Soviet Foreign Minister (Bessmertnykh), in quest of a Middle East settlement, foreshadowed the restoration of full diplomatic ties, achieved six months later with the appointment of Aleksandr Bovin as Soviet (later Russian) ambassador.

**IVANOV**, Nikolai Veniaminovich (1952– ). See 'Gdlyan, Telman'.

**IVASHKO**, Vladimir Antonovich (1932– ). Surprise figure of the Twenty-eighth Party Congress* in 1990, where he was elected Second Secretary with the complicity of Gorbachev. The promotion obliged him to resign the position of First Secretary of the Ukrainian party, to which he had just been elected. A leading 'de-Brezhnevizer' (though he demurred at this description), he was employed by Gorbachev to put order into the Ukrainian party, mired by scandal and stagnation. Working in the shadows, he had prepared the removal of Shcherbitsky.*

**IZBA**. Traditional village house, romanticized by townsmen, who really prefer week-ending in its latter-day successor, the *dacha*. Knowing foreigners' attachment to the Hollywood version of *Doctor Zhivago* – and their certain shock on finding the real thing, with its dark and airless interior – some entrepreneurs have built 'modern' *izbas* for use as 'country restaurants' where hard currency buys so-called traditional meals served by waiters dressed as *mujiks*. For residents fed up with Moscow hotels, a Soviet-German joint venture offers 'cottages for rent in a real Russian village only 40 miles from the Kremlin'. In hundreds of abandoned villages real *izbas* are meanwhile going for nothing – but not to foreigners.

**IZMAILOVO PARK**. Successor to Bitsa* as a Mecca for tourists seeking indifferent art and stolen antiques.

**IZVESTIA.** Formerly the daily newspaper of the Soviet government, as opposed to *Pravda*, formerly the paper of the Communist Party. Circulation in 1991 was 4.7 million, a drop of more than 7 million from the previous year, and slightly less than in 1985. In 1990 its registration as the organ of the presidium at the Supreme Soviet caused a war of words, both within the paper and in parliament, about the degree of its dependency. But as long as the editor-in-chief, Nikolai Yefimov, was balanced by Igor Golembyovsky (his deputy and the candidate of the journalists for the editorial job), it supported moderate reformers, with sharper commentaries than *Pravda*'s and factual reports on the state of society. The fight for editorial control reached a climax during the August 1991 *putsch*,* when the staff refused to put out the coup leaders' announcements. With the collapse of the *putsch*, Golembyovsky took over. The paper is now owned by its staff.

# J

**JACKSON-VANNIK AMENDMENT**. Decision of the US Congress in 1974 denying the Soviet Union 'most favoured nation' trading status so long as it imposed restrictions of emigration. The status was restored in July 1991.

**JAMMING**. 'Iron curtain' of the airwaves once supported by a network of 3,000 stations, aimed mainly against the Russian-language broadcasts of the BBC, Voice of America and Radio Liberty. It was gradually dismantled from September 1987 and ended the following year.

**JAPAN**. Natural partner in the development of Eastern Siberia if only it would drop the Kuril Islands★ question. Despite Tokyo's coolness, Japanese firms regularly traded indirectly with the USSR through subsidiaries in the Philippines, Australia and South-East Asia. They even quietly used South Korean firms before the latter became competitors. In 1991 a visit by Gorbachev to Japan was presented as a turning point in relations, but neither side was prepared to relent on the Kurils, and Japan failed to make a much hoped-for offer of economic and technological aid. In December 1991 Japan was quick to recognize Russia, despite disappointment over earlier rumours that Yeltsin was prepared to make a deal.

**JEWS**. According to Soviet figures in 1990, 1,811,000 Jews remained living in the Soviet Union despite steady emigration, but only 100,000 were active religious believers, mostly in Georgia, Bukhara and the Caucasus. The same year, with the ending of the anti-Zionist campaign, the number of synagogues increased from sixty to a hundred. In 1991 the Moscow Choral Synagogue had a *yeshiva* for rabbis and cantors, and several communities had suppliers of kosher food. After two decades of religious harassment in the 1920s and 1930s, in World War II hundreds of thousands of Soviet Jews perished as a result of the Nazi occupation. In the 1950s a new persecution followed the founding of the state of Israel★ (with which the Soviet Union at first had good relations). For the next thirty years Jews applying to emigrate were charged with 'Zionism' and refused exit visas. The 'refuseniks',★ who included a large proportion with high qualifications, eventually numbered tens of thousands. Over the years Jewish emigration followed a very uneven pattern. In 1972, with the signing of SALT 1, 32,000 Jews were allowed out. In 1974 the number fell to 21,000. With the 1978 US-Soviet wheat deal, it rose to 29,000, only to fall back again to 21,000 with the wheat embargo imposed after the invasion of Afghanistan. During the 'Reagan' arms race the number dropped to less than 1,000 annually. Persecution continued until 1987, when an abrupt change of policy caused visas to be granted to nearly all who wished to leave. Between 1988 and 1989 the number leapt from 8,000 to 71,000, and in 1990 to 150,000. The only Jews held back were victims of family disputes involving legal battles. With moves towards a freer economy, even in the worsening conditions of 1991, many Jews remaining were prepared to give the Soviet future a try. Their attitude was partly conditioned by the disappointing experience of emigrants in some host countries. Another factor affecting emigration was tougher Western (especially US) visa requirements. See also 'Anti-semitism'.

**JOBS**. See 'Work'.

**JOGGING**. Way to impress neighbours with one's Western-style fitness training, boosted in 1990 when Jane Fonda, followed by cameras, led 500 Moscow joggers on a traipse along the river. A chance to 'demonstrate friendship between peoples' – and promote cassettes.

**JOINT STOCK COMPANY**. *Deus ex machina* of Soviet reformers seeing privatization* as the only way to avoid complete economic collapse. In 1990 huge monopolies, including Intourist,* Aeroflot* and the Kamaz truck plant, were 'privatized'. The same year saw the opening of the new Moscow stock exchange (bourse*). But real joint-stock companies, as opposed to enterprises simply turned over to the ownership of their work collectives, are still rare.

**JOINT VENTURE**. Commercial association for mutual benefit, commonly founded on a grave misunderstanding of the other party's aims. In the worst case, the Soviet side wants Western technology and a share of profits without making any investment; the Western side sees only a site and a market, and cheap labour with which to make outdated goods unsaleable at home. But a number of joint ventures have taken root, most promisingly when the Western partner is a large organization prepared to wait for conditions to mature. At the beginning of 1991 there were some 3,000 registered joint ventures, compared with 1,000 a year before. The commonest foreign partners, in order of numbers of enterprises, were German, Finnish, American, Austrian, British, Italian, Swiss, Swedish, French, Canadian, Japanese and Dutch. Nearly a third specialized in consultancy, public relations and staff training. Half were registered in Moscow and nearly a fifth in Leningrad and the Baltic republics. But only 4.2 per cent were producing goods or services. Their output amounted to only 0.6 per cent of home sales, and 0.3 per cent of exports. With only three such enterprises involving investments of more than $20 million, they contributed only 0.2 per cent to the GNP. In May 1991 the government admitted that joint ventures had failed to become new models of technology and management, or to attract the hoped-for large amount of foreign investment. This could now only come from direct foreign ownership of enterprises, as provided for in a new privatization* law.

**JOURNALIST**. Citizen needing only ten published articles to qualify for accreditation and a coveted press card. Now respectable, after years of being scorned as insignificant power-seekers, Russian journalists tend to take themselves very seriously, writing didactically and at great length. Their new prestige enables them to take revenge on the literary intelligentsia* that used to look down on them. Numerous journalists became deputies in the first freely elected parliament, where they proceeded to combine two professions. Before the Soviet break-up there were 86,000 members of the Confederation of Journalists' Unions, set up as a successor to the Union of Journalists after the 1991 *putsch*.* The new organization elected as its chairman Edgard Sagalayev, a parliamentary deputy and deputy director of Gostelradio.*

**JUDGE**. Professional magistrate, usually sitting with two locally elected 'assessors' who in theory have an equal say in the verdict but in practice tend to defer to the judge's experience. A new law, under study since 1990, envisages changing the number of assessors or even introducing real juries. The panel of judges was weeded out in 1986 when the Minister of Justice sacked fourteen of them, moved seventy-six to different jobs, and declared 837 administratively unfit for having sentenced people to prison, and even death, for crimes they had not committed. In 1987, judges, leading attorneys and senior law officials became liable to easier dismissal in case of incompetence.

**JUSTICE**. System radically reformed in 1988 when the Supreme Soviet gave individuals the right to appeal against the actions of officials. The same law gave defence lawyers the right to be present at pre-trial investigations. It was followed by the appointment of a new procurator-general (Sukharev*) and a new corps of investigators independent of the police. In 1987 the Nineteenth Party Conference endorsed the doctrine of the presumption of innocence, and the principle that everything not explicitly forbidden is permitted. On the eve of the Soviet break-up in 1991 three obnoxious articles of the criminal code awaited the legislative axe: Article 71 on 'Anti-Soviet agitation and propaganda', and Articles 190−1 on 'defamation of the Soviet state and social system'.

# K

**KABAKOV**, ALEKSANDR ABRAMOVICH (1943– ). Journalist and author of *The Defector*, a heavy satire set in a Moscow torn by civil war. Its cynicism reflected the mood of the time, when intellectuals spent morbid evenings devising worst-case scenarios for civil war and military coups. As a pro-reformist, writing in *Moscow News*, Kabakov was nevertheless one of the first to question the unsettling social aspects of political and economic change.

**KAGARLITSKY**, BORIS. Creator of a succession of *ad hoc* informal groups* – Supporters of *Perestroika*, Group for Social Initiative, the Electors' Club, Socialist Federation, etc. A one-time Party member expelled from the State Arts Institute for anti-Soviet activity, he attempted to found a Labour-style workers' movement, an unusual thing for an intellectual at the beginning of *perestroika*. The idea was to mobilize grass-roots discontent behind calls for further reform and to prevent its exploitation by reactionaries. This went down badly in the Moscow of 1986–87, and Kagarlitsky attracted hostility when he accused deputies like Stankevich* and Rumyantsev, elected in 1989, of using the movement as a personal springboard and then forgetting their promises to voters. As a result, he ended up as the target of both his former brothers-in-arms and the conservative press. In 1990, as a member of the Moscow city council, he helped to found the small (300 members in 1991) Socialist Party.

**KALUGIN**, MAJOR-GENERAL OLEG DANILOVICH (1937– ). Former KGB* section head turned, in 1990, a supporter of Democratic Russia.* In a thirty-two year career he worked in the Soviet embassy in Washington and as head of counter-espionage in the Ministry of Foreign Affairs. He claims to have attracted the hostility of his peers for defending an innocent Soviet scientist. In 1989 he criticized the KGB in the journal *International Life*, and in June 1990, more sensationally, in *Komsomolskaya Pravda* and *Moscow News*. In these he accused it of being obsessed with 'political enemies', incapable of change, and scheming against both Yeltsin* and Ryzhkov.* He also attacked Gorbachev for depending on its leaders, who were old and 'out-of-touch'. He was promptly stripped of his rank and honours by a Presidential decree and charged with divulging state secrets. Like Gdlyan* and Ivanov before him, he used the 'persecution' to get himself elected a deputy, in Krasnodar in August 1990, and so acquired parliamentary immunity. The charges against him were dropped after the failure of the 1991 *putsch*.*

**KAMPUCHEA**. See 'Cambodia'.

**KARELIA** (pop. 780,000). Autonomous republic, formerly part of Finland, since 1945 within the Russian Federation.* In August 1990 it was the first autonomous republic to claim precedence for its laws over those of both the Russian Federation and the Union. In December 1991 Finland ended speculation by renouncing all claim to the territory.

**KASHPIROVSKY**, ANATOLI. Miracle-worker and faith-healer, who temporarily ousted Gorbachev from TV popularity charts. His performances in 1990 had to be stopped when one viewer fell into a coma and hospitals nationwide reported admissions for heart attacks, kidney failure and acute insomnia after each appearance. Churches attacked him as an instrument of the Devil.

**KASPAROV**, GARI (1963– ). Grand master at 17, Soviet chess champion at 18, world champion at 22, tyro politician at 27. In 1990 he began by bankrolling the Democratic Party of Russia, then started a faction in the so-called Centre Bloc.* In 1991 he was a supporter of Democratic Russia.* A brilliant player with playboy looks (and an ever-watchful mother checking his visitors and timetable), he repeatedly gripped world attention in his matches with the more orthodox Anatoli Karpov. Especially abroad, he turned their encounters into a contest between the Jewish-Armenian genius (himself) victimized by discrimination and the industrious *apparatchik* (Karpov) protected by the Chess Federation. For years the darling of his native Azerbaijan, with a permanent apartment in its Moscow representation, he was obliged to leave Baku at the time of the anti-Armenian riots in September 1989. In Moscow he violently attacked Gorbachev, first in the name of Armenians in Baku, then of Azeris massacred when the army came to restore order. In December 1990 he retained his world title against Karpov in a match decided after a tie.

**KATYN**. Byelorussian forest village near Smolensk, for years a focus of embarrassed contention between the Soviet Union and Poland. In 1943, the occupying Germans disinterred the bodies of some 4,000 Polish officers, who they said had been shot by the Soviets. An Allied inquiry upheld the Soviet version – contested by the Poles – that they had been massacred by the Nazis. In 1989 the Polish government pressed for a truthful explanation, and Katyn began to be mentioned in the Soviet press. Finally, in August 1990, the Polish Minister of Justice obtained permission from the Soviet procurator-general, Sukharev, to interrogate Pyotr Soprunenko, a former major of the NKVD, who according to the Poles had signed the list of 4,200 officers to be executed at Katyn in the

spring of 1940. Visiting the USSR about the same time, President
Jaruzelsky went to see the common grave. By degrees the Soviets came to
accept, and endorse, the Polish version. It remained to find the bodies of
more of the 15,000 Polish officers interned in three Soviet camps after the
occupation of Poland in 1939; and soon afterwards a mass grave was
discovered near Kalinin. The same year − on September 2nd, the
anniversary of the massacre − a Polish delegation was for the first time
allowed to place flowers on the spot. More flowers were laid to commemo-
rate Polish war dead elsewhere in the Soviet Union (while Poles were
destroying memorials to Soviet soldiers who died driving the Germans
from Poland in 1944).

**KAVERIN**, VENYAMIN ALEKSANDROVICH (1902−89), real name Zilber.
Novelist of many talents, responsible in 1986 for calling on the Central
Committee to allow publication of Rybakov's\* *Children of the Arbat*.

**KAZAKHSTAN** (pop. 16.5 million). Second largest republic (by area) after
Russia, having, under its president, Nursultan Nazarbayev, a powerful
voice in the debate about a successor to the former Soviet Union. Its
distinctive features include mineral wealth, particularly gold,\* and the
submergence of its indigenous inhabitants in a population comprising 41
per cent Russians, 36 per cent Kazakhs, and 23 per cent other nationalities. In 1991 a proposal by Yeltsin\* to re-draw Russia's boundaries with
republics having large Russian populations caused angry demonstrations
by Kazakhs and a sharp response by the President. The proposal was not
new. For years there were proposals (supported by, among others,
Solzhenitsyn\*) to split Kazakhstan and annex the north − the main area of
the Russian, Ukrainian, Cossack and German population − to the Russian
Federation, of which it was part until 1936. The large 'foreign' presence
arose partly from the need to import workers for the mines, and partly
from Kazakhstan's use as a place of deportation. The industrial cities of
Ust Kamenogorsk,\* Chimkent, Karaganda and Pavlograd are among the
worst polluted in the USSR; and environmental protests, led by writers
like Olzhias Suleimenov, have helped to ferment nationalism. In October
1990, in a parliament still dominated by the Communist Party, opposition
deputies founded 'Democratic Kazakhstan', calling for sovereignty within
a Soviet federation and more power to the soviets. This was followed, in
September 1991, by the founding of the Republican Party of Kazakhstan,
devoted to a reformed system of government, full Kazakh statehood,
territorial integrity and economic integration. By deciding to join the new
Commonwealth\* founded by the Minsk agreement,\* the republic helped
to avoid a serious split between the Muslim republics and the Slav. But its
insistence on keeping an estimated total of up to 1,800 Soviet nuclear
warheads on its territory created problems for Russia (and the West),
which argued for their transfer under central control to the territory of the
Russian Federation.

**KAZAN** (pop. 4.5 million). Capital of the Tatarstan,* with the double burden of two cults – of Gorky and Lenin. Gorky worked in a local bakery (its facade still visible); Lenin was a rebellious student at the university, where he is now commemorated by a rare beardless statue with a luxuriant quiff of hair. This promising past has not saved Kazan from becoming the capital of Soviet juvenile delinquency. In 1988 a special police task force identified 150 gangs with a membership of 1,500 adolescents. Ninety leaders were arrested; the remainder took to descending on Moscow, where in 1991 they continued to rob and terrorize people in the vicinity of the Kazan railway station.

**KGB** (*Komitet Gosudarstvennoy Bezopaznosti* – Committee of State Security). Chief intelligence and security organ, supposedly reformed and depoliticized by *perestroika* but continuing to wield great power until turned inside out as a result of the 1991 *putsch** of which the KGB chief, Kryuchkov,* was a chief organizer. While Kryuchkov was investigated in prison for treason, the reform of the KGB, and the job of purging it of tainted elements, was put in the hands of Yeltsin's nominee, Bakatin.* In October the organization was split into three divisions – a Central Intelligence Service (under Primakov*), an Inter-Republican Security Service (under Bakatin), and Border Troops (under the Army). It was also relieved of the Government Communications Service, the Protection Service (Kremlin guard etc.) and the 'Alpha' anti-terrorist group. The changes reduced its manpower strength from half a million to 35,000–40,000. Then in a second stage in November it gave up military intelligence and technical services, and the KGB collegium (command council) was replaced by a co-ordinating council composed of the heads of republican organs. With the end of the Soviet Union in December 1991, Bakatin's organization was taken over by Russia and merged with the former Soviet Ministry of the Interior in a new Russian Security and Internal Affairs Ministry. The move was made against protests from the Russian parliament, where many deputies feared the creation of a body 'beyond parliamentary control'. At the time the feeling was voiced in some republican circles that while independent states, with different laws, might have different systems of law-enforcement, there would still be a need to co-ordinate activities by republican secret services and police forces.

**KHASBULATOV**, Ruslan Imranovich (1942–   ) Chairman of the Russian parliament, finally appointed after the 1991 *putsch.** As deputy chairman, he was seen as the natural successor to Yeltsin when the latter became President. But his appointment was delayed by a split among 'democrats'. In 1992 he fought to uphold parliament's rights against the growing power of presidential aides. A Chechen by nationality, he has been used to settle disputes in his native autonomous republic.

**KHOZRASCHET**. Literally cost-accounting; principle advanced as from 1987 that an enterprise receiving state funds must produce goods or services at a profit. It could use its income as it wished, subject to guidelines ('normatives') as to the proportions assignable to basic wages, capital amortization, and the state budget.

**KHRUSHCHEV**, Nikita Sergeyevich (1894–1971). Nostalgically remembered author of the deceptive 'thaw' of 1956–64 (but also of the Cuban missile crisis, a fierce crackdown on religious belief, and the suppression of the 1956 Hungarian uprising). He emerged on the death of Stalin (March 6, 1953) as one of the three competitors for leadership, with Georgi Malenkov (chairman of the Council of Ministers) and Lavrenti Beria (Minister of Internal Affairs and secret police chief). Already a Central Committee Secretary, he quickly became *de facto* Party head and within six months First Secretary. Four months later Beria was arrested and executed. Malenkov resigned in February 1955, after admitting economic mistakes. In February 1956, at a closed session at the end of the Twentieth Congress, Khrushchev made a four-hour speech denouncing the crimes of Stalin. In 1958 he became head of government as well as of the Party, defeating and expelling a group of conspirators against him (the so-called 'Anti-Party Group') including Molotov* and Malenkov. His greatest fault as a national leader was to rush headlong into ill-considered schemes, such as that for creating a huge 'instant' granary in the virgin lands of Kazakhstan. His policy towards the arts was liberal but inconsistent: he personally approved publication of Solzhenitsyn's* *One Day in the Life of Ivan Denisovich* but forbade Pasternak's* *Doctor Zhivago*. Despite his faults he is still remembered by ordinary people for having improved daily life, particularly in the cities, with the mass building of five-storey apartment blocks (still called 'Khrushchev' buildings) which, though architecturally undistinguished, are much preferred to the gargantuan blocks built later. As Party leader his mistake was to alienate his early supporters and ignore them when making decisions. In 1964 he was ousted by the conspiracy of a majority in the Politburo and obliged to retire on grounds of age.

**KIEV** (pop. 2.5 million). Capital of Ukraine, an important cultural and religious centre; cradle of Russian Orthodoxy through the baptism in A.D. 998 of Prince Vladimir. On the occasion of the Millennium,* the Soviet government restored the church's ownership of the Kievan Monastery of the Caves (1051); but Kievans were aggrieved that the main celebrations were held in Moscow. In 1990, the Russian Orthodox church returned the cathedral of Saint Sophia to the new Ukrainian Orthodox church. The transfer took place in an atmosphere of violence because of an inter-church war over property with the Uniates.* Following Ukrainian independence (1991) the city became a fully-fledged state capital with the installation of Western embassies, a full foreign ministry, a defence ministry, and other departments appropriate to a sovereign country.

**KIRGHIZIA/KYRGYSTAN** (pop. 4.9 million). Republic in Tien Shan/ Pamir mountain area of Central Asia. All the land is above 4,500 feet, making it an attraction for climbers and skiers. The Kirghiz are only 48 per cent of the population, and in the capital, Bishkek (formerly Frunze), up to 1991 only three of the seventy schools were Kirghiz. Twenty-six per cent of the population are Russians, 12 per cent Uzbeks, and 12 per cent members of smaller groups speaking eighty different dialects. In June 1990, a row between Uzbeks and Kirghiz over the distribution of building land resulted in a series of pitched battles. From Osh the violence spread to the whole of the area boarding Uzbekistan,* which was put into a state of emergency. The Kirghiz writer Aitmatov* (a member of Gorbachev's presidential council) and the Uzbek writers Yabukov and Kadyrov intervened to stop war between the two republics. The riots in Osh left 78 dead, over 300 wounded and over 200 houses destroyed. Earlier clashes had occurred between local people and Caucasian immigrant workers at Uzgen. The troubles contributed to the rise of a militant nationalist movement and caused the flight of 34,000 Russians and Uzbeks. In 1990, at the insistence of the 'Kyrgystan Democratic Movement', parliament renamed Kirghizia the 'Socialist Republic of Kirghizistan', omitting 'Soviet'. The Movement was formed by Osh region intellectuals and technical cadres who, alarmed by the riots, wanted to keep the republic multiracial and within the Union. But in 1991 it split on the question of turning into an Islamic movement in favour of a 'Turkestan'* confederation. In October 1991 Askar Akayev (the only candidate) was 'democratically' re-elected president and two months later, following the Soviet break-up, led Kyrgystan to join the Commonwealth of Independent States.*

**KIROV** (theatre). Leningrad/St Petersburg rival of the Moscow Bolshoi and first to lose dancers like Natalia Makarova, who in 1970 sought political asylum in Britain. In 1988 she rejoined the company in London for a performance of *Swan Lake*.

**KISHINEV FORUM**. Association of the six republics – Estonia, Latvia, Lithuania, Georgia, Armenia and Moldavia – who refused to sign a new Union treaty* in 1991 at Novo-Ogarevo.*.

**KLIMOV**, ELEM GERMANOVICH (1933– ). Film director, elected head of the Film-Makers' Union* at its fifth congress in 1986. Instigator of radical changes, he secured the release of many important films shelved during the Brezhnev period, beginning with Abuladze's *Pokayaniye* ('Repentance'). His departure, with that of the secretary Smirnov, at the sixth congress (1990) marked the end of an epoch. His films include *Sport, Sport, Sport* (1971–76); the epic *Agony* (1973–75), about relations between Nicholas II and Rasputin; *Farewell to Mother* (1982); and *Come and See* (1985), about the German occupation of Byelorussia.

**KOBETS**, General Konstantin Ivanovich (1939– ) Putative Russian Defence Minister; in 1991 imposed by Yeltsin on Gorbachev as head of a committee studying army reform.

**KOHL**, Chancellor Helmut (1930– ). Architect, with Gorbachev's agreement, of German reunification. Their relations began on a false note when in October 1987 Kohl compared Gorbachev with Goebbels. Kohl later apologized handsomely, but the gaffe froze Soviet-German contacts for several months.

**KOLKHOZ**. Collective farm, theoretically the result of a voluntary association of villagers who agreed to share their land and agricultural equipment. In 1988, 27,000 *kolkhozy*, with 12.5 million members and occupying 53.6 per cent of the cultivated land, still produced half the country's food. In March that year Gorbachev called a congress of *kolkhozniki*, the first in twenty years. The congress approved the draft of a law authorizing the setting up of family farms and defining their legal rights. It also elected a 'national council of collective farms' with 125 members, but failed to tackle basic problems, with the result that in 1991 the *kolkhozy* remained as bureaucratized as the state farms, under permanent management by agricultural and local Party *apparatchiks*. The latter always meddled more in agriculture than in industry, causing seasonal events such as harvests to be governed more by obedience to slogans than by serious agricultural considerations. The congress avoided one of the great taboos of Soviet politics, a law permitting land ownership. For this it was necessary to wait until 1990, when radicals called for the collective farms to be broken up (without knowing how to replace them). In the spring of 1992 *kolkhozy* were caught in a crisis of uncertainty, without directives or knowing where their budget would come from. Ordered to become profitable or close, many were expected to declare bankruptcy, with serious implications for the next harvest.

**KOMSOMOL** (Young Communist League). Former Party 'nursery' and movement for young people aged 14–28. (Youth lasted a long time in the Party.) Its activities were suspended, like those of other Party organizations, after the 1991 *putsch*,* and in October 1991 it was disbanded. Before *perestroika*, membership was a 'must' for any young person wanting to stay out of trouble, as well as a social security card for aspirants to a Party career and a ribbon to tie round one's *kharakteristika* (a kind of political curriculum vitae). Its appeal shrank with its social utility. By 1991 several republics had already dissolved their Komsomols and replaced them with national or religious youth organizations.

**KOMSOMOLSKAYA PRAVDA**. Former Komsomol daily newspaper serving a young adult audience; also preferred to *Pravda* by many older readers because of its livelier make-up and frequently radical tone. It had the second largest all-Union circulation. In 1985−90 subscriptions rose from 13.2 million to 21.9 million, falling back to 16.3 million in 1991. In 1991 the editor was Vladislav Fronin.

**KORAN**. 'Dangerous' religious text once printed and distributed under strict supervision of the Committee for Religious Affairs.* Now, like the Bible, freely available (at a stiff price) from co-operative bookstands.

**KOREA**. See 'North Korea', 'South Korea'.

**KOROTICH**, VITALI ALEKSEEVICH (1936− ). Kiev-born poet and writer, for five years editor of *Ogonyek*★ (succeeding the conservative Anatoli Safronov in 1986). He previously edited the Ukrainian magazine *Vsevit* and travelled widely abroad as a deputy of the Ukrainian parliament and member of the Soviet Peace Committee. In 1989 − still a member of the Communist Party, which he joined in 1967 − he was elected a member of the Congress of People's Deputies from the Kharkov region. As well as transforming *Ogonyek* politically, he showed himself an astute business manager. In August 1991 he accepted a US university teaching post and was replaced by his deputy, Oleg Gushin. The move coincided with a widening division from his staff who, while respectful of what he had done for the magazine, felt the need of a less political style. He remained a board member.

**KOZYREV**, ANDREI VLADIMIROVICH (1951− ). Russian Foreign Minister, made responsible for launching Russian diplomacy under the existing Soviet Union, then appointed to take the place of Shevardnadze★ when Russia took over the Soviet Foreign Ministry. Born in Brussels, the son of a diplomat, he took a Ph.D in history before taking up a career as a Foreign Ministry *apparatchik*. His command of foreign languages and loyalty to Yeltsin made him a high-flyer within the Russian president's circle.

**KRAI** (territory). Name taken from Imperial times. A large administrative area differing from a region (*oblast*★) by the presence of non-Russian minorities, which the *krai* is designed to protect by locating them in separate autonomous regions.★ There are six, all in the Russian Federation.

**KRAIKOM**. Krai Party committee.

**KRASNODAR SPEECH**. Discourse by Gorbachev in September 1986, in which he alarmed Party officials by his first use of the word 'democratization' in relation to Soviet society and by declaring war on bureaucracy and resistance in ministries. The key passage read: 'The Party is at the service of the people; its directing role [in society] does not represent a privilege.'

**KRASNOYARSK.** Site of a giant space-tracking radar station 500 miles from the Mongolian border. The US alleged that it was intended for a second ABM* complex, contravening the ABM treaty. The uncompleted structure was dismantled in 1988, following discussion in the SALT Standing Consultative Commission. Foreign Minister Shevardnadze said later that the military had misled the Soviet government about its purpose. Krasnoyarsk is also the centre of a vast military and nuclear industrial area (Krasnoyarsk-26) and in 1992 became one of the two points, together with Khyshtym (in the Urals), to which nuclear warheads were expected to be taken for destruction under Commonwealth* denuclearization agreements.

**KRAVCHUK**, LEONID MAKAROVICH (1937– ). Ukrainian President, elected in December 1991. Though handicapped by long membership of the Communist Party (he resigned from the Politburo* only on August 24, 1991), he managed to construct an increasingly nationalist team together with the prime minister, Vitold Fokin. While, under his leadership, pre-independence Ukraine was negotiating an economic union, the republic parliament was voting for a Ukrainian currency, the restoration of a Ukrainian defence ministry, and the subordination of military units in the Ukraine to Ukrainian jurisdiction.

**KREMLIN**. Journalists' shorthand for the Soviet government, never properly for the leadership of the Communist Party, whose Moscow headquarters were on Old Square. The word 'Kremlin' means any kind of fortress, usually on a hill and a river bend. Since the dissolution of the Soviet Union the Moscow Kremlin has been the seat of the Russian president and parliament. It also contains the large building known as the Hall of Congresses. The last is used for major state assemblies, and on alternate evenings, in season, for performances of the Bolshoi ballet and opera. (Artists deplore its vastness.) The original Kremlin was of wood. Stone walls were built in the fourteenth century and replaced by the present brick walls and towers in the fifteenth century.

**KREMLINOLOGIST**. Western academic species, threatened with extinction until offered new pastures by the fragmentation of the Union in 1991.

*KROKODIL*. Humorous weekly, founded 1922. Though often wickedly funny in its social comments and cartoons, *Krokodil* never lampooned the Party or government, or domestic or foreign political figures. In 1991 it suffered a disastrous 80 per cent circulation loss.

**KRUISE**. Leading 'pop' group, given a mass audience, with others, at Moscow's first 'pop' concert in 1986, for the victims of Chernobyl.

**KRYUCHKOV**, VLADIMIR ALEKSANDROVICH (1924– ). First head of the KGB* to address the Soviet public on television, in December 1990. He joined in 1967, after serving as a Komsomol *apparatchik*, then as a diplomat (probably already in Intelligence). At the time of his appointment in 1988 in succession to Chebrikov,* he headed the department in charge of intelligence and counter-intelligence abroad. He was later promoted from candidate to full member of the Politburo. His career in the foreign, rather than the 'home', side of the KGB led some optimists to consider him 'liberal'. One of his first actions was to set up a KGB 'public relations' department and announce a shift of direction towards suppression of organized crime. In December 1990 he told the Congress of People's Deputies that foreign forces were trying to impose 'questionable ideas' on the Soviet Union. Accused by the Western press of using dangerous rhetoric, he denied a move to return to the Cold War. More alarm followed when in February 1991 the KGB was given powers to investigate companies suspected of 'economic sabotage', and when in June 1991 Kryuchkov again paraded his paranoia before a parliamentary commission. Two months later he was arrested for his part in the August 19 *putsch*,* which he was considered to have master-minded, and charged with treason.

**KULIKOV**, MARSHAL VIKTOR GEORGYEVICH (1921– ). Commander of Warsaw Pact forces, 1977–89. Despite formal acceptance of Gorbachev's 'new political thinking',* a conservative military outlook led to his replacement by Lushev.*

**KUNAYEV**, DINMUKHAMED AKHMEDOVICH (1911– ). Former Politburo member (1971–87) and for sixteen years Party chief in Kazakhstan, where he succeeded his patron Brezhnev. For years Kunayev plied Brezhnev with cash and other gifts, as did his counterpart in Uzbekistan, Sharaf Rashidov.* During his term of office he left politics in the hands of Party officials in order to concentrate on the affairs of his large and corrupt clan. In December 1986 his replacement as Kazakhstan First Secretary by a Russian, Kolbin, led to the Alma-Ata* riots. The loss of the First Secretaryship entailed his departure from the Politburo in January 1987. In 1989, with the help of his clan, he was unexpectedly returned to office as a deputy in the Kazakhstan parliament.

**KURDS**. Despised minority, estimated to be 153,000-strong, in Central Asia and Transcaucasia. In July 1990, the Kurdish 'Yakbun' ('unity') committee called for a Kurdish autonomous territory to replace the autonomous *raion** which had existed in Azerbaijan until 1931. It asked Gorbachev for 'zones in the south of Russia' to be set aside for Kurdish refugees. Some

18,000 from Armenia and 2,000 from Uzbekistan gathered in Krasnodar *krai* hoping to hear the result of the Yakbun's plea (which was not granted), while Kurds in Kirghizia and Kazakhstan were forced to abandon their homes because of local nationalism.

**KURIL ISLANDS.** Volcanic archipelago lying between the Soviet Kamchatka peninsula and Japan. Two parallel groups (the Greater and Lesser Kurils) were ceded to the Soviet Union on the defeat of Japan in World War II. In 1991 Japan's demands for their return remained an obstacle to much-wanted Japanese participation in the development of the Soviet Far East. A visit by Gorbachev to Tokyo failed to break the deadlock. In September 1991, there were reports of a deal being prepared by Yeltsin; but after a visit to Tokyo, Khasbulatov* said any discussion would have to depend on the establishment of satisfactory relations between Japan and Russia.

**KUROPATY.** Village in Byelorussia recalling Poland's Katyn.* In 1988 it was found to contain a large number of common graves. A Byelorussian official inquiry concluded that they contained the bodies of tens of thousands executed by the NKVD (forerunner of the KGB) in 1937−41. But in 1991 Mikhail Bezrukov, chairman of an independent investigation, said that the tragedy happened in 1941, when the Germans drove Jews from Hamburg and Poland into Byelorussia for extermination.

**KUZBASS.** Major coalfield in the Kemerovo region; centre, with the Donbass,* of an important strike* in 1989 against conditions of work and the disappearance of coal earnings in the maze of ministerial budgets. An even more serious strike occurred in 1991, with demands for better pay and conditions and for the resignation of Gorbachev. Six weeks' interruption of coal supplies threatened to close large sectors of industry. The strike was called off after an agreement between Gorbachev and Yeltsin transferring the mines to the ownership of the Russian republic and allowing managements to keep foreign exchange earned by exports. In 1990 the Kemerovo region declared itself a special economic zone* with the blessing of Yeltsin, who, as future Russian president, blessed anything that could embarrass Gorbachev. The two centuries-old Kuzbass coalfield was vigorously developed in the 1930s, half the production going to local coking plants (Leninsk-Kuznetsky and Prokopievsk).

# L

**LACOSTE**. Coveted crocodile fashion label, enabling wearers to look down on those still at the stage of T-shirts, Coca-Cola and Adidas.

**LADOGA**. Lake north of St Petersburg supposed to ensure drinking water for one of Russia's most heavily populated regions. It contains the largest reserve of fresh water in Europe but is close to biological death due to the industrial discharge of phosphates. Since 1986 moves to protect it have set the urban intelligentsia at loggerheads with the workers of the riverside industrial town of Prioziorsk. In 1990 searchers discovered the wreck of a ship that had lain for thirty years on the lake bed, leaking radioactivity.

**LANDSBERGIS**, Vytautas Vytautovich (1932– ). Lithuanian musicologist turned leader of the Soviet Union's first 'independent' republic (an independent *state* from September 1991). A founder of Sajudis,★ elected to the Soviet parliament in 1989, he became chairman of the Lithuanian parliament in 1990. In 1991 the ultimate in a series of crass and brutal acts by troops of the Soviet MVD★ – an assault on the Vilnius television station – raised him to a moral eminence surpassing even that achieved ten months earlier during Moscow's heavy-footed (but successful) economic blockade. Within Sajudis he owed his ascendancy more to a flair for romanticism than to practical statesmanship. Barricaded at the height of the crisis in his heavily defended parliament building, he would receive visitors with a brief recital (and a few false notes) on his office piano and a quick peek at the adjoining chapel, with its madonna and candles. Later, having failed, like other presidents, to deliver prosperity at the same time as independence, he took to seeing the hand of the former KGB behind every expression of disappointment and opposition, and accused Poland of stirring up trouble among Lithuania's Polish minority.

**LANGUAGE**. Focus of struggles for national identity. In 1990 several republics passed laws imposing the official language of the republic on all their inhabitants. The move caused friction between Russian-speaking and 'national' populations, and no less between 'national' majorities and non-Russian minorities who wanted Russian to remain as a *lingua franca*. Until the advent of post-*perestroika* nationalism there was a laudable fiction that the 130 or so different languages spoken in the Soviet Union (seventy-seven of them literary) were all equal.

**LATVIA** (pop. 2.7 million). Baltic republic finally recognized as an independent state after four years of struggle in September 1991. Its holiday landscape conceals poor soil and an industry heavily dependent on imported materials. In 1991 the population comprised only 54 per cent Latvians, 33 per cent Russians, 5 per cent Byelorussians, 3 per cent Ukrainians and 3 per cent Poles. At independence it was not clear what would happen to the Russians, who lived, like two-thirds of the whole population, in the capital, Riga. Young Latvians were one of the first groups anywhere to assert their national identity, mainly through rock* music. Organized nationalism was touched off by a free-speaking cultural exchange with American academics, daringly permitted by the new Soviet leadership, at Jurmala, near Riga, in 1987. Later, Latvia fell behind its Baltic neighbours, probably because the native Latvians were weak in relation to the rest of the population (being outnumbered in the cities) and because its economy was poorer than those of Estonia and Lithuania. But with the approach of the elections of 1989–90 nationalism gained strength. The Latvian Communist Party split from the Soviet party, leaving only a splinter group loyal to Moscow; and the elections were won by the Latvian Popular Front. The new government followed Estonia and Lithuania in declaring independence* and in October 1990 set up customs posts on the borders with Russia and Byelorussia. Meanwhile tension developed between the local population and Soviet 'occupation' troops. On January 20, 1991 OMON* forces attacked a building of the republic's Interior Ministry. Four people died in the shooting and a fifth in a separate incident. The affair caused anti-Moscow feeling that transcended ethnic divisions.

**LAW**. Concept revived in 1986 with an undertaking to observe the rule of law. The first innovation was to declare as lawful everything not expressly forbidden. But for this it was necessary to acquaint the public with the contents of the legal code, in a country where copies were harder to find than a bible. When it came to legislating, there was a lack of lawyers among parliamentary deputies and little experience in drafting. (From 1938 to 1985 the Supreme Soviet passed only seventy laws, less than the British parliament in a year.) From 1986 until 1989 the country continued working with 'legislative acts' (*zakonodatelniye akti*) and decrees.* After 1989, deputies went to the opposite extreme, putting rushed drafts to rushed votes, until government by decree again became general after the 1991 *putsch** and in the period surrounding the Soviet break-up.

**LAW ON CITIZENSHIP** (April 1990). Law providing that in the USSR every person had the right to citizenship. No person could be arbitrarily deprived of citizenship or the right to change it. In addition:
- Any citizen of a Union republic was also a citizen of the USSR, and any citizen of an autonomous republic a citizen of the appropriate Union republic.

- A Soviet citizen might not be extradited abroad, nor was foreign citizenship recognized for USSR citizens.
- Where parents had different citizenship and one was a Soviet citizen at the time of a child's birth, the child was a Soviet citizen even if born abroad.
- Renunciation of citizenship was allowed by petition, unless the person had (a) unfulfilled obligations to the state or 'significant private interests', or (b) was subject to criminal proceedings.
- Renunciation might be disallowed if renunciation by the person making it 'contradicted the interest of state security'.
- An action 'causing significant damage' to state security might justify revoking the citizenship of a person living abroad. (Full text in the Soviet press, June 1, 1990.)

**LAW ON CO-OPERATIVES** (1988). Law allowing co-operatives to engage in any form of activity, including banking and foreign trade. Among its provisions:

- Co-operatives might sell shares and set up joint ventures with foreign companies, without restriction as to participation, size or the type of production or service.
- Earnings might be distributed in relation to participants' financial investment and not merely work input.
- No special permission was needed from local authorities (though in many places compulsory registration continued).

When the law became effective in July 1988, an earlier one imposing crippling taxes was rescinded. (Co-operatives were first made possible by the Law on Individual Economic Activity; see below.)

**LAW ON ENTERPRISES** (June 1990). Law governing the creation, registration and (in case of bankruptcy) liquidation of enterprises; still in force in 1991 but liable to modification in independent republics. Among its provisions:

- Enterprises might be owned by individuals, co-operatives or joint-stock companies, if necessary with foreign participation.
- Associations might be formed with other enterprises, subject to restrictions on monopoly.
- Funds might be raised through loans or the sale of securities.
- Workers might own shares and participate in management decisions through a general meeting.
- Labour disputes might be resolved under either Soviet or republic law (one of several points left imprecise).
- The council (i.e. board) of the enterprise should include both workers' and owners' representatives.
- If the enterprise held a monopoly or near-monopoly of supply, prices might be set by the state.
- The enterprise might hold a hard-currency account, but only for

payments to union, state and local budgets.
- Enterprises were expected to provide housing, medical care, welfare and pensions.
- In case of bankruptcy, a liquidation commission had to value the property and settle claims, giving priority to state and union budgets, with investors and workers in second place. (Full text in the Soviet press, June 12, 1990.)

**LAW ON INDIVIDUAL ECONOMIC ACTIVITY** (November 1986, effective May 1987). Law permitting 'individual' or co-operative activities in twenty-nine trades, including hairdressing, dressmaking, motor-car maintenance, catering, photography, house-decoration, household appliance repairs and taxi-driving. Beneficiaries were required to obtain a licence and pay taxes, and were limited to pensioners, housewives, students and others without full-time jobs, or state workers 'in their spare time'. In September 1987 the law was extended to include owning and managing shops or taking space in state shops to sell goods or produce. In April 1988 its operation suffered a temporary setback when tax changes (cancelled three months later) made co-operatives★ liable to up to 90 per cent on their profits. Later provisions allowed one-man businesses to employ relatives, hire apprentices (paid workers or partners), obtain bank credit, rent work space, and procure goods and materials from state enterprises. The law was really meant as a guide for more detailed legislation by republics. It initially fell short of expectations due to bureaucratic obstruction, e.g. over issuing licences, and frictions arising from people's resentment of private 'profits'.

**LAW ON PROPERTY** (1990). Product of two Presidential decrees: one in August establishing a State Property Fund and one in September guaranteeing ownership. The Fund was designed to facilitate the transformation of state property 'into other forms, and ensure conditions for [its] rational utilization'. Its powers would be framed with a view to developing a single Soviet market★ (which most republics opposed). The second decree forbade 'illegal' seizures and ordered courts to safeguard the titles of citizens, public organizations and the state. Gorbachev was thinking of recent seizures of Party property and rows between rival claimants.

**LAW ON THE PRESS** (effective August 1990). Law ending censorship★ and Party or state monopoly of the media by allowing anyone to found a publication. It also required the registration★ of titles (in September 1990), under the names of the owners. There were numerous disputes, as in the case of *Ogonyek*, whose ownership was contested between production staff and editorial staff, and *Sovietskaya Rossiya*, where there was a tug-of-war between Yeltsin's 'reformist' Russian government and Polozkov's★ conservative Russian Communist Party. At the time of enforcement, four-fifths of Soviet newspapers were still owned by the Party; but it was no longer a united Party, and many of its organizations were demanding their own journal. The law ignored professional questions, such as the mixed roles of the many journalists in parliament. Nor did it address problems that might arise in the future from concentrations of ownership or the purchase of newspapers (and even more broadcasting stations) by foreign interests.

**LAW ON STATE ENTERPRISES** (June 1990). Law covering all economic activity by state-owned industries, including changes due to have been completed by the end of the year. Except for important products subject to state purchasing orders (*goszakazy*), enterprises were free to decide their own production plans, based on contracts with other units. Fulfilment of state orders, with guaranteed supplies of material, was obligatory; material for other contracts might be procured at prices allowed to move within limits. All enterprises were required to be self-financing (*samofinansirovaniye*) – a stricter condition than *khozraschet* (cost accounting), which allowed the state to bail out loss-makers. (In the words of the law they had to 'maximize revenues after meeting the cost of supplies, contributing to local and central budgets and paying interest on loans or credits.') There was also provision for declarations of bankruptcy. Profitability was to come from the greater involvement of the work collective (all workers plus an elected council and manager). Allocation of funds between investment, product innovation, social benefits etc. was at the council's discretion. And there was a uniform rate of taxation, replacing the previous progressive rate. But restrictions remained. In 1991 planners still set 'guidelines' for the division of 'retained earnings' between investment and social consumption, and could decide what 'major' projects were safe to start. Ministries stayed responsible for 'ensuring the satisfaction of demand' in their field, and for 'improving productivity, innovation and maintenance of a progressive capital structure'. Arguments between a manager and an enterprise council were supposed to be settled by a general meeting of the collective, and decisions to hire or transfer workers to be approved by the appropriate brigade council.

**LAWYER (ATTORNEY).** Member of a profession restored to respectability since *perestroika* made laws matter. Since 1979, lawyers have been organized in 'colleges' (*advokaturi*) based on geographical and administrative boundaries, for the purpose of consultation. In 1989 they began to press for a professional union, independence from the Ministry of Justice, and working conditions less degrading to clients (sometimes obliged to sit ten on a bench when explaining their circumstances).

**LEFT-WING.** See 'Wing'.

**LENIN,** alias VLADIMIR ILICH ULYANOV (1870–1924). Author of the 1917 October revolution, claimed by Gorbachev to be the inspiration of his own. In numerous ways — NEP,* Party 'internal democracy', his policy on nationalities — Lenin offered Gorbachev precedents with which to fend off Party conservatives and concede almost anything while remaining ideologically coherent. When the time came to 'rewrite history', Stalin served as the villain, the man whom Lenin rejected as his successor and who spirited away his 'testament' in order to grab power. But gradually the attacks moved on from Stalin to take in the whole system, and thus its creator. Lenin's critics began gently, pointing out that he was only a man and as such happened often to change his mind and even get things wrong. But in 1989 the niceties began to be dropped and Lenin joined the symbols of communism that had to be destroyed. In places across the country his portraits and statues were taken down by delirious crowds; and in 1991 it was proposed to remove his body from the Red Square mausoleum. But deleninization was not like destalinization: it was more intellectual and political. It required an explanation, whereas with Stalin it had been enough just to condemn.

**LENINGRAD/ST PETERSBURG**. Ancient capital of Peter the Great formally restored to its old name by the Russian parliament in September 1991. The move followed a 54 per cent vote in a referendum the previous June. The regional elections of 1990, won by the Democratic Front, marked the start of a process distancing it from Moscow. Its television became more daring, its intelligentsia* more radical, its conservatives (led by Boris Gidaspov) more conservative. Even its 'democrats' are more divided than those anywhere else; in October 1990 it took weeks to choose a mayor, Anatoli Sobchak,* who was to distinguish himself ten months later by his handling, in Leningrad, of the attempted Moscow *putsch*.* The city's architectural magnificence hides serious environmental problems. One of Sobchak's first moves was to obtain a vote cancelling a project for a barrage across the Gulf of Finland. The barrage was supposed to protect Leningrad from flooding, but a commission of the USSR Academy of Sciences advised that in fact it would endanger the city by worsening the already deplorable ecological condition of the river Neva. Sobchak suggested diverting the funds (R1 billion, less two-thirds already spent) to an ecological clean-up. But in 1991 work had yet to begin. Faced with an equally serious unemployment problem (most of its industries depended on the Defence Ministry), the great metropolis finally persuaded the Russian republic to declare it a special economic zone.*

**LIBERAL**. Any kind of partisan for the 'market', or against communism.

**LIBERAL-CONSERVATIVE UNION**. 'Thatcherite union' (*sic*) launched by Gari Kasparov* and Arkadi Murashev* in July 1991, after breaking with the Democratic Party of Russia.* They accused the latter's chairman, Nikolai Travkin,* of departing from rigid anti-communism.

**LIBERAL DEMOCRATIC PARTY OF THE SOVIET UNION**. Maverick party founded in 1990 by Vladimir Zhirinovsky,* suspended from activity after the 1991 *putsch*.* Claiming to have 15,000 members and active contact with liberal parties in Germany, Japan and South Korea, it pursued a strange mixture of policies: privatization of property combined with demands for military action in the Baltic region and a refusal to 'join in anti-communist hysteria'.

**LIBERTARIAN PARTY**. Minuscule group of young men proclaiming sexual and other liberties. Distinguished by a demonstration in Red Square in 1990 at which they handed out condoms to deputies leaving parliament.

**LIBRARIES**. Decayed reminder of early campaigns for literacy and popular culture. Across the country barely used libraries are filled with books of the day before yesterday. In 1990 staffs joined other cultural workers in protests at budget cuts and deteriorating conditions. National libraries are in the same sorry state as community libraries. In 1991, in the Lenin Library in Moscow, thousands of irreplaceable books were stacked in disorder, some even standing on the floor. (In 1986 the foundations were damaged by construction of a Metro station.) In 1988 the Leningrad library of the Academy of Sciences was severely damaged by a fire, described by Academician Likhachev* as a 'cultural Chernobyl'. After a nineteen-hour blaze, extinguished with tens of thousands of gallons of water, firemen used bulldozers to disperse the debris. Losses included 400,000 books, an irreplaceable collection of seventeenth-century medical literature, a quarter of a unique collection of newspapers, and the entire reference section.

**LIFE EXPECTANCY**. Gloomy indicator of national well-being (in 1991 the USSR was said to be forty-fifth in the world table). Causes range from poor diet to environmental pollution and alcoholism, the last accounting for one of the world's largest life expectancy gaps — ten years — between women and men. Statistics released in 1986 showed that in the mid-1950s men's expectancy was 63 years, in the mid-1960s only sixty years, and in the mid-1970s 62.3 years. For women the respective figures were 69, 74 and 73 years. Expectancy varies greatly among regions. In 1990 the average for both sexes was 69.3 years.

**LIGACHEV**, Yegor Kuzmich (1920– ). Conservative leader of consistent views. In June 1987 he set them out in the *World Marxist Review*, indicating what for him were the limits of reform (which he supported): 'Our course is aimed not at a liberalization of the Western type, which conceals the omnipotence of capital, but at a deepening of socialist democracy and the socialist self-government of the people.' A man of rigidly puritan principle, during the latter years of a long career he repeatedly condemned past mistakes, acknowledging that in the years before *perestroika* socialist ideas became 'clotted'. But he also condemned 'hasty' self-reproach and an 'over-large' rewriting of history. In his own words, new generations could range themselves against the old and people could 'lose faith and a sense of morality'. As a resolute defender of Leninist principles, he was so devoted to Party unity as to vote for majority-approved measures with which he personally disagreed. He retired from the Politburo in August 1990 but remained an important voice in politics.

**LIKHACHEV**, Dmitri Sergeyevich (1906– ). Academician and first chairman of the Soviet Cultural Fund;* rare example of a Russian patriot untainted by chauvinism. In the 1930s he did time in Stalin's camps for holding a private seminar in which he criticized the contemporary reform of the Russian alphabet. His disclosure of this hitherto unknown fact in a 1986 television interview caused a deep moral shock, particularly among young people. One of the first public men to declare himself a Christian.

**LIMITCHIKI**. Outsiders attracted to Moscow by unskilled industrial jobs. In return for doing the least popular work they receive permission to live just outside the city limits; hence their name. After seven years they are entitled to a residence permit (*propiska**). Their claim on scarce housing and reputation for criminality are sources of conflict with Muscovites. In 1991 there were proposals to move factories employing *limitchiki* to the city periphery, to reduce the housing problem, as well as pollution.

**LINKAGE**. Political jargon word for coupling an international agreement in one policy area to that in another. Examples have included (unsuccessful) Soviet demands that the US drop 'Star Wars'* as a condition for agreeing on the INF treaty,* and later START.*

***LITERATURNAYA GAZETA*** (*Literary Gazette*). Reformist weekly, required reading for the intelligentsia.* In 1985–88 circulation doubled to 6.2 million before falling back to 4.4 million in 1990, and only 1 million in 1991. A front section deals with subjects ranging far beyond literature. In 1990 it came under the editorship of Fyodor Burlatsky,* a former senior writer. The same year, with the requirement to register the title and its ownership under the new Law on the Press,* Burlatsky persuaded the paper's editorial staff to vote to take it away from the Union of Writers* and into staff ownership. Recrimination followed when journalists found they had lost access to social benefits, such as the Union's polyclinic – a serious matter at a time of depleted services. They were also unhappy about the paper's espousal of political themes at the expense of its literary function, which they blamed for the fall-off in readership. And in 1991 Burlatsky was voted out by the collective.

**LITHUANIA** (pop. 3.6 million). Former Union republic bordering Poland and the Baltic, 60 per cent dependent on industry and the Ignalina nuclear power station. In September 1991, as a result of the defeat of the Moscow *putsch*,* it gained the independence it had formally proclaimed for the previous eighteen months. At the time the population was 80 per cent Lithuanian, 9 per cent Russian, 7 per cent Polish and 2 per cent Byelorussian. Although initially slower than Estonia and Latvia, Lithuania had soon become the spearhead of Baltic independence. In 1988 the process was speeded by two events: the formation of Sajudis* by Algirdas Brazauskas and normalization of state relations with the Roman Catholic church. The nationalists emerged victorious from the 1989 elections, and in March 1990 the parliament declared Lithuania independent. This led Moscow to impose a blockade* which would show everyone what economic independence entailed. Three months later independence was 'suspended' to permit negotiations with Moscow. In agreeing to these the Lithuanians were thinking of independence, whereas Moscow thought only of a new union treaty.* According to President Landsbergis,* in October 1990, the outcome would depend on the type of treaty offered. The nationalist common front meanwhile showed signs of a split. Government ministers, mostly ex-communists, complained of pressure and impatience by parliament; and the prime minister, Mme Prunskiene* (more realistic than the romantic Landsbergis), warned against the danger of an 'authoritarian and dictatorial republic'. A law making Lithuanian the only official language caused deep resentment among Russians and Poles. Russians, with a municipal majority in Klaipeda – a major Soviet port – rejected application of the law there on the ground that Klaipeda (formerly Memel) was never Lithuanian. Poles unilaterally declared an autonomous region south of the capital, Vilnius, which was Polish-occupied from 1921 to 1940. Adding to the tension, the Polish government spoke of a return to 1939 frontiers if the Polish minority should be mistreated, and Byelorussia threatened the same if Lithuania continued to withhold its products from 'foreigners'. To calm the atmosphere on the eve of new negotiations with Moscow in November 1990, a Lithuanian parliamentary commission proposed postponing application of the language law until 1995. Nevertheless, 1990 ended in confusion and with hostility mounting towards Soviet 'occupation troops'. The government cancelled military families' residence permits, depriving them of access to schools, hospitals and shops; barracks were attacked by a nationalist action group, the League of Freedom; and a further law banned 'parties directed from abroad', indicating the Communist Party. In January 1991, Mme Prunskiene resigned after a refusal by parliament to approve price increases. On January 13, Soviet tanks attacked the Vilnius television station which, in a new situation of tension vis-à-vis the Soviet 'occupation', was being guarded by a large civilian crowd. Fourteen civilians and a Soviet officer were killed in the shooting (which a Soviet military investigation later unconvincingly claimed had all come from the crowd). Barricaded against attack in the Lithuanian parliament building, Landsbergis called for a plebiscite; and on February 9, Lithuanians voted overwhelmingly for a 'free and democratic Lithuania'. Post-independence politics have been marked by the brusque treatment of ethnic minorities, a drift towards authoritarian presidential rule, and disappointment with Western economic aid.

**LOBOV**, GENERAL VLADIMIR NIKOLAYEVICH (1935– ). Strategic theorist appointed Deputy Chief of the Soviet general staff after the 1991 *putsch*.* (His superior, Shaposhnikov,* was appointed simultaneously.) During the *putsch*, as head of the Frunze Military Academy, he refused an order from Yazov* appointing him commandant of Moscow's Leninski *raion*.* Earlier, as commander-in-chief of Warsaw Treaty forces, he advocated developing contacts with NATO. Never a political general, he was seen to have been appointed as a gesture of reassurance towards the professionally-minded officer corps. In December 1991 he was abruptly retired, apparently due to differences with Shaposhnikov over methods of reforming the armed forces. He was replaced by Gen. Viktor Samsonov (50), former commandant of the Leningrad Military District.

**LOPATIN**, VLADIMIR NIKOLAYEVICH (1960– ). Retired major, founder of 'Shield'.* In 1990 he left the army in order to have greater freedom to attack the military bureaucracy as a deputy of the Soviet parliament. In 1991 he became First Deputy Chairman of the Russian Federation State Committee for Public Security and Collaboration with the USSR Ministry of Defence and the KGB.

**LUBIMOV**, YURI PETROVICH (1917– ). Legendary stage director of the Taganka* theatre, exiled to the West and stripped of his citizenship in 1983 for criticizing the authorities. After first refusing to seek political asylum, he later applied for Israeli citizenship together with his Jewish wife. When in 1988 the authorities invited him back, he insisted on returning to his old theatre, and was later helped to do so by the Minister of Culture, Gubenko.* Back in Moscow, he recovered the inspiration that evaded him in exile.

**LUKYANOV**, ANATOLI IVANOVICH (1930– ). Former Chairman of the USSR Supreme Soviet, accused of involvement in the 1991 *putsch** and charged with treason. A lawyer and old friend of Gorbachev from their Moscow University days, in 1987 he was made a Central Committee Secretary, and in 1988 a member of the Politburo. The same year he was elected First Vice-President of the old Supreme Soviet, and in 1989 of the new, where he proved an able day-to-day business manager. He became full chairman in 1990, with Gorbachev's move to an executive Presidency; but in 1991 he was increasingly accused of conservative bias. A few days before the *putsch* he published a highly provocative letter, declaring that the new union treaty,* due to be signed on August 20, meant 'the end of the USSR'. After the *putsch* Gorbachev took nearly a week to be persuaded of Lukyanov's complicity — which Lukyanov strongly denied — and order his arrest. In gaol, awaiting trial for treason, Lukyanov, almost alone among those similarly accused, refused to answer questions put to him by investigators and threatened to make 'sensational revelations' about current political leaders if and when brought into court.

**LUMUMBA UNIVERSITY**. Recipient of Third World students with scholarships in any subject from farming to tropical medicine, where boredom breeds rabid anti-communism. Courses start with a year's language teaching. In 1990 there were more than 100,000 students from 149 countries at Lumumba and 500 other Soviet training establishments, including Moscow State University.* Soviet citizens complained angrily at the expense. In February 1992 Lumumba was renamed the Russian University of Friendship of Peoples. See also 'Blacks'.

**LUSHEV**, GENERAL PYOTR GEORGYEVICH (1923– ). Pro-Gorbachev officer (deputy Defence Minister and former commander of Soviet forces in Germany) appointed chief of Warsaw Pact forces in February 1989, in succession to Kulikov.* His command disappeared fourteen months later.

**LUTHERAN** church. Force active in Estonia and Latvia, but much less so than Catholicism in the third Baltic republic, Lithuania. In 1991 it had 600,000 members.

**LYUBERITES**. Youths of the Moscow working-class suburb, Lyubertsi, who in 1986 took to descending on the capital. Their violent physical attacks on 'snob' Muscovites and 'rubbish' (punks, hippies and anyone 'offensively' dressed) caused a public outrage. In February 1987, 500 young Muscovites marched down Kalinin Avenue in protest, one of the city's first public demonstrations.

# M

**MCDONALDS**. Corner of America on Pushkin Square, with three-hour queues until the wait was shortened by price rises. Opened in February 1990, Moscow's first fast-food restaurant began by selling its 'Big Macs' for 3.5 roubles, thanks to a contract allowing it to buy meat at subsidized prices (2.5 roubles, compared with 20 roubles in the market).

**MAFIA**. Term long given a specious romance, thanks to *perestroika*'s most popular TV series, *The Octopus*. In May 1990 mafias ceased to be entertainment. The police announced that in eighteen months they and the KGB had busted 1,200 gangs. Petrovka 38, Moscow's counterpart of Scotland Yard, makes a distinction between mafia groups and ordinary gangs. Whereas ordinary gangs are local, mafia groups are distinguished by geographical mobility, inter-regional or international connections, and, commonly, ethnic-group specialization. Within the last category, Chechen mafias specialize in gold, a Jewish mafia in computers, Moldavians in stolen cars, etc.

**MAIN POLITICAL ADMINISTRATION (OF THE ARMED FORCES)**. Former body responsible for political work in the Army and Navy, having dual status as a department of the Central Committee and a directorate of the Ministry of Defence. From 1985, under Aleksei Lizichev, it was supposed to be the principal channel for advancing *perestroika* in the armed forces. It was abolished in 1991 with military 'de-politicization'. The move released 92,000 persons, not including 20,000 on courses at political-military colleges. The latter were turned into 'armed forces humanitarian academies' giving officers psychological and sociological instruction.

**MAKASHOV**, GEN. ALBERT MIKHAILOVICH (1938– ). Soviet deputy and candidate last in the 1991 Russian presidential election, with only 3.74 per cent of the votes. He was embittered because Soyuz★ backed Ryzhkov★ and the barracks voted Yeltsin. In June 1991 he used his defeat to form the Movement for a Communist Initiative, aiming to rally orthodox communists behind a call for the 'sovietization' of industry (transferring ownership to work collectives).

**MANDELSTAM**, OSIP EMILIEVICH (1891–1938). Legendary figure of

Russian poetry of the first half of the twentieth century, who died in a camp near Vladivostok seven months after his arrest. (He had previously spent three years' administrative exile in Voronezh, when his poetry was committed to memory by his wife, Nadezhda.) He was rehabilitated in 1956, but for most of the time copies of his work, republished in 1977, were kept under the table. In 1988 *Yunost** published the first twenty-four chapters of the memoirs of his widow, which she completed after her return to Moscow in 1964. She died without seeing them in print. The book appeared in the West in 1970, but in its entirety (eighty-three chapters) in the USSR only in 1989.

**MANPOWER**. Under the Union a potential force of 164 million people, about 60 per cent of the total population. In 1990 (the last year for which there are statistics) the number actually employed was 138.4 million — a drop of nearly a million from 1989, officially explained by more leave for mothers, earlier retirement and greater unemployment.* The state sector employed 114.6 million and the co-operative sector 19.3 million (of whom 11.5 million were in collective farms, 3.5 in consumer co-operation and 4.3 million in co-operatives proper). The individual sector engaged 4.5 million. About 1 million left state enterprises and organizations during the year. A major problem was the restriction of labour mobility by the *propiska** system, particularly in big cities.

**MARCHENKO**, ANATOLI TIKHONOVICH (1938–1986). Martyred human rights activist and author. His death in prison, in circumstances suggesting foul play, provoked worldwide protest and cast a shadow over *perestroika*.

**MARCHUK**, GURI IVANOVICH (1925– ). President (1986–90) of the Academy of Sciences. His election, at the age of 61, to succeed 83-year-old Anatoli Aleksandrov resulted from the Academy's first secret ballot. A mathematician, Marchuk was responsible in the 1960s for installing an important computer centre at Novosibirsk. In 1980 he became a Soviet vice-premier and head of the State Committee for Science and Technology. Marchuk is considered an expert on nuclear reactors. His choice as president reflected Gorbachev's impatience to speed up Soviet scientific research and develop its industrial applications.

**MARKET** (1) Space (still sometimes listed in guidebooks under 'local curiosities') for the sale of produce from collective farms and family plots.* By the late 1980s 'peasant markets' had become indispensable to urban existence, with prices mounting in parallel with the shortages in state shops. By the winter of 1990–91 their stock had become affordable only by foreigners and the Soviet 'new rich' produced by reforms or living on the 'parallel economy'. Which did not stop their being crowded, especially at weekends.

**MARKET** (2). Magic formula for instant riches. For producers, always a sellers' market; for consumers, a buyers' one. At least until a more thoughtful mood set in, with 1991–92 price increases.

**MARRIAGE**. Institution supposed to make for social stability but discredited by rising divorce figures and marriages of convenience. The latter, once a favourite method of emigrating with the help of foreigners, came to be used to get round the problem of obtaining *propiskas*★ for big cities.

**MARTIAL ARTS**. Sport born in secret and long forbidden by law. In the mid-1980s its underground clubs became nurseries for young hoodlums (see 'Lyuberites'), attacking punks, demonstrators, drunks and prostitutes. No longer illegal, they now help train bodyguards for 'businessmen' and politicians.

**MARXISM-LENINISM**. Repository of religious texts handed down by Karl Marx (1818–1883), Friedrich Engels (1820–1895) and Vladimir Ilich Ulyanov, *alias* Lenin (1870–1924). It proclaimed that by virtue of its principles the Communist Party would lead the USSR to its final destination: communism. Lenin set out to accelerate the process imagined by Marx, whereby, thanks to an interlude of bourgeois rule, a proletariat forged by class conflict would become the force needed to introduce communism. He declared that by a union of the proletariat with the peasantry it was possible to skip the bourgeois stage and pass directly to the socialist revolution. But, being aware of the workers' inertia, he created a strictly controlled party in order to arrive there more quickly. Lenin believed that the Russian revolution would spread; he was wrong. Stalin drew the lesson, and on Lenin's death proclaimed 'socialism in one country', before launching a campaign of terror against his own people. In 1988 the authorities ended the obligatory study of Marxism-Leninism in universities and institutes (in medical faculties it had added a year to the training of doctors). Meanwhile at the Party-controlled Institute of Marxism-Leninism in Moscow, a reformist director, Georgi Smirnov, began trying to reassemble the pieces of the puzzle in a way that could rationalize the transition from Soviet socialism to democracy and the market. In 1991 Marxist political inspiration was effectively killed by Gorbachev's introduction of a new 'social-democratic' programme at the June plenum of the Party Central Committee. Its coffin was nailed by the failure of the August 1991 *putsch*.★

**MARXIST PLATFORM** (CPSU). Programme presented by Party conservatives at the Twenty-eighth Party Congress★ in opposition to the 'Democratic Platform'★ and the pro-Gorbachev centre.

**MARXIST WORKERS' PARTY**. Party with Trotskyite tendencies founded in March 1990. It campaigns for 'decentralization of power' and in 1991 claimed to have 5–7,000 members in eight republics.

**MASLENNIKOV**, ARKADI AFRIKANOVICH (1931– ). Senior journalist, formerly *Pravda* correspondent in London, in 1989 recalled to head the Soviet parliament press centre and become Gorbachev's press secretary.

**MASSES**. Vague bodies with floating opinions supposed to express 'the will of the people'. In the early phase of street demonstrations, 1990–91, political opponents could be forced to resign for having 'lost the confidence of the masses'.

**MATRIMONIAL CLUB**. Early idea for bringing 'lonely hearts' together, especially young people far from home and young divorcees. They were sometimes organized by the Komsomol.★ In 1988 a racket began when newspapers started accepting advertisements from foreign matrimonial agencies, playing on the myth of rich foreign suitors. In 1991 it continued to flourish, despite exposure of the advertisements as a confidence trick with their invitations to send a 'curriculum vitae, photo and $20' to a Canadian or American box number.

**MAXIMALIST**. Young person 'all-out' for *perestroika*; especially numerous when reform was still green. Maximalists were pledged to respect socialist values while working for changes that would bring a better life, end corruption, give a better picture of the USSR abroad, and provide opportunities to young cadres.★ They were usually recruited in universities or among newly returned soldiers from Afghanistan. The flame was soon extinguished.

**MEDIA ('MEDIATIZATION')**. Brutal innovation for a society living for years on the principle that happiness depended on keeping a low profile. With elections and power struggles, 'being known' suddenly became important. Deputies grabbed journalists' microphones and even got out 'press kits' with pictures and biographies. Television created overnight 'star performers'; and people started to ask how they 'came over'. For the first time the private lives of artists, politicians and even scientists became 'newsworthy'. Prudently, newspapers began the new journalism gently, with profiles of foreign personalities (from Britain's Prince Charles to Princess Caroline of Monaco). In September 1990 Gorbachev's new press officer went so far as to give details of his master's day: work in the office from nine until eight, before going home with an evening's paper-work.

**MEDICINE**. See 'Health service'.

**MEDVEDEV**, ROY ALEKSANDROVICH (1925– ). Soviet historian and twin brother of Zhores (see below). He first attained fame with his seminal work on Stalinism, *Let History Judge* (New York, 1974). In the same period he became one of the editors of the *samizdat* journal, *Chronicle of Current Events*, which reported acts of persecution under the Brezhnev regime, and in 1970 co-signatory, with Sakharov* and Churchin (another physicist) of an open letter to Brezhnev containing a twelve-point proposal for the democratization of society. The unauthorized publication of his book abroad caused him to be expelled from the Communist Party and undergo a twenty-year period of harassment. Yet he remained a Marxist and preserved his freedom by skilful observance of Soviet law. Through-out the period, and for several years after the arrival in power of Gorbachev, Roy Medvedev remained one of the principal sources of objective information to foreign journalists in Moscow. In 1988 the chairman of the commission responsible for opening up the *Spetsfond*\* ruled that Roy Medvedev's works were not for public reading; yet a year later Medvedev was regularly writing in the Soviet press on the period of Stalin. In 1989 he was chosen in the first free elections to represent a Moscow constituency in the Congress of People's Deputies, and by the Congress as a Deputy of the Supreme Soviet,* where he chaired the commission investigating allegations of misconduct by the prosecutors Gdlyan* and Ivanov. The same year he was invited to rejoin the Communist Party, and in 1990 elected to a place in the Central Commit-tee. In December 1991, objecting to the 'illegality' of the Party's dissolution after the August *putsch*,\* he became a co-founder of the Socialist Party of Russian Working People.\* The Medvedevs' father, a Civil War communist, died in a prison camp in 1937.

**MEDVEDEV**, Vadim Andreevich (1929– ). Party official responsible for ideology since 1984 and member in 1990 of the Presidential Council.\* After graduating from Leningrad university in 1951, he followed an academic career until 1968 when he became Gorkom* secretary for Leningrad. From 1978 to 1983 he was rector of the CPSU Academy of Social Sciences. He was a member of the revision commission of the Twenty-fifth and Twenty-sixth Congresses, and at the Twenty-seventh Congress was elected a member of the Central Committee. The same year (1986) he was elected a Secretary, and in 1988 a member of the Politburo. In 1989 he became a parliamentary deputy.

**MEDVEDEV**, Zhores Aleksandrovich (1925– ). Soviet biochemist and writer, twin brother of Roy (see above), now living in London. An early victim of the use of 'psychiatry' to confine dissidents to mental hospitals, he was freed by the efforts of his brother, helped by Sakharov* and other friends. He later exposed psychiatric abuse in his book *A Question of Madness*, published abroad. In 1969 he gamely offended the authorities by the foreign publication of his book *The Rise and Fall of T.D. Lysenko*, exposing the work of the regime's charlatan geneticist, with the result that in 1973 he was deprived of Soviet citizenship while on a year's secondment to the National Institute of Medical Research in Britain. He subsequently took British citizenship. In 1979 he became the first person to tell the outside world about the 1957 Kyshtym (South Urals) nuclear disaster. In 1990 Medvedev's Soviet citizenship was restored by a presidential decree, and he started to be published in the Soviet press. As a scientist, he is best known for his research into the process of ageing.

**MEETINGS SYNDROME.** Disease that struck the USSR during the 1989 election campaign and then spread with alarming speed. The street became the place for making (and breaking) political careers. In many places the authorities capitulated to the pressure of crowds, who in fact were doing less to defend democracy than to satisfy the rancour accumulated over years of silence. Among the officials sacrificed to the mob to get it to end round-the-clock demonstrations in 1990 was the Ukrainian prime minister Vitali Massol.

**MEMORIAL.** Society founded in 1988 on the initiative of representatives from widely differing groups (Sakharov,* Afanasiev,* Klimov*) to preserve the memory of Stalinist repression and its victims. First meetings revealed a difference of view between those who wanted to limit the field to Stalinist repression and those who wanted to extend it to include *all* repression, from the Revolution up to 1985. Local sections across the country collected historical evidence and helped families find traces of relatives who had disappeared. They were specially active in cities like Vorkuta, which had been built by political prisoners. In October 1990 the society unveiled a monument, consisting of a stone from the Solovetskiye* Islands, to the victims of totalitarianism, in front of the KGB headquarters. The ceremony included a benediction by a priest.

**MEN**, FATHER ALEKSANDR (1935–1990). Orthodox priest assassinated as he left his home near Zagorsk early one morning. Widely respected, even in some circles close to power, he was not a dissident, as some people hastily concluded; and certainly not a potential political martyr like Poland's Father Popielucsko. But he was an unusual and charismatic man, coming from a family of Jews converted to Christianity under Tsarism. As a theologian he offended the Patriarchy by founding an 'Orthodox University of Moscow'. But he consistently opposed any attempt to create a schism. Theories about his killing included a suspicion against Pamyat.* But it could well have been an act of purposeless violence.

**MERCHANT FLEET.** Ageing asset. In 1992, half the Soviet merchant vessels were fifteen years old or more, and replacement was not keeping up with obsolescence. Foreign ports were reported to have turned away some of the oldest ships as environmentally dangerous.

**MESKHETIAN TURKS**. Muslims of Turkish origin, living in the south of Georgia\* until deported by Stalin to Central Asia in 1944. In June 1989 they were attacked by Uzbek rioters in the Fergana valley (105 dead, more than 1,000 wounded, 1,000 homes destroyed). The Uzbeks besieged them even in refugee camps, which had to be defended by the army. Most Meskhetians subsequently left the region and took up residence in deserted Russian villages, where they could keep their communities together. In 1991 the Georgian government obstinately refused to let them come home, following popular demonstrations against their return at Borzhomi. The same year they founded an 'all-Union society' named *Vatan*, under the presidency of Yusuf Savarov.

**METRO**. Urban transport system established in every city with more than a million inhabitants. In 1991, operating and financial responsibility was transferred from the state to republics and regional authorities. Moscow city council demanded special treatment in view of the Moscow Metro's national function (one third of each day's ten million passengers are from outside the city). When no central government subsidy was forthcoming, fares were increased from 5 to 15 kopecks. In 1992 they were raised to R0.5.

**MID**. See 'Foreign Ministry'.

**MILITARY DOCTRINE**. See 'Defensive Defence'.

**MILITARY-HISTORICAL JOURNAL** (*Voenno-Istoricheskyi Zhurnal*). Ultra-right journal (circulation 227,000 in 1991) read mainly by the officer corps. In November 1990 the editor, Maj.-Gen. Viktor Filatov, was reprimanded by Defence Minister Yazov for publishing excerpts from Hitler's *Mein Kampf*. The magazine was prominent in attacks on Shevardnadze.\* In 1991 it promised publication of the anti-semitic 'Protocols of the Elders of Zion'.

**MILITARY-INDUSTRIAL COMMISSION** (VPK, *Voenno-Promyshlennaya Kommissiya*). Soviet governmental agency for co-ordinating military and government organizations involved in weapons production and procurement. Defence-related industries were required to submit proposals to the VPK, where they were studied for technical feasibility and impact on other parts of the economy.

**MILITARY SERVICE**. Under Soviet law, up to 1991, obligatory service for all young men from the age of 18. Military reforms after the 1991 *putsch*\* provided for a cut in the service term from two years to 18 months, and for the general exemption of students. Since 1989 the latter had been allowed to postpone service, and in many cases to forgo it, leading to a lower intellectual level in the forces and increasing the proportion of Asians (two men out of three). In 1990 some republics voted to suspend Soviet military service law and allow instead a period of service in the republic (as in Armenia); others disrupted the call-up or in some cases encouraged their nationals to desert. The Ukraine decided that service outside the republic should be purely voluntary. As part of a transition to more professionalism, beginning in the Air Force, Air Defence Force, Strategic Nuclear Forces Command and Navy, in September 1991 plans were announced to extend opportunities for contract service. After independence, republics kept military service, but with their own terms and regulations.

**MILITIA**. Name given to the police after the revolution (since 'police' was associated with Tsarist repression). But after the 1990 regional and republic elections, 'militia' sounded too communist and there were moves in some republics to revert to the old name. Until the elections, all militia were legally controlled by the Ministry of the Interior* in Moscow. After them, non-communist city councils replaced the militia with city 'police'* under their own control. Otherwise law enforcement came under republics' interior ministries, and forces of the Soviet Ministry of the Interior (MVD) could be used only with republic approval. Gorbachev continued a clean-up of the militia begun by Andropov.* In March 1988 the Interior Minister, Vlasov, revealed that in five years 170,000 police officers had been dismissed for indiscipline or law-breaking. Since 1989, 38 Petrovka Street (Moscow's 'Scotland Yard') has held regular briefings for the press. See also 'Militias'.

**MILITIAS**. In the late 1980s, in advance of republics' independence, a number of nationalist movements raised irregular armed forces, which quickly showed a tendency to escape from the control of their creators. In Armenia the authorities managed to disband them and restored order for a while, but the trouble broke out again in 1991. Elsewhere non-communist governments emerging from the 1990 elections maintained ambiguous relations with self-appointed security forces. In the Baltic states and the western Ukraine militias were presented as the foundation for a republican gendarmerie, but in practice were used by Popular Fronts against the Communist Party and other opponents. In Moldavia the nationalist government incited the militias of the Popular Front to 'restore order' among the Gagauz* and other ethnic minorities (but quickly retreated after the first fatal casualties). Estonia saw the reconstitution of the Katiselita militia, a 'bourgeois' police that hunted down pre-war communists. A new development in early 1991 was the recruitment by republic governments – Georgia, the Baltic republics – of so-called 'national guards'* to protect 'symbols of independence' (parliaments, TV stations etc.) against the Centre. Confusion about their role caused a number of incidents.

**MILLENNIUM** (1). Thousandth anniversary of Russia's conversion to Christianity by Prince Vladimir of Kiev; turning-point in state-church relations. Its celebration in Moscow (June 1988) dismayed Ukrainians who wanted the event to be centred on Kiev. The city of Novgorod – historically the second Russian city after Kiev – organized an 'alternative' millennium in protest at its exclusion. The Uniates* held their millennium in Rome with Pope John Paul II. During official preparations a series of interior power struggles led to fears that the festival would see the Orthodox church hit by a schism, but this did not happen. The state marked the event by giving back the Danilov monastery in Moscow and the Pechersky monastery in Kiev (a museum since 1961), bringing the number of religious buildings returned to the church over a period of three years to thirty-five. It also ended restrictions on importing bibles and liberated remaining religious prisoners. Participating in the millennium were 171 newly registered religious communities (compared with sixty-seven in 1986, 104 in 1987). Not all had churches, and in February 1988 thousands of believers came to Moscow to ask for the reopening of their parish church. At the time of the millennium there were 7,000 active churches, a tenth of the number before the Revolution.

**MILLENNIUM** (2). Last stage of society predicted by Marxism, when the state was supposed to wither away and socialism to be replaced by real communism.

**MINERS**. Toilers in a field as dangerous as it is unhealthy (fifty deaths per month in 1990, 7.5 per cent more than ten years earlier). In 1990 miners were the first workers to organize a national strike.* They went back to work after the government agreed to improve work conditions (longer holidays, earlier retirement) and living conditions (more housing and nurseries, better supplies), and to recognize the industry (no more ministerial control, autonomy* for each coalfield). At the end of 1990 they gave notice of a strike for full realization of the plan, which had been suspended because of the general economic situation. The second congress of their official union, the Union of Mineworkers, saw a revolt against state and Party control and a vote to set up an independent union. In March 1991 the latter launched an overtly political strike, backed by Boris Yeltsin, demanding the resignation of Gorbachev. In six weeks it came close to paralysing industry, and was only called off when Yeltsin announced that the Russian mines would be transferred to Russian ownership and allowed to keep part of their foreign exchange earnings.

**MINISTRY**. Scapegoat for economic setbacks and 'saboteur' of reform. Ministries became the first subjects for staff cuts. In February 1988 Aganbegyan* announced the ending of half the jobs in ministries and state committees* and a 30 per cent cut in Gosplan.* In March 1988 the Ministries of Light Engineering, the Food Industry and Household

Appliances were abolished. Next, three separate education ministries and a state committee for Professional and Technical Education were replaced by a single Education Ministry. But although ministries contracted at the centre (from seventy-one to fifty in 1990—91) their numbers multiplied in each of the fifteen republics. In November 1991 all Union ministries still in existence ceased to operate by a decision of the USSR State Council,* making 36,000 staff redundant, and their functions were taken over by Inter-Republican Councils until the dissolution of the Union at the end of the year. Temporary exceptions were the Foreign and Defence Ministries.

**MINISTRY OF THE INTERIOR** (*Ministerstvo vnutrennikh del* — *MVD*). Until 1991, co-guardian, with the KGB,* of internal security, with thirty divisions of troops for internal security.* The MVD was also in overall control of all the Union's militia* (police) forces. But even before the republic elections of 1990 the constitutionally separate MVDs of several republics, most notably the Baltic republics, Georgia and Armenia, had ceased to take orders from the Centre. Another modification of MVD police powers in republics where they still operated was the 1989 transfer to the Ministry of Justice of the officials responsible for conducting pre-trial investigations in criminal cases. In December 1990, a change of Ministers (Boris Pugo* for Vadim Bakatin*) signalled a return by hard-liners. After the 1991 *putsch** Pugo was replaced and the very much weakened MVD passed under the direction of the former Russian Interior Minister, Viktor Barannikov.* In December, Barannikov was appointed head of a new Russian super-ministry, the Ministry of Security and Internal Affairs, which absorbed both the MVD and the remnant of the former KGB* — a move then reversed under parliamentary pressure.

**MINORITY.** (1) Members of an important ethnic community living in a foreign republic (Russians in Estonia, Ukrainians in Moldavia, etc.). (2) Members of a small ethnic community living on its own territory (Nenets in Siberia) or dispersed across a wide area (Koreans in Siberia and the Kuban). See 'Small Peoples'.

**MINSK**. Capital of Byelorussia (Belarus), chosen as the co-ordinating centre of the Commonwealth of Independent States (CIS) by the 'Minsk agreement' of December 8, 1991. The agreement was signed after thirty-six hours of discussion – actually in a hunting-lodge near Brest, 120 miles away – by the presidents of Russia, Byelorussia and Ukraine. In it they agreed, as heads of founder states of the original USSR, that 'the USSR has ceased to exist as a subject of international law and geopolitical reality.' It was said that Yeltsin* had first proposed the meeting as a chance to 'find a new way' of keeping Ukraine within a common political and economic structure, after its vote for independence in the December referendum. He later claimed that, since this showed that Gorbachev's proposed union treaty* would not work, he was obliged to look for a new solution. But subsequent statements by his close advisers, and expressions of surprise by the Byelorussian leadership, made it clear that from the beginning he had something much larger in mind. Among the factors fuelling accusations of a political *coup d'état* was the role played by his advisers, to the exclusion of the Russian parliament and vice-president Rutskoi.* It was also constitutionally questionable whether the USSR could be dissolved by its founder members alone. Further fuel was added by Yeltsin's humiliating treatment of Gorbachev (informed of the agreement only after President Bush was told) and by the by-passing of the Soviet parliament. But the fact remained that the USSR was finished, and, using the subsequent Alma-Ata* agreement to avoid a split between the Slav and the Muslim republics, Yeltsin went on unilaterally to dismantle central structures and to bury the Soviet Union and Gorbachev before the end of the year. See also 'Alma-Ata', 'Commonwealth of Independent States'.

**MIR** ('Peace'). Space station launched February 20, 1986 to provide a base for the first permanently manned vehicle in orbit. In 1992 it was up for sale to anyone ready to bail out the economy.

**'MISS'.** Young women or teenagers chosen in beauty competitions sponsored by Russian or foreign firms. Thanks to the novelty, Tass* now publishes pictures of legs instead of the humourless faces of Politburo members. But Russia is still a prudish country. To show that even on the path of progress it remains attentive to moral qualities, newspapers emphasize juries' regard for the winner's 'brain' as well as her body. Since the first election of Miss Moscow in 1987 (a financial disaster), beauty contests have spread throughout the country. Inflation of numbers has reduced the value of prizes, and yesterday's 'contract with a Western model agency' now tends to be replaced with some token of mediocre quality.

**MOISEYEV**, GEN. MIKHAIL ALEKSEEVICH (1939– ). Chief of staff of the armed forces, 1988–91, in succession to Akhromeyev.* He was replaced after the 1991 *putsch*\* (in which he took a neutral position) by Lobov,* and took early retirement. The first chief of staff not to have seen active service in World War II, his relatively junior position at the time of his appointment was seen by some experts to suggest a move by Gorbachev to reduce the role of the general staff in national decision-making in the Defence Council,* where he and Yazov* became the only military representatives. In fact he showed vigour in restructuring the armed forces at a time of administrative problems following the withdrawals from Eastern Europe, and in applying the new doctrine of defensive defence* to create a leaner, more professional army in line with international agreements and economic realism.

**MOLDAVIA/MOLDOVA** (pop 4.1 million). Former union republic existing in its present form since 1940, when it absorbed Bessarabia (Russian in 1812, Romanian from 1918). In 1989 the new Popular Front\* sought to restore cultural links with Romania\* and the use of the Latin alphabet; and in December 1989 the death of Ceaucescu removed any obstacle to a Romanian rapprochement. But Moldavians are only 64 per cent of the republic's population and less than half that of the capital, Chisinau (formerly Kishinev). The rest of the inhabitants (14 per cent Ukrainian, 13 per cent Russian, 4 per cent Gagauz,\* 3 per cent gipsy and, before emigration, 2 per cent Jewish) became alarmed when, in July 1990, the Moldavian parliament passed a law making Moldavian the sole official language. On the principle that 'all power in Moldavia belongs to the people', the Popular Front-dominated parliament took absolute power, limiting freedom of association and the right to strike or hold organized demonstrations. Conscious of non-Moldavian agitation, it rejected proposals for the creation of autonomous\* entities. Nevertheless, in October 1990 the republic's Slavs\* proclaimed an autonomous republic east of the river Dniestr. The Gagauz did the same in the south. In November 1990 both announced the holding of 'republic' elections, whereupon the Kishinev government called on the population to blockade the rebel districts, and sent police to prevent voting. After a weekend of clashes (eight dead and thirty wounded in the 'Dniestr republic'), Gorbachev summoned the Moldavian president, Snegur, together with Gagauz and Dniestr representatives, and the setting up of a conciliation commission was agreed. In December 1990 Gorbachev declared the constitution of the self-proclaimed republics illegal while simultaneously ordering the Moldavian parliament to re-examine the nationalist legislation that had been so explosive. In June 1991 the Moldavian Ministry of Culture and Religion issued a decree banning Marxist-Leninist books from the republic's libraries. A 'blacklist' went on to include books by Russian writers and poets such as Pasternak, Akhmatova, Tsvetayeva, Solzhenitsyn, Rasputin, Astafiev and Belov. Priority was henceforth to be given to Romanian and religious literature. Two months later the republic authorities took advantage of the August *putsch*\* to accuse minorities of supporting the putschists and to arrest their leaders. At the same time they claimed the right to reunite Moldavia with Romania. In the autumn of 1991 fresh clashes, and some deaths, occurred when the Gagauz and Dniestr republics decided to push ahead with plans for independence. Tensions were unabated when in December Moldova joined the new Commonwealth.\*

*MOLODAYA GVARDIA.* Anti-reformist monthly magazine, edited by the conservative, Anatoli Ivanov.

**MOLOTOV**, Vyacheslav Mikhailovich, born Skriabin (1890–1987). Only high-ranking Bolshevik to survive the purges. As Minister of

Foreign Affairs (1939–49 and 1953–57) he signed the 1939 German-Soviet* non-aggression pact. Removed from power in 1957 with other members of the 'anti-Party group' which attempted to get rid of Khrushchev, he ended his career as ambassador in Mongolia. Among Soviets he is remembered as having been willing to do anything to please Stalin, even signing the order that sent his own wife to a camp. For Westerners, he became the embodiment of the Cold War. He ended his life in bitterness, shocked by detente and the denunciation of Stalin, continuing to pay his Party dues, which were methodically returned, until 1985, when he was readmitted to membership. His burial was officially described as the 'private burial of a retired person'. But he received a place among other historic figures in Novodevichi cemetery.

**MONARCHIST**. Nostalgically inclined supporter of one of numerous small movements campaigning for a restoration of the Romanov dynasty or its trappings. In 1991 only one such group had managed to get representatives elected – the Russian National Monarchist Party,* with council seats in eighteen cities. In Moscow, popular romanticism and yearning for mementoes of the past are seized on by pavement vendors offering photographs of the imperial family and family trees of the Romanovs. The monarchist is readily seduced by 'revelations' like those of Geli Ryabov, journalist and storyteller, who claims to have identified the remains of the imperial family found in a swamp near Sverdlovsk (now again Ekaterinburg). The site of the house where the Tsar and his family passed their last moments is now subject to a cult. (The house itself was blown up in 1977.) In 1990 the Orthodox hierarchy invited contributions towards building a church on the site. A separate movement exists among Georgian monarchists, some of whom want to bring back the reluctant heir to the Georgian throne, the racing driver David Bagration, now living in Madrid.

**MOON**, REV. SUNG MYUNG. Apostle of anti-communism turned admirer of *perestroika* in the name of friendship among peoples. In 1988 he acted as an intermediary in establishing relations between the Soviet Union and South Korea.* A 'Moonie' company, the World Media Association, let it be known that it was ready with capital whenever the Soviet media were open to foreign investment; and Moon himself donated $100,000 towards restoring the fire-damaged building of *Moscow News*.* In 1989 he invited the first of thousands of Soviet guests to his sect's American headquarters. Journalists were delighted, but the students found life in 'Moonie' centres unexpectedly reminiscent of Soviet army barracks.

**MOSCOW**. Double capital, of the USSR and the Russian Federation (RFSR), relieved of its identity crisis by the former's dissolution and Russia's take-over, in December 1991, of Soviet offices and ministries. For years the city was a crossroads for travellers from all parts of the Union. After the 1990 elections, the city authorities asked for Moscow to be given a special status (something like Washington, D.C.), and an extraordinary budget to meet the enormous costs of its double function. The request was to have an untoward consequence (see below). In its desperate quest for funds the council often acted without thought for the consequences. In 1990 there was talk of a municipal tax on a private sector that did not yet exist. All shops were to be 'privatized' by January 1991, when in fact there was a shortage of buyers. In 1991 the city talked about selling land, but without any means of valuation. The mayor, Gavril Popov,* confirmed in office by a popular vote in June 1991, proposed to reduce industry (and thus the *limitchiki** problem), and at the same time to increase 'intellectual' activity, with research centres, specialist hospitals and large universities. This would limit expansion and pollution. The 1991–2000 development plan was passed in bland disregard of the fact that no one had observed the previous plan. Population should have levelled off at 8 million; but in 1988 there were already 8.9 million. The housing problem seemed likely to be seriously worsened by proposals to end the *propiska** system. In July 1991 tensions arose between Popov and the council when the city's thirty-two *raions* were replaced by a system of nine prefectures, with a separate prefecture for the satellite city of Zelenograd, the prefects being appointed by the mayor. More came with his appointment of a new police chief, Murashev.* In December 1991, the city's application for a special status was rewarded by the Russian Federation taking over many of the responsibilities of both the mayor and the council, causing Popov to offer (but then withdraw) his resignation.

**MOSCOW ECHO**. 'Independent' radio station, set up August 1990, with funds from the city of Moscow and the support of the Russian government, as an alternative to Gostelradio*. It won fame during the August 1991 *putsch** by operating an improvised short-wave transmitter from inside the Russian parliament building.

*MOSCOW NEWS*. Previously dull weekly for promoting the official Soviet image, now recycled as a standard-bearer of *glasnost*. Its foreign-language editions still outrun the Russian editions, obliging Russians to read the copy displayed outside the editorial office. Its best sales plugs came from conservatives like its arch-enemy Yegor Ligachev,* who before the Nineteenth Party Conference complained of its 'ersatz information'. When its offices were damaged by a fire next door, a rebuilding appeal brought donations from the unlikeliest people, among them Western press magnates, like the Rev. Moon,* with an eye on the Soviet market. The response made it possible to found the 'first newspaper belonging only to its readers', and ended with the editor-in-chief, Yakovlev,* signing a joint-venture agreement with *Paris Match*. In September 1991 Yakovlev was appointed director of Gostelradio* and replaced by his deputy Len Karpinsky.

**MOSCOW STATE INSTITUTE FOR INTERNATIONAL RELA-TIONS (MGIMO).** Foreign affairs school formerly reserved for sons of members of the *nomenklatura*.★ Its diploma was a passport to a foreign appointment. In 1986 the rector was expelled for irregularities. It was restored to respectability under *perestroika*.

**MOVEMENT FOR DEMOCRATIC REFORMS.** Movement 'to unite forces for building a new civil society', launched in July 1991 by former allies of Gorbachev, such as Shevardnadze★ (elected chairman), Yakov-lev,★ Popov,★ Sobchak★ and Volsky.★ Differences of opinion obliged the organizers to postpone its founding congress until October. When it met, in the new situation caused by the *putsch*,★ discussion centred on whether to form an all-Union political party. Despite the reluctance of Democratic Russia★ to participate, it was agreed to form the Democratic Reform Party.★

**MOVEMENT FOR SOCIALIST RENEWAL.** Shadowy movement apparently subscribing to a declaration in favour of reform in 1986. The document was widely suspected of being a provocation by the KGB. But Medvedev and Chiesa (see Bibliography) say it could have come from a radical reformist group 'immediately below the *nomenklatura*'.★

**MULTI-PARTYISM.** Democratic ideal that lost some of its glamour when 'multi' became synonymous with splintering. In March 1991, according to official figures, there were 11,000 political parties and movements in the USSR, of whom 1,500 aspired to a nationwide role. In 1990 the country's first multi-party elections, in Georgia, were contested by thirty-six parties – and ended by producing a dictatorship. Real multi-partyism only became possible with the ending of the special position of the Communist Party after the 1991 *putsch*.★

**MURASHEV**, ARKADI NIKOLAYEVICH (1957– ). Russian deputy, founder-member of Democratic Russia★, appointed Moscow police chief by Popov,★ against the advice of the city council, which wanted a profession-al, General Vyatcheslav Komisarov. The appointment, which also went against a nominee of Yeltsin, Barannikov,★ caused a furore. Popov, asserting municipal independence, argued for the need for a non-professional (Murashev is a physicist). Some staff refused to serve under him.

**MUSLIMS.** See 'Islam'.

**MVD.** See 'Ministry of the Interior'.

# N

**NABOKOV**, VLADIMIR VLADIMIROVICH (1899—1977). Reckoned by many the greatest Russian man of letters, he emigrated to Paris in 1917. Extracts of his writing, dismissed by Soviet critics as 'pornographic', first appeared in a chess magazine, then in *Znamya*, in 1986.

**NADEZHDA** (Hope) (1). Association of parents of soldiers missing in Afghanistan★ (see 'Prisoner of War').

**NADEZHDA** (2). Independent radio set up in Estonia by Inter-Front,★ using military transmitters; declared illegal by the Estonian government. Closed down after the 1991 *putsch*★ and Estonian independence.

**NAGORNO-KARABAKH AUTONOMOUS OBLAST (NKAO)**. Mainly Armenian enclave ('Artsakh' to the Armenians) attached by Stalin to Azerbaijan on the division of Transcaucasia in 1923. Before refugee movements in the late 1980s, there were 174,000 inhabitants. In 1987 Armenians began agitating for the territory's restoration. On February 11, 1988 internal relations between Armenians and Azeris broke down when the Armenian-dominated NKAO parliament voted for integration with Armenia. Disturbances caused the demand to be taken up by a mass rally in Yerevan. A Politburo team was sent to investigate, and the NKAO Azeri first secretary was replaced by an Armenian. Gorbachev pacified Yerevan by appearing to promise what was demanded, but failed to deliver for fear of provoking Azerbaijan. His failure discredited the Armenian Communist Party, and the campaign for annexation was pursued by the intellectuals of the so-called Nagorno-Karabakh Committee. In March 1988 the situation was electrified by the Sumgait★ massacre, and for weeks Armenia and Azerbaijan stood on the brink of war. When the Nagorno-Karabakh Committee sought an emergency meeting of the USSR Supreme Soviet, Moscow replied by dispatching troops to 'take all necessary steps to restore order'. In December 1988 Gorbachev sought to end an impossible situation by proposing to attach the NKAO 'temporarily' to the Russian Federation. The move, made too late, was denounced by both sides, and in 1990 his special commissioner, Arkadi Volsky, who had been sent to the NKAO to restore confidence, resigned his commission. In the summer of 1990, the president of the new Armenian parliament, a former member of the Karabakh Committee, Levon Ter-Petrossian, spoke for the first time of the possibility of direct negotiations with Azerbaijan to give the NKAO the status of a truly autonomous republic. Troubles returned in May 1991, when Armenians attacked Soviet convoys and Soviet and Azerbaijan MVD troops raided Armenian villages in the NKAO and border districts, purportedly to disarm Armenian paramilitary groups. 1991 also saw large-scale Armenian terrorism against representatives of 'foreign' authority in the enclave. In October 1991 a joint mission of Nazarbayev* and Yeltsin managed to get an agreement between the Armenian and Azerbaijan presidents, allowing more autonomy to the NKAO while keeping it part of Azerbaijan. The problem was to impose order on the ground. Two months later, following the withdrawal of Soviet troops, shooting recommenced between Armenian groups and detachments of the Azerbaijani MVD.

**NAKHICHEVAN** (pop. 267,000). Autonomous republic* of Azerbaijan,* enclaved by the carving up of Transcaucasia in 1923. In 1988 it was blockaded by Armenia, causing Azerbaijan to blockade Armenia in revenge. In 1990 the Nakhichevan Azeris, unable to leave their enclave except by air, sought aid from across the Iranian frontier. There were scenes of 'fraternization' with Iranian Azeris after the destruction of frontier posts. For a week the Soviet authorities leaned over backwards to avoid undoing their recent work of reconciliation with Teheran. *Ogonyek** published an amusing photograph (without commentary) of veiled women looking sadly at their brothers beyond the frontier fence. The veils did not quite hide a number of male moustaches. In 1991 Nakhichevan was chosen by Geidar Aliyev* for his political come-back as a member, then chairman, of the republic's supreme soviet, which was renamed the *majlis*.

**NARCOBUSINESS**. Soviet media word *circa* 1989 meaning a new form of delinquency made possible by freedom to travel and open a bank account in hard currency.* The criminal narcotics industry, with clandestine laboratories and factories, international markets and channels for laundering profits, grew steadily from 1986. Internationalization extended to the Soviet interior: in 1990 two-thirds of the people found involved in the Moscow 'narcobusiness' were not Muscovites. Hoping to break up the networks, police that summer launched the first all-Union operation, 'MAK-90', followed the next year by 'MAK-91'.

**NASH SOVREMENNIK** ('Our Contemporary'). Russophile review founded in 1956, turned anti-semitic at the end of the 1980s. The deviation was blamed on its editor, Sergei Vikulov, but it also reflected the view of several members of the editorial board (Vasili Belov, Yuri Bondarev, Valentin Rasputin*). Not that the 'line' brought it many readers. In 1991 circulation was under 250,000, a tiny figure for a Soviet publication.

**NATIONAL GUARD**. Republican paramilitary force first set up by Georgia (January 1991), followed by the Baltic republics. With the Union break-up, plans for a similar organization were discussed or adopted by most other republics, including Russia, in each case under the jurisdiction of the President.

**NATIONAL SALVATION COMMITTEES**. Faceless bodies formed by pro-Moscow communists to oppose Popular Front movements in separatist republics, e.g. Latvia. They claimed to speak 'for the people' and were used to legitimize military intervention.

**NATIONALITY**. Ethnic status determined by parentage and entered in every Soviet citizen's passport.* In the case of differing nationalities, children had to choose at the age of 16. With the splitting of the Union into independent republics, nationality commonly coincided with citizenship.*

**NATIONALITY POLICY**. Policy launched after the 1917 revolution to preserve and develop cultural differences within a federal framework. Elimination of illiteracy made it possible to rescue doomed languages and get unwritten ones on to paper. A campaign of de-Russification in the Ukraine and Byelorussia encouraged the revival of national languages that had formerly been prohibited or discouraged. The process was interrupted in the 1930s, when industrialization led to centralization and the use of only one language (Russian). Under Khrushchev there was a reversal, and local intelligentsias* were revived. Brezhnev adopted a non-ideological approach in nationality matters, flattering or reprimanding for the sake of peace. Andropov* liked the old idea of a 'commonwealth', and ordered Ligachev* to encourage the shuffling of cadres* (which also helped against corruption). Gorbachev underestimated the complexity of the nationality question, believing that everything could be settled by *perestroika* and *glasnost.* In fact these were the very things that, helped by the economic crisis, led republics, then regions, to demand autonomy and independence – after 1990 using the law and elections to their advantage.

**NATO**. Old foe indispensable to socialist cohesion until the Warsaw Pact* organization fell apart in 1989. As well as using the 'threat' of Western aggression to hold allies together in the Cold War, Moscow often found it helpful to engage in dialogue with a single Western voice. When a new-model NATO, with a different doctrine and changing force structure, came out of the London summit in July 1990, Moscow expressed the hope that it would merge with the dissolving Warsaw Pact organization to form a pan-European security body via CSCE.* With the dissolution of the Soviet Union in 1991, several republics, including Russia, went further and made noises about applying to join NATO itself as part of the process of 'entering the civilized world'. Reactions within NATO were noticeably cautious.

**NAVY.** Strategic arm developed by Admiral Gorshkov★ to project Soviet strength and influence across the globe. The creation of an ocean-going surface fleet in the 1960s and 70s was intended to match America's. In 1991 the navy had five aircraft-carriers, 38 cruisers, 29 destroyers, 146 frigates and 317 submarines: the result of untold inroads into precious industrial resources which had done nothing, in the end, to extend geopolitical power. With the end of the Cold War★ nearly all submarines, including sixty-three carrying nuclear-armed missiles, were withdrawn to bases in the Baltic and the Sea of Okhotsk, where they were less susceptible to appalling accidents. In January 1992 the newly independent Ukraine claimed ownership of the powerful Baltic fleet (28 submarines, 43 surface warships). Azerbaijan took the Caspian flotilla, including four frigates.

**NAZARBAYEV,** NURSULTAN ABISHEVICH (1940– ). President of Kazakhstan. A respected economist, he was offered the post of Soviet Vice-President, but declined to serve as Gorbachev's office boy. Appointing instead the treacherous Yanayev,★ Gorbachev missed a unique chance to have as his deputy both a much needed specialist and a senior representative of the country's 50 million Muslims. In 1991, Gorbachev renewed the offer jointly with Yeltsin. Too late. Nazarbayev was now an internationally known figure, sought out by Westerners and invited to Beijing to discuss border questions. His sights were set on developing Central Asia with specific programmes and the help of South Korea.

**NECROPHILIA.** Term of mockery applied by conservative members of the Writers' Union★ to a national preoccupation with previously banned books. Its murky paternity compromises the position of young critics who fear that the priority given to undoing the work of censorship may lock Russian culture into an obsession with the past.

**NEKRASOV,** VIKTOR PLATONOVICH (1911–1987). Unhappy novelist who even had a problem with his obituary. The editor of *Moscow News* had to threaten to resign before being allowed to publish an appreciation by the poets and writers Grigori Baklanov, Bulat Okudzhava, Vyacheslav Kondratiev and Vladimir Lakshin. Nekrasov became famous with his war classic, *In the Trenches of Stalingrad* (1946), followed by his first book on the shock of returning to civilian life, *Home Town* (1954). But emigration killed his talent. In Paris he fell out with Maximov, who refused to let him collaborate on *Continent*, and with the émigrés Bukovsky and Plyushch.

**NENASHEV,** MIKHAIL FYODOROVICH (1929– ). Mediator of the media. In 1986 Gorbachev plucked him from *Sovietskaya Rossiya* to head the State

Committee for Publishing and prepare the way for *glasnost*. He made a less favourable impression on his later appointment to head Gostelradio,★ where he was accused of obstructing over-bold journalists. In December 1990 he was made chairman of the State Committee for the Press and given two weeks to draw up a plan for restructuring the mass media.

**NEO-NAZIS**. Young (average 20 years old) hoodlums with ideological pretensions: 'Hitler was the only one brave enough to take on communism.' They used to take it out on Soviet insignia – which they daubed with swastikas – war memorials, bemedalled veterans and members of Party youth organizations. In the mid-1980s, fights with communist youths developed into annual battles on Moscow's Pushkin★ Square, where the neo-Nazis celebrated Hitler's birthday. Only later did they single out Zionism, with the encouragement of clandestine literature from an émigré publisher, Nikolai Tetenov.

**NEO-STALINISTS**. Solid citizens pining for the days of the 'iron rod', when everyone worked, youngsters gave up their seats in the Metro, and there was none of this talk about drugs, strikes, rape, robbery etc. Usually evasive when asked how they would keep order if in power. Mostly found among women over 40, but with a new 'neo-Stalinist' tendency among young blue-collar workers hit by the economic crisis.

**NEP** (New Economic Policy), 1922–28. Policy permitting some forms of private enterprise, introduced by Lenin to restore productivity after the Civil War and the period of War Communism; claimed as a model by latter-day reformers, including Gorbachev, wanting to give the 'market' Lenin's approval. It ended with Stalin's reversion to a centralized 'command' economy. The question was: did Lenin mean it to be temporary or permanent?

**NEPMEN**. *Nouveaux riches* of the NEP, speculators profiting from the return to a free market. The word was revived to describe *bizinesmen*★ who did well out of *perestroika*, often with a vulgar display of bad taste.

**NEVZOROV**, ALEKSANDR GLEBOVICH (1958– ). Leningrad television presenter, creator and producer of the popular show '600 Seconds'. Naively adopted by 'democrats' simply because he was a lively investigator. In December 1990 he was shot and wounded at a rendezvous with a mystery informant. The incident was seen as an attack on the liberal media. (A few weeks later he escaped another attack in Riga.) Soon afterwards his activities caused him to be branded a Russian chauvinist and reactionary.

**NEW THINKING**. Gorby-word derived from *perestroika* and *glasnost*, essentially meaning a non-adversarial foreign policy. Once described as an ideological handle for managing institutional change.

**NEZAVISSIMAYA GAZETA**. Newspaper launched in 1991 by Vitali Tretyakov, former right-hand man of Yegor Yakovlev* at *Moscow News*. It marked a break by a younger, more pragmatic, generation from the attitude of the 'Khrushchevists' who inaugurated *perestroika*.

**NOMENKLATURA**. Caste with strong survival instincts. Technically the list of candidates suitable to fill posts within the control of the Party (otherwise the list of goods for sale in a shop). Launched on the West by a defecting nomenklaturist, the word came to symbolize political nepotism in the 'stagnation'* of the 1970s. In the late 1980s it coexisted with 'bureaucrat', *chinovnik** and apparatchik as a stick-word for beating the system.

**NORTH KOREA**. Neighbour dramatically down in affection since Moscow discovered the South Korean economy. Frictions first appeared when Pyongyang objected to Soviet participation in the Seoul Olympics. Then North Korea insisted on keeping up ideological tension, after Moscow turned to a 'balance of forces' policy (alias 'new thinking'*) and invited South Korea* to help develop the Soviet economy. Following the formalization of South Korean trade relations in 1988, Moscow's chief worry was that China might exploit North Korean bitterness to set up an anti-Soviet socialist camp with North Korea, Cuba and Vietnam.

**NORTH OSSETIA** (pop. 612,000). Autonomous republic of North Caucasus, part of Russia since 1774 and now an autonomous republic of the Russian Federation. The capital, Vladikavkaz, was until 1990 Ordzhonikidze. A mosaic of nationalities (Ossetes, Russians, Armenians, Ingush,* Germans and immigrant Koreans), it has experienced cyclic violence between Ossetes and Ingush since 1921. In 1991 tension rose with the arrival of Ossetian refugees from South Ossetia.*

**NOVAYA ZEMLIA**. Group of islands between the Karsk and Barents Seas used for nuclear tests. In October 1990 the government authorized a test that had been held up for nearly a year in hope of bringing America into a unilateral moratorium. The decision caused a foray by Greenpeace,* protests from Arkhangelsk council and the Komi autonomous republic. In 1992 it was disclosed that for twenty years the sea in the area had been used for dumping nuclear waste.

**NOVODVORSKAYA**, Valeria Ilinichna (1950– ). Rare case of a woman heading a political group, the Democratic Union.* She was arrested in September 1990 for 'insulting the President' and sent to a psychiatric hospital, but was released after the 1991 *putsch.** Her extravagant behaviour damaged the democrats more than their adversaries. She had a sad personal history. In 1967, as a young student, she had written a bitter poem called 'Thank you, Party' (for the camps, the famine, etc.) and showered copies from the balcony during an interval at the opera. She was then interned for two years in a psychiatric hospital in Kazan. She helped found her group while working as a translator in Moscow.

**NOVO-OGAREVO.** Suburb of Moscow that gave its name to the 'Nine-plus-One' agreement of June 1991, whereby nine presidents undertook to defend the new union treaty★ in their parliaments, using the title 'Union of Sovereign Soviet Republics'. At the time, the agreement was hailed as a dramatic move to stop the Union's drift towards a break-up. Only the Baltic republics, Georgia, Armenia and Moldavia abstained. But further discussions got nowhere and all question of a new Union was killed six months later by the Minsk★ agreement. See also 'Kishinev forum'.

**NOVOSTI PRESS AGENCY (APN).** Official news agency, in 1990 renamed 'Novosti Information Agency' (IAN) and required to operate commercially. In distinction to TASS★, which supplies home and foreign media with spot news, Novosti specialized in supplying foreigners with feature material and (for hard currency) arranging interviews and television facilities. Until internal changes in 1987 its worldwide network was a regular cover for KGB operations. In 1991 a tight budget, and customers' resistance to paying extravagant fees for services normally given gratis by government information services, resulted in 40 per cent staff cuts. After the 1991 *putsch*★ Novosti was merged with the Russian Information Agency under Albert Vinogradov.

*NOVY MIR.* Literary monthly still best remembered for the editorship of the great Tvardovsky (1950–54 and 1958–70). In the late 1980s, under that of Sergei Zalygin, it forsook its role as the discoverer of new writers for profitable publication of books that were once forbidden. In 1989 its circulation rose from 425,000 to 2 million, thanks to its coup of the works of Solzhenitsyn.

**NUCLEAR DISARMAMENT.** As 'total' nuclear disarmament, still Moscow's official goal for the year 2000, at the time of the Union's break-up. The ultimate zero was first proposed by Gorbachev in January 1986. At the Reykjavik summit★ nine months later he suggested a 50 per cent cut in Soviet and US strategic missiles within five years, and total abandonment within ten. Progress was blocked by 'Star Wars' (see Strategic Defence Initiative), which also delayed cuts in intermediate-range weapons. But in 1987 a compromise led to the INF Treaty,★ scrapping SS-20s and US cruise missiles. The Soviet government was now hard pressed to cut arms spending, and Gorbachev needed an international success for domestic reasons. He may also have guessed that 'Star Wars' was unlikely to survive in the US Congress. The INF treaty cleared the way for the much more complicated START* negotiations. Finally signed in July 1991, START committed the US and the USSR to cut their combined stock of nuclear warheads by nearly one third, and to reduce substantially the number of their delivery vehicles (missiles and bombers). By and large it favoured the United States, by cutting land-based intercontinental ballistic missiles (ICBM), in which the Soviets had their greatest strength, more drastically than submarine-based missiles (SLBM), which were considered less 'offensive'. But it would leave the Soviets in possession of 154 'heavy' SS-18s.

The START negotiation had been so laborious that no more disarmament moves were expected from the US for some time. But the Soviet internal situation after the August 1991 *putsch** provided an unexpected opportunity.

In September 1991 President Bush unilaterally announced the US intention to:
- end the alert status of 40 US strategic bombers;
- end the alert status of all long-range missiles due to be deactivated under START;
- destroy all nuclear artillery shells and short-range warheads;
- remove all nuclear cruise missiles from ships and attack submarines;
- remove all nuclear weapons for use with land-based naval aircraft;
- drop plans to deploy a mobile MX missile and the smaller Midgetman missile.

At the same time he asked Moscow to:
- begin talks on eliminating all intercontinental missiles with multiple warheads;
- start discussions on improved command-and-control arrangements and the security, safe storage, transportation and dismantling of warheads;
- destroy all ground-launched short-range nuclear weapons, including nuclear land mines and nuclear air-defence warheads;
- remove all short-range nuclear weapons from surface ships, attack submarines and land-based naval aircraft;
- confine all mobile intercontinental missiles to their garrisons;
- speed up elimination of weapons due for destruction under START;
- limit modernization programmes to single-warhead missiles;
- permit limited deployment of anti-missile defences against limited nuclear strikes.

A week later Gorbachev responded by proposing to:
- destroy all nuclear artillery ammunition and nuclear warheads for Soviet tactical weapons;
- remove all tactical warheads from surface ships and multi-purpose submarines;
- remove and partly destroy all nuclear warheads of anti-aircraft missiles;
- take strategic bombers off standby and put their nuclear weapons into storage;

- stop development of compact mobile intercontinental ballistic missiles;
- freeze rail-mobile intercontinental ballistic missiles at present levels and keep them at permanent sites;
- remove 503 intercontinental ballistic missiles from alert status;
- cut Soviet armed forces by 700,000 men to 3 million 'in the coming years';
- end nuclear tests for 1992.

He also proposed:

- negotiation of a further 50 per cent cut in strategic weapons;
- creation of a joint US-Soviet early warning system against nuclear attack;
- joint liquidation of all tactical nuclear weapons in both sides' navies;
- removal of all nuclear weapons from forward tactical air units.

In December 1991 Russia undertook all the obligations of the USSR under START and other arms treaties. Other republics similarly pledged their obedience, often stealing Gorbachev's initiatives.

**NUCLEAR ENERGY.** Miracle of technology that came apart at Chernobyl. The catastrophe necessitated extensive modifications to all Chernobyl-type RBMK reactors and a drastic rewriting of safety procedures. (Researchers were also asked to accelerate work on a safer type of reactor, the Tokamak 15, using controlled nuclear fusion − a process thought far distant by most experts in the West.) Meanwhile plans to expand the nuclear energy programme continued, with a 40 per cent cost addition for new safety measures. The first new station to be opened after Chernobyl was at Zaporezh (Ukraine) in December 1986. But growing awareness of environmental and health risks caused nationwide protests − long before more general political movements. In 1988−89, these caused a whole series of cancellations or closures, including: the station at Medzamor (18 miles from Yerevan), closed after 150 malfunctions in less than ten years; a third reactor at Ignalina in Lithuania (26 miles from Minsk); new stations at Chigirinsk (Ukraine), Krasnodar (southern Russia), Odessa, Rostov, Minsk and Ulyanovsk; and, after a local referendum, a station about to come on stream at Voronezh. By 1991, according to the Soviet power authorities, construction and design had stopped at some sixty sites. In the first six months of the year nuclear plants were working at only 67 per cent of capacity. There were fifty-nine stoppages, twenty caused by human error. But local moves to restrict nuclear development were not followed everywhere. Though Byelorussia stuck to a year-old decision to stay 'nuclear-free', the Ukraine and Russia had to resume construction of 'advanced safety' plants in order to meet serious power shortages. And Armenia reopened Medzamor. See also 'Electricity'.

**NUCLEAR TEST MORATORIUM.** Unilateral cessation of nuclear tests instituted by the Soviet Union in February 1986. It was maintained for a year in the hope of US reciprocation (which would have stopped work on

'Star Wars'*). Tests were resumed in 1987 after two prolongations. A second cessation was declared in 1989, but ended at Novaya Zemlia* in October 1990 when, after eleven months, other countries failed to respond. By then, according to a Foreign Ministry spokesman, there had been 2,050 nuclear tests worldwide: 1,080 by the United States, 714 by the Soviet Union, 180 by France, 42 by Great Britain, and 34 by China. A new moratorium – for 1992 – was among offers made by Gorbachev in response to an initiative by President Bush in September 1991 (see 'Nuclear Disarmament').

**NUCLEAR WEAPONS.** At the time of its break-up the Soviet Union possessed 28,000 nuclear warheads, of which 11,000 were 'strategic', for launching by long-range missiles or bombers, and the rest 'tactical', i.e. short-range or battlefield weapons. Its principal intercontinental ballistic missiles were the SS-17, SS-18, SS-19, SS-24 and SS-25. The SS-18, SS-24 and SS-25 were mobile, and the others 'fixed' in underground silos. As well as the 3,600 warheads in ICBMs, 3,672 warheads were carried by submarines. Bombers formed a relatively small part of the strategic forces. Up to 4,000 warheads were in Ukraine, 1,250 in Byelorussia, and 1,800 in Kazakhstan. 19,000 were in Russia. With the formation of the Commonwealth,* it was agreed that the nuclear weapons in Byelorussia and Ukraine should be transferred, under central control, to Russia, to be scrapped, as appropriate, under START* or later agreements. But Kazakhstan insisted on keeping its weapons. In the end all the nuclear weapons were put under central control (in the person of Gen. Shaposhnikov,* the interim C-in-C of joint forces), with each republic having a finger on the nuclear safety-catch. But whereas strategic weapons are technically controllable by a system of electronic locks, tactical weapons have mechanical locks which can be broken. In the new conditions of republican independence the worry was that tactical weapons could pass into the possession of outsiders or criminals. More immediately worrying was the possibility of outsiders acquiring nuclear materials or weapons technology (a likely case was Iraq) from scientists hit by programme closures or inflation.

# O

**OBKhSS** (*Otdel borby s khishchenyem sotsialisticheskoi sobstvennosti* – Department for Combating Misappropriation of Soviet Property). Branch of the Soviet Ministry of the Interior. In 1989 it declared war on co-operatives★ which were pilfering from state enterprises the materials unobtainable on the market.

**OBKOM.** Party committee of an *oblast*.★

**OBLAST** (region). Major administrative subdivision of a Soviet republic, comparable to a province.

**OCCIDENTALIST.** Hereditary enemy of Russophiles. Suspicion of Western ideas took a new turn in the late 1980s when propaganda on behalf of private advancement was seen by traditionalists as undermining the old Russian sense of community.

**OCTOBER.** Month of the great Revolution, now often referred to as the 'coup d'état of 1917'. The November 7 anniversary (dated by a switch in 1918 from the Julian to the Gregorian calendar) was formerly marked by a military parade in Red Square. Its observation was abolished, together with May Day, by a decree of the Russian parliament in December 1991.

**OGARKOV**, Marshal Nikolai Vasilyevich (1917– ). Chief of the General Staff, 1977–84, privately critical of Brezhnev's abandonment of nuclear superiority and cynical towards arms agreements.

*OGONYEK.* Weekly standard-bearer of *glasnost*, sometimes excessive in its presentation. Like *Moscow News*,★ it sprang to life from an existence of conservative insipidity. Taking over as editor in 1986, the writer Vitali Korotich★ plunged into subjects formerly taboo. He launched a campaign against Stalin and his heirs, and opened the paper's columns to protestors both inside and outside the Party. A strongly Jewish editorial staff, coupled with its denunciations of anti-semitism and its rehabilitation of Jewish public figures and artists, made it the *bête noire* of Pamyat.★ After doing much good, in 1990 it became increasingly combative on the side of Yeltsinite 'democrats' against Gorbachev, and devoted large amounts of space to personal vendettas. On the management side, it set up a profitable department selling video-cassettes, which helped to meet the cost of financial autonomy* and the abandoning of dependence on its former owner, *Pravda*. In 1991, sharing in the general collapse of circulations due to price increases, it lost a third of its 1.5 million readers. The subsequent departure of Korotich signalled a new editorial policy.

**OGORODNIKOV,** Aleksandr (1950–   ). Religious militant liberated by the 1987 amnesty.* In 1989 he unsuccessfully proposed an 'alternative' to the official Orthodox millennium* celebrations with a display showing churches closed by the state and a mass by unfrocked priests who accused the church of having left Christians to be persecuted. Since 1987 he has edited the *Bulletin of Christian Society*, a magazine concerned with the current life of the church, whereas the other Christian journal, *Vybor* (Choice), is more historical and philosophical.

**OIL.** Gradually diminishing mineral wealth. The former USSR may still be the world's biggest producer, and oil its main source of foreign exchange, but the industry is in decline. After an erratic decade, output reached a peak in 1988 then turned downward. In 1990 a sharp drop prevented the USSR from deriving profit from the higher prices caused by the Gulf crisis. In 1991, for the first time in forty-five years, it turned towards becoming a net importer. Falls have been caused mainly by geological conditions and exhaustion of the most accessible fields. The main producing areas, in Western Siberia, have shifted north and east, where conditions are more difficult and transport more costly. Production in 1990–91 was also affected by the breakdown and obsolescence of equipment. Pipeline accidents (900 in the first four months of 1991) became an ecological disaster. If things continued as they were, it was estimated that by mid-1993 all foreign currency profits would be absorbed by the need for imported replacements. In the first year of *perestroika* steps were taken to arrest a serious decline by opening up new wells in the Tyumen* field. As a result production went up from 595 million tonnes in 1985 to 626 million tonnes in 1988, in which year the greater domestic use of natural gas allowed more oil to be exported. In 1989, it was down 17 million tonnes, and in 1990 another 37 million. In 1991 production was not expected to exceed 500 million tonnes. In peak years exports reached 100–125 million tonnes, but only 30–40 million tonnes earned hard currency. In 1992 some Western experts forecast that with the fall of GNP (an estimated 50 per cent in 1989–95) a 30 per cent reduction in domestic energy demands could leave a margin for export. The same applied to gas.* Longer-term prospects were likely to depend heavily on the success of Western investments in Siberia (see 'Tyumen').

**OLD BELIEVERS.** Schismatic group formed in 1688 in opposition to moves to bring the Russian church into conformity with other Orthodox communions, notably the Greek. Still active.

**OLYMPIC GAMES.** Ancient celebration whose high ideals were supposed to have been uniquely preserved by the socialist countries – till Soviet athletes learned that sport* can be both professional and profitable. The Moscow Olympics of 1980 are still remembered as a shoppers' Eldorado, a time of well-stocked shelves and smiling assistants; and of forbidden fruits like talking freely with foreigners. The city was cleaned up, in every sense – prostitutes, tramps, alcoholics and dissidents being safely moved elsewhere. There was less excitement when in 1990, in Seoul, Soviet athletes took 142 medals (against 94 by the United States). The games were the last to include an all-Union team.

**OMON** (*Otdel Militsii Osobovo Naznacheniya* – Special Purpose Militia Detachment). So-called 'black berets', volunteers from the regular army transferred to the Ministry of the Interior for use against separatists and other 'law-breakers'. In 1991 there were thirty units with a total strength of 9,000. In January 1991, OMON troops killed five civilians in Latvia.* Without any clear indication as to who gave them orders, their existence became a menace to every attempt to solve the problem of separatism by negotiation. OMON units of the Soviet Interior Ministry were disbanded after the 1991 *putsch*,* but some republics kept their own units.

**ORTEGA,** DANIEL. Longtime Nicaraguan hero whose defeat in the 1990 elections took Soviets by surprise. Commentators finally decided that Nicaragua was going through a *perestroika* and that the people had passed judgement on a regime that had ruined them economically. The 'reformist' Soviet version made no mention of the US blockade; the Contras were made to look like patriots (admittedly going a bit too far); and the new President, Mrs Chamoro, appeared as the champion of democracy, rewarding the peasants with the land that had been taken from them for collective farms.

**ORTHODOX CHURCH.** Popular refuge of intellectual orphans of Marxism, having for years been monopolized by old people; for young Russians, one of the few honourable links with the past. Yet the entry of religion into politics has also caused some neophytes to embark on religious and national chauvinism. The Russian Orthodox Church is the country's largest (there is also an Autocephalous Georgian and a Ukrainian Orthodox Church). It is governed by the Patriarch of Moscow and All Russia, elected by a Synod. In 1991 there were more than 7,000 Orthodox churches serving 8,200 parishes in seventy-four dioceses, and twenty-eight functioning monasteries, including the Holy Trinity-St Sergius *lavra* (major monastery) in Zagorsk,* the *lavra* of the Assumption of Pechora (Pskov), and the *lavra* of Pochaev in the Western Ukraine. Seminaries exist in Zagorsk, Leningrad and Odessa. The Patriarchate is based in the Danilov monastery in Moscow. The Patriarch, Aleksei⋆ (chosen 1990), has brought a new, more active style to his function than his predecessor Pimen,⋆ particularly by visiting his dioceses. Within a year of his election, in an opinion poll asking 'In what political force or social movement do you have the most confidence?', 60 per cent of Russians said the Church, 10 per cent the Army.

**OSSETES.** Ethnic group of 542,000, of whom 299,000 live in North Ossetia⋆ and 65,000 in South Ossetia,⋆ separated by the Caucasus chain. The Ossetes speak an Indo-European language and are Christians.

**OVIR.** Office issuing passports and visas, for years the heartbreak of *refuseniks*⋆ and others applying for permission to emigrate. Still a cog in the machinery of bureaucracy, devouring hours of everyone's time.

# P

**PACIFISM.** Long-applauded principle for Western 'peaceniks', but rank
heresy for defenders of the socialist motherland (outside the platitudinous
and subservient Peace Committee\*). The unofficial 'Confidence Group'
formed in the 1970s to add an honest Soviet voice to the international
peace movement was mindlessly derided as a puppet of the CIA. In May
1988 *Pravda* tempered the chauvinism a little by telling readers that
communists had no monopoly of the struggle for world peace and that the
fight against nuclear armaments was too important for anyone to be
'wasting time in sectarianism and power struggles'. But conscientious
objection\* was beyond the comprehension of Soviet law, and in 1991
refusal to do military service was still legally punishable by imprisonment
– if heavy-footed military snatch squads were ever able to catch up with
the offender.

**PALESTINE LIBERATION ORGANIZATION (PLO).** Aggrieved party
since the restoration of Soviet relations with Israel\* and the lifting of all
brakes on Jewish emigration, part of it to the West Bank. The PLO called
Moscow's policy during the 1990–91 Gulf crisis a 'betrayal of promises to
the Arab world'. In August 1991 it was ill-advisedly quick to give approval
to the *putsch.*\*

**PAMYAT** ('Memory'). Society formed with honourable intentions, before it
veered towards chauvinism and anti-semitism.\* It began in 1982 with the
publication in *Nash Sovremennik*\* ('Our Contemporary') of a book called
*Pamyat* by Vladimir Chivilikhin. A student circle gathered round the
author with the idea of safeguarding the memory of the past. It continued
to grow after his death, caring for monuments and cultivating historical
associations, until a group of adherents, led by a prominent supporter,
D. D. Vasilyev, took off on a flight of chauvinism and anti-semitism. By
1988, when it began to make news, its 90,000 members could be divided
between harmless defenders of Russian culture (about two-thirds) and
dangerous fools like Vasilyev (who later turned out to have served a prison
sentence for murdering and dismembering his wife). In the winter of
1988–89, Pamyat organized meetings in Leningrad, distributing lists of
the early communist leaders responsible for collectivization and terror. On
the lists it indicated Jewish participants, like Trotsky,\* by their real names
(lesson no. 1: it was the Jews who destroyed our churches, culture and

peasantry). It then gave out other lists naming Jewish intellectuals supporting *perestroika* (lesson no. 2: we have been infiltrated by Jews who are destroying our past). In 1989, the movement experienced a humiliating election defeat and split into three parts: the Vasilyev faction, a more intellectual faction led by the present (1992) leader, Sychov, and a violently anti-semitic faction led by a disturbed individual called Smirnov-Ostashvili. In January 1990 Smirnov-Ostashvili was given a two-year sentence for shouting racist propositions at a meeting held in the House of Writers. In 1991 he committed suicide in prison and Pamyat all but disappeared from the news pages.

**PANKIN**, Boris Dimitrievich. Diplomat made Foreign Minister, replacing Bessmertnykh,* after the 1991 *putsch*.* As ambassador in Prague, he denounced the *putsch* as illegal, albeit only on the third day. After a period as a journalist, his ten years in diplomacy included seven as Soviet ambassador to Sweden. In November 1991 he was appointed ambassador in London.

**PARALLEL DIPLOMACY.** Best way to free foreign travel, short of hijacking a plane. In 1991 Soviet deputies, academicians and *bizinesmen*★ secured invitations enabling them to pursue their mutual recriminations in front of bewildered foreigners. Some *bizinesmen* proposed deals so breathtakingly naive that the Westerners suspected a trap. And 'parallel' diplomacy could cross with state diplomacy. In 1990 the head of the Central Committee International Department had to calm down the Chinese ambassador after the mayor of Moscow, Gavril Popov, took off on a visit to Taiwan. Republican independence has not changed things.

**PARALLEL ECONOMY.** See 'Black market'.

**PARLIAMENT.** See 'Supreme Soviet'.

**PARTY CONFERENCE.** See 'Conference'.

**PARTY OF CONSTITUTIONAL DEMOCRATS.** Party formed in 1990 among the Moscow intelligentsia★ to 'promote human rights, including the right of property'. Almost immediately deserted by a splinter group, the Constitutional Democratic Party (People's Freedom Party★).

**PASSPORT.** (1) Document entitling Soviet citizens to travel abroad. Until 1990 a passport had to be issued for each journey; later made valid for several years and costing R200-1,000. (2) Internal passport serving as a means of identification, with the holder's nationality,★ and *propiska*.★

**PAST.** A 'happier' time under (a) Brezhnev, (b) Stalin, (c) the Tsar.

**PASTERNAK,** Boris Leonidovich (1880–1960). For foreigners the author of *Doctor Zhivago*; for Russians a poet. *Doctor Zhivago*, a love story set in the time of the Revolution and Civil War, was published in Italy in 1957 and immediately considered anti-Soviet by the authorities. Pasternak was expelled from the Writers' Union* and in 1958 obliged to refuse nomination for the Nobel Prize for Literature. He died in official disgrace in 1960 but was posthumously rehabilitated in February 1987. *Doctor Zhivago* was finally published in the Soviet Union in 1988, in *Novy Mir** (which had planned to bring it out in 1956). His house in Peredelkino is now a museum.

**PATRIARCHATE.** Supreme authority of the Russian Orthodox church. The patriarch of Moscow and all the Russias, Aleksei,* was elected in 1990. His predecessor, Pimen,* was accused of subservience to the political authorities.

**PATRIOTISM.** Un-Leninist '-ism' born of the Great Patriotic War* and sustained by its constant commemoration, from the kindergarten to the grave. Patriotism was supposed to go hand in hand with 'international-ism'. But both have been replaced by a third '-ism' − nationalism.

**PAVLOV,** Valentin Sergeyevich (1937– ). Dim but ambitious Prime Minister caught up in the August 1991 *putsch*.* Eight months earlier Gorbachev had picked him to succeed Ryzhkov, after a short spell as Finance Minister (1989). Deputies still suffering from another mediocrity imposed on them by Gorbachev − Vice-President Yanayev* − had their fears confirmed when he abruptly withdrew all R50 and R100 notes from circulation. Action was badly needed to mop up the excess amount of money in circulation, mostly from the black market; but Pavlov's ill-organized measure hurt small savers much more than speculators. To deflect public anger, he announced that he had thwarted a Western plot to destroy the economy by flooding the country with fake currency. This bizarre allegation was a construction on events in the Russian republic, where it had just been found (by the KGB) that Gennadi Filshin,* a deputy premier and Yeltsin's close economic adviser, had countersigned authority for a huge sale of public property to foreign interests. On the eve of the July 1991 G-7* summit, Pavlov told the Soviet parliament that Gorbachev had too much power and not enough time to fulfil all his duties; he asked for a constitutional amendment giving more authority to the cabinet. Parliament turned down the request, which was later seen as having foreshadowed the attempted coup. On August 19 he appeared as one of the *putsch* leaders, having almost certainly been enlisted by Kryuchkov* and Pugo,* who needed the Prime Minister's name to give their action legitimacy. Next day it was announced that he had resigned from their eight-man 'emergency committee' due to problems of blood pressure. But this did not save him from subsequent arrest and a charge of treason.

**PAY.** So-called reward for so-called work. In 1991 the failure of the Soviet government to deal with the economic crisis caused pay demands to coincide with a disastrous fall in production. Anomalies in pay went back to the last years of Brezhnev, when there were concessions to workers unbacked by productivity. In 1986 the Ryzhkov★ government announced plans to link pay to performance, simultaneously with a general increase of 25–30 per cent to cover increased living costs. The same year there was a 30–40 per cent increase in the pay of qualified workers, including engineers, technicians and medical staff. This was to rectify an anomaly whereby many young specialists earned less than unskilled workers; for example, a skilled engineer earned only R120 a month, R75 below the national average, and a doctor only R100–130. But real pay rates were complicated by the distribution of social consumption funds,★ commonly adding a third to the value of pay itself, through the provision of housing, polyclinics, holiday vouchers etc. It was therefore impossible to stimulate productivity simply by pay increases. With the 'privatization'★ of state enterprises, pay became linked to profitability. In 1991 the average monthly wage of employees in the national economy rose from R240 to R270, whereas the average for people working in co-operatives was R450. From January 1992, Russia adopted a legal minimum of R342.

**PEACE COMMITTEE.** Tame body used to project the image of peace-loving USSR and highlight the warlike designs of all countries 'unfriendly' to it, starting with NATO countries. The inclusion of church representatives helped to give foreigners a picture of peaceful co-existence between communism and religion. Rejuvenated with *perestroika*, the committee showed a trace of independence by condemning the restarting of tests at Novaya Zemlia,★ but it continued to be held at arm's length by much of the Western peace movement.

**PEASANTS' PARTY OF RUSSIA.** Party founded in 1991 'to advance the position of individual farmers and accelerate the transformation of *kolkhozy*★ into truly voluntary co-operatives.' The Soviet writer and deputy, Yuri Chernichenko, was elected chairman.

**PEASANTS' UNION.** Organization founded in 1990 by collective and state farm representatives. A year later it adopted a political stand against private land sales. Discredited when chairman Vladimir Starodubtsev joined the *putsch*.★

**P.E.N.** Affiliate of the international writers' association, authorized in the Soviet Union in 1989. Anatoli Rybakov★ was elected the first chairman for a term of two years.

**PENSIONERS.** Social category hardest hit by the economic crisis. At the time of the Soviet collapse there were 61 million pensioners, of whom three-quarters were old-age pensioners, 6.2 million war pensioners, and 1.2 million disabled. Pensioners of all kinds formed nearly one fifth of the total population. Under Soviet law, taken over by most republics, most retirement pensioners receive 50-75 per cent of their former pay. But in the case of many older ones, this may have been very low (collective farmers received no pensions at all before Khrushchev). In 1991 the minimum pension was fixed at R70, raised at the end of the year to R110, but inflation quickly put the majority of pensioners below the poverty line. Retirement starts at 55 for women, 60 for men (50 in the case of some classes of workers, such as miners).

**PEOPLE'S FREEDOM PARTY**. Party founded under Mikhail Astafiev by members leaving the Union of Constitutional Democrats (May 1990) and wanting to revert to the pre-revolutionary Constitutional Democrats (Kadets). In 1991 it allied with Travkin's* wing of the Democratic Party of Russia to found the People's Concord Group.

**PEPSI-COLA**. Western pioneer of the Soviet soft drinks market. In 1974 Pepsico started shipping syrup to Soviet-based plants and selling bottled product, taking out profits in Stolichnaya vodka. In April 1990 a new agreement enabled it to modernize and double its bottling capacity and take out profits in the form of ten Soviet merchant ships worth $300 million. The deal included a monopoly to sell Soviet vodka in the US until 2000. In 1991, twenty-five plants produced 40 million cases a year.

**PEREGIB** ('Excess'). Weakness for overdoing things – polemic, protests, praise, promises – forever complicating Soviet social and political life.

**PERESTROIKA**. Literally 'restructuring': launched on the country at the April 1985 plenum of the Communist Party Central Committee. The next plenum, in June, adopted a scientific, technological, investment and structural policy for 1986–90 (the period of new Five Year Plan). The broad ideas of *perestroika* were then approved by the Twenty-seventh Party Congress of February 1986, which also considered the question of *perestroika* in the social sector. The Congress decisions were recorded in a document, 'Main Directions of the Economic and Social Development of the USSR in the period 1986–90 and the Prospects up to the Year 2000'. Afterwards *perestroika* came to have a broader meaning, its social aspect being boosted when it was seen that progress depended on popular support against conservative forces in the administrative and industrial bureaucracy. Crucial decisions on economic reform were next taken at the June 1987 plenum of the Central Committee. In preparation, experts had drafted a Law on State Enterprises,* which purportedly drew on a nationwide debate in which 180,000 suggestions, additions and proposed amendments were put forward. In line with the Law, the government submitted eleven resolutions on planning, prices, finance and banking, supplies and technology, social and labour questions, and ministerial responsibilities in the Union and republics. These were accepted and their main points included in a document entitled 'Radical *perestroika* of Management and the Economy', enshrining the principles of 'self-financing' (*khozraschet*\*) and 'self-management'.\*

**PERESTROIKA 88.** Informal group created in 1988 to uphold reforms. It put out petitions in support of Boris Yeltsin when he lost his job as head of the Party in Moscow.

**PHILANTHROPY.** Innovative Soviet word, together with 'charity'.\* The first 'philanthropic' event was in 1986, a Moscow rock concert in aid of Chernobyl\* victims.

**PHILBY,** KIM (1912–1988). British-born double agent, representing the most successful penetration of British intelligence by the KGB. After nearly thirty years working for Moscow, Philby came under positive suspicion in 1962 and, evading surveillance, fled to the Soviet Union from Beirut in 1963. In 1988 he spoke about his career in a series of Soviet television programmes, and in an interview with the London *Sunday Times* – the first intimation of a major change in KGB public relations policy.

**PIMEN,** Patriarch SERGEI MIKHAILOVICH IZVEKOV (1910–1990). Russian patriarch accused of political subservience. A sick man during his last years, he rejected pleas to give way to a younger man. Gleb Yakunin,\* a leading clerical critic, accused him of having made compromises which over seventeen years turned the church into a state department for religion. Pimen replied that it had grieved him to see churches closed, but he had acted diplomatically to avoid worse.

**PIONEERS.** Communist Party youth organization, for ages 10–14, lying between Young Octobrists (7–10) and the Komsomol.\* It survived in Russia and some other republics as an organizer of summer camps and hobby centres, despite being formally suspended by anti-Party measures after the 1991 *putsch*.\*

**PLAN.** Overall co-ordinator of the economy, until reduced in scope (but not eliminated) by reforms in 1988. The crucial vote of the Central Committee ended the practice by which all industrial and agricultural activity was subordinated to achieving the 'plan' for the enterprise or sector. Annual plans ceased to be made after 1990. Five-year plans\* were to have continued.

**PLENUM.** Plenary meeting of the Party organization, most often meaning the CPSU Central Committee. Under the rules up to August 1991, Central

Committee plenums had to be held at least twice a year, to consider a report by the General Secretary and to approve changes in the Politburo and the Secretariat. From April 1985 Gorbachev used plenums to increase his hold and push through reforms. The most important were in January 1987 (three times postponed because of its heavy agenda of social and economic reform), June 1987 and March 1989 (on agriculture), and in July 1989 (on democratic elections and the internal organization of the Party). With unexpectedly little opposition from conservatives, the plenum of July 1991 adopted a social-democratic direction proposed by Gorbachev. It was followed by the August *putsch** and was the last.

**PLO.** See 'Palestine Liberation Organization'.

**POGROM.** Historically, a punitive expedition against Jewish communities; now used to mean an attack involving bloodshed against a particular nationality. In May 1990 the Jewish community in Moscow took serious notice of a rumour of a pogrom planned for that month. The Foreign Ministry described it as 'something hatched by people wanting to add to the number of émigrés to Israel' — one way or another almost certainly the truth.

**POKLONNAYA.** Small hill in Moscow narrowly saved from becoming a patriotic Disneyland. The fortieth anniversary of victory over fascism was to have been commemorated by the erection of a 250 feet-high statue supported by a host of allegorical figures. The site had already been levelled (and more than a quarter of the R184 million budget consumed by its preparation) when, in August 1986, the Politburo cancelled the project.

**POLAND.** Ally freed of dependence on Moscow when Bonn underwrote its post-war frontiers and laid the ghost of revanchism. Relations improved with the admission of the truth about Katyn,* and Moscow's establishment of relations with the Vatican. Poland and the former USSR are condemned to stay trading partners. In 1991 they signed an agreement towards a solution of their respective energy and food problems. The USSR would supply nearly 1.5 billion cubic metres of natural gas in exchange for Polish food products worth $100 million. In March 1990 it was agreed that the last of 50,000 Soviet troops would be out of the country by mid-1994, but in October 1991 the date was advanced to the end of 1992.

**POLEMIC.** Means of learning among intellectuals,* the purpose being not to deliver the truth but to provoke thought and argument. Thanks to polemic, each side widens its understanding a little. But what is supposed to enrich intellectual life is also destructive of informative political debate.

**POLICE.** In 1990 the city council of Lvov took the step of establishing its own police force in place of the local militia,* who were indirectly subordinate to the Moscow MVD.* The idea was copied by other local authorities, who saw it as a way to put the police 'under popular control', i.e. to impose their own order. The move was fiercely but impotently resisted by Moscow, as well as by local communist parties.

**POLITBURO** (Political Bureau of the Central Committee). For years the most powerful Soviet institution, running the country as well as directing the work of the Party between Central Committee plenums.* In 1990 its role was drastically changed by the Twenty-eighth Congress,* which approved the transfer of power to parliamentary institutions. It then became concerned only with Party matters. Elections by the new Central Committee raised its membership to twenty-four, but its loss of authority was marked by the departure of leading members to the new (and short-lived) Presidential Council.* Resignations included those of Prime Minister Ryzhkov, Foreign Minister Shevardnadze, KGB chief Vladimir Kryuchkov, leading reformer Aleksandr Yakovlev, State planning chief Yuri Maslyukov and Defence Minister Marshal Dmitri Yazov. The only members staying in place were General Secretary Gorbachev and (a new appointment) Deputy General Secretary Vladimir Ivashko.* The Politburo ceased to function with the suspension of Party activities in August 1991.

**POLITICAL CONSULTATIVE COUNCIL.** New nine-member body created in September 1991 as replacement, more or less, for the former Presidential Council. First members included Bakatin* (chairman), Academician and physicist Yevgeni Velikhov, Nikolai Petrakov (director of the Market Institute), Yuri Ryzhov (head of the Supreme Soviet Committee for Science and Technology), Anatoli Sobchak,* Edvard Shevardnadze,* Aleksandr Yakovlev* and Yegor Yakovlev.* It finished with Gorbachev.

**POLOZKOV,** Ivan Kuzmich (1935– ). Unsuccessful competitor with Yeltsin* for the presidency of Russia. His election in 1990 as First Secretary of the Russian Communist Party showed the grip of the conservatives on the most important communist party in the country. His appointment caused the flight of 800,000 members. He resigned in August 1991 and was made USSR Deputy Minister of Agriculture.

**PONTINE GREEKS.** Community of 350,000 living for centuries on the shores of the Black Sea until dispersed in Central Asia and Siberia by 1949 deportations. In July 1989 an Association of Soviet Greeks was founded in Moscow under Gavril Popov.* It called for a return to 1938, before Stalin suppressed Greek schools, theatres and presses. A wave of emigration in 1989 caught Greece quite unprepared for the sudden arrival and assimilation of tens of thousands of often unskilled people, speaking a form of Greek incomprehensible in Athens.

**POPOV**, GAVRIL KHARITONOVICH (1936– ). Obscure economist until reform called attention to his bold 'market' theories. In 1989 he was elected to the Soviet parliament and, more importantly, the Moscow city council, where he became chairman. As such he made a cautious reform of public services, probably remembering the explosion caused three years before by Yeltsin's sweeping changes. But when he spoke in favour of more autonomy for city districts, these districts took him so literally as to declare themselves 'sovereign', with the result that he was always having to settle disputes over authority. Soon tiring of managing the huge city with its decaying infrastructure and hybrid status as Soviet and Russian capital, he took to parallel diplomacy★ and rushed round the world on the pretext of seeking foreign investors. His absences, showmanship and inability to achieve miracles led to calls for his resignation; and his young and ambitious deputy, Sergei Stankevich,★ was not always zealous in defending him. In 1991 he nevertheless succeeded in securing his popular election as mayor. At the same time a revived interest in a 'presidential' form of city government led him to become increasingly embroiled in what was frequently a three-cornered fight between himself, the large city council (more like a parliament) and the dominant Russian Federation. In December 1991 he offered to resign, but retracted. See also 'Moscow', 'Murashev'.

**POPULAR FRONTS.** Informal groups formed in several republics before the 1988 Party Conference to stop conservative leaders promoting anti-*perestroika* delegates. Several called themselves groups 'for the defence of *perestroika*' or 'for the support of Gorbachev'. After the conference they turned increasingly nationalist, gathering under the name 'Popular Front' all those – including communists – who wanted a change in relations with the centre. At the 1989 elections, the Fronts presented themselves as the alternative to central control from Moscow and the dictatorship of the Communist Party. It was hard to classify them as 'right' or 'left', since their degree of internal democracy varied from republic to republic. Arrival in government often proved fatal to their cohesion.

**POPULATION.** At the beginning of 1991, according to the USSR State Committee for Statistics, the Soviet population was 290.1 million – an increase of 1.4 million over twelve months, against 2 million in 1989. The reduction was due to a lower birth rate (60.8 per 1,000 against 67.6 in 1989), a higher death rate (10.4 per 1,000 against 10.0 per 1,000) and emigration.★ A more detailed breakdown is available from the census of 1989. This showed a population of 286,717,000, a ten-year growth by 24.3 million (9.3 per cent). The fastest growth was in the Turkmen, Uzbek and Tajik republics, the slowest in the Ukraine, Latvia, the Russian Federation and Estonia. There were 15.7 million more women than men, due largely to lower male life expectancy and also, still, to the effect of World War II. The ratio of city dwellers to country dwellers was 2:1, reflecting *inter alia* an increase in the number of new industrial towns and a ten-year 11 per cent growth in the population of Moscow. The difference of birth rates between Central Asia and the European parts of the country provoked thought among Slavs, who till recently had appeared to dominate society. Two-thirds of Army recruits were now Asiatic, and half the young men in Central Asian regions without jobs.

**PORNOGRAPHY.** Salacious culture introduced under cover of 'art exhibitions', art-of-love manuals and 'Freudian studies'. In 1991 a Moscow exhibition of 'feminine beauty and poetry of the female form' was simply a show of dirty photographs.

***POSTFACTUM.*** Economic and political news service, victim of over-ambition and a satiated market. Co-founded by Commersant* and the Menatep private bank, it lost heavily when it launched a separate economic bulletin, *Zakanadatelstvo i Ekonomika* ('Legislation and Economy'). In September 1991 it owed Menatep R1.5 million.

**POVERTY.** Malady making no distinction between capitalist and Soviet society. In 1991, 100 million Soviet people, more than one person in three, were in households with incomes below the minimum tolerable subsistence level. Economists accurately predicted that with 1992 price increases the figure in Russia could double.

***PRAVDA*** (Truth). Daily newspaper of the Communist Party, founded in exile by Lenin in 1912. In 1987 an editorial in its 25,000th issue recalled that its history was 'inseparable from that of the heroic history of the CPSU'. So much the worse: between 1985 and 1989 circulation fell from 10.5 to 9.7 million, when that of all other newspapers was going up. In 1990 it had only 6.8 million subscribers, and in 1991 barely 2 million. The editor-in-chief, Ivan Frolov, said he had no intention of changing *Pravda* or of resigning. On the contrary, there was talk of starting a *Pravda International*, with the participation of 'press magnates in America, Britain and France'. Nemesis came in 1991 when *Pravda* was temporarily closed by Yeltsin at the time of the *putsch.** The three-day closure (the eighth in its history, all others having been under the Tsar) was bitterly contested; not only was Yeltsin's authority confined to Russia, but a week earlier the staff had severed the Party connection by declaring *Pravda* a 'general political newspaper'. It reappeared with a masthead shorn of Lenin's portrait and communist insignia. With no money coming from its legal owner, the Central Committee, and no property or material of its own, the paper faced bankruptcy. A letter to Gorbachev, appealing for the release of paper supplies, to enable it to compete in the market, went unanswered.

Subscriptions for 1992 were down to 100,000, and the new editor, Gennadi Seleznev, was hard put to keep it alive as a paper 'for the ordinary people, the rank and file communist'.

**PRESIDENCY.** Formerly decorative office, infused with authority and cut to Gorbachev's personal measurements in 1990–91. In 1990, under new constitutional arrangements, he was voted executive President by the Congress of People's Deputies,* combining the office with leadership of the Party 'as a temporary necessity'. In September the same year, after a stormy debate, he obtained special powers enabling him to rule by decree* for eighteen months (until March 31, 1992). The step had a practical justification but was highly controversial. For a long time, the often sterile debates of an inexperienced parliament had shown that the move to a market economy could not be realized without greatly strengthened executive powers. But as early as 1989, deputies like Sakharov* had taken to warning against the effect of too great a concentration of power. Supporters with unshaken confidence in Gorbachev personally were nevertheless afraid that he might be ousted and replaced by a less democratic successor ready to profit from earlier legislation. Republics on the road to autonomy would have liked a presidency loftily detached from the debates over nationalities and parties. But Gorbachev could never have considered such a eunuch-like role. On the contrary, at the end of 1990 he carried constitutional amendments concentrating even more executive power in the hands of the president. Having earlier been accused of indecision, he now ironically leaned to the right, appointing ministers who were later to betray him for 'breaking up the Union'. In 1992 republican presidents came under the same kind of criticism for resorting to authoritarian rule. And 'presidencies' erupted in a variety of former autonomous republics and territories.

**PRESIDENTIAL COUNCIL.** Short-lived consultative body composed (1990) of leading political figures, academics and scientists. It died at the end of the year with changes in the constitution.*

**PRESIDENTIAL ENTERPRISE COUNCIL.** Body created in September 1991 to advise the President on economic reform. Appointments included Aleksandr Vladislavlev, vice-president of the Soviet Scientific and Industrial Union (chairman); economist Pavel Bunich; and Konstantin Borovoi, head of the Russian commodity exchange. It died with the Soviet presidency.

**PRESS.** Touchstone of democracy, as everywhere. The 1991 *putsch** showed the fragility of *glasnost* (all but eight newspapers closed overnight) but also its resilience: the refusal of *Izvestia** staff to print *putsch*ist announcements, continued production of *Moscow News*,* broadcasts by radio 'Moscow Echo'.* The post-*putsch* closure of *Pravda** and other 'communist' papers proved temporary. The previous two years had seen momentous changes, including the ending of Party control of the press (but not, alas, the vocation of all newspapers to 'educate' and moralize). In his campaign of reform Gorbachev regularly called meetings of editors to associate the press with high spots, but in 1988 – a sign of the times – the Deputy Foreign Minister Yuli Vorontsov had to tell foreign ambassadors that signed articles in the Soviet press should not be taken as the official viewpoint. In 1989 Soviet citizens were for the first time allowed to subscribe to some forty foreign newspapers from capitalist countries. At the same time their own newspapers lost part of the circulation they had so spectacularly put on with their new freedom. This was due partly to price increases (see below), but also to fresh competition: 800 new titles among the 1,500 registered in 1991. At the same time in parts of the country there were instances of a revival of censorship* that recalled aspects of the previous regime. The worst came not from the central authorities but from new 'democratic' and nationalist governments. Curbs on reporting included the expulsion of 'foreign', i.e. Soviet, reporters, the imposition of news blackouts, the cutting of telephone links (especially after disturbances), and physical and psychological violence against anyone, especially communists, expressing disagreement with the official line.

In the autumn of 1990, when the time came for registration under the new Law on the Press,* there were struggles for the ownership of titles affected by election changes. Fights were particularly bitter where a newspaper was tied to a soviet* that had fallen to non-communists (as with *Sovietskaya Rossiya,* *Moskovskaya Pravda*, etc.). Many newspapers now called themselves independent, on the ground that they were independent of the Communist Party, but the term was misleading when, as most often happened, they were owned or financed by other parties. In 1991 nearly all Soviet newspapers suffered a landslide in circulation (80 per cent in the case of *Krokodil**). The main reason was the rise in subscription prices: 65 per cent higher for dailies and 45 per cent for periodicals. This was due in turn to the imposition of financial independence, obliging them to pay for accommodation and technical services, such as printing, at 'market' rates. With the worsening of conditions in the winter of 1991–92 the Russian government instituted tax relief and other measures to help papers through the period of transition to a market economy.

**PRICES**. Capitalist regulator turned the headache of Soviets en route to the 'market'. In the last year (1990) of the Gorbachev-Ryzhkov partnership, price reform was repeatedly postponed for fear of social disturbances. The problem was how to fix prices nationwide, to prevent anarchy and stop republics setting up customs barriers to preserve their own market. In April 1991 the government finally acted, and the prices of nearly everything from bread to tractors went up by an average of 300 per cent. To cushion the effect on people with low incomes and on large families the central government introduced a scheme of compensation. Republics added their own measures. A greater shock came in 1992 when on January 2, Russia – quickly followed by other republics – freed prices to reach their market level. Foodstuffs rose 300 per cent, energy 300–500 per cent, medicines 400 per cent, rail fares 200 per cent and air fares 300 per cent. The move opened the way to the Western economic aid that Gorbachev had been unable to secure, and (see 'Humanitarian Aid') shipments of food were rushed to big cities to relieve shortages and help stave off social unrest.

**PRIMAKOV,** YEVGENI MAKSIMOVICH (1929–   ). Academician appointed as Gorbachev's special envoy during the 1990–91 Gulf* crisis. As a historian and economist, he specialized in economic policy and social change in the Arab states and Egypt. He was also a member, since 1986, of the Central Committee.* In the general reorganization after the 1991 *putsch** he was appointed head of the new organization taking over foreign intelligence activity from the KGB, and later of its successor, the Russian Foreign Intelligence Service.

**PRISON.** As part of the general awakening to social questions, in 1986 the press took up the matter of prison conditions, printing reports by ex-prisoners. There was special interest in the conditions of women prisoners and young offenders, and in overcrowding, recidivism and problems of returning to society. In 1989–90 prisons were shaken by a wave of revolts, often involving hostage-taking. The authorities blamed part of this on the 1987 amnesty* which, by freeing petty delinquents, had left a dangerous concentration of hardened criminals. Increased remissions in the case of first offenders had contributed to the same result. In less than two years, violence caused the death of 126 guards.

**PRISONER OF WAR.** Victim of circumstance, dependent on history. After World War II, 2 million Soviet prisoners (surviving out of nearly 4 million) came home in dishonour, often going straight into the *gulag,** and in 1991 were still the forgotten figures of the war. Prisoners of the Afghan *mujaheddin*, though at first forgotten, were later considered to have paid the price for other people's mistakes. This was so even in the case of deserters, and of small sad groups acquired from the *mujaheddin* by Western politicians and presented at press conferences like performing monkeys. In 1988 a dozen former prisoners returned from Canada after all had been amnestied, regardless of circumstances. At the end of the 1980s the association of relatives of the missing, Nadezhda* ('Hope'), held meetings with *mujaheddin* in Pakistan, hoping to obtain a complete list of names (the last one given contained 306, but the Afghans said the total was a military secret). Later the Russian vice-president Rutskoi,* took a lead in the negotiations. Early in 1992 Afghan sources spoke of 'some eighty' Soviet POWs still hidden, often by field commanders, with their release requiring difficult individual negotiation. In July 1991, apropos of a debate about the Soviet treatment of German PoWs after World War II, Tass published statistics from official archives. In 1945–50, 122,671 passed through a total of ten camps. Some were exchanged for Russian PoWs, 45,262 were released, about 14,000 were handed over to the East German Interior Ministry, 756 were condemned to death by military tribunals, and 43,000 died of sickness, often tuberculosis.

**PRIVATE BUSINESS.** *Deus ex machina* in the triumphal advance to a market* economy. In 1990 optimists saw millions of potential private proprietors; pessimists saw millions of simpletons confusing private business with the good old black market. Moderates perceived the need to create a network of small to medium-sized private businesses alongside a reorganized state sector, giving the country time to adjust itself. But, moderation being in deficit, the famous plans of 1990–91 for transition to the market envisaged an almost overnight switch. The juridical basis of private business is the Law on Property,* taken over by most republics. In 1991, 80,000 people were employed in joint ventures,* and 2,100 indust-rial firms had a work force of 1.5 million. In addition there were 150 privately owned construction businesses, 23,000 shops and restaurants, 200 firms selling food or services to consumers at their workplaces, 1,500 studios and boutiques, and 400 garages of all kinds.

**PRIVATE PLOT.** Small parcel, in 1990 still averaging half an acre, allocated to collective farm families for their own use, usually to raise a pig or chickens or grow fruit and vegetables. Introduced in the Brezhnev period to make country life more attractive, they were initially restricted to serving family needs. Free sales were not allowed until 1986, and then were sabotaged by bureaucrats and *kolkhoz** directors, who had the police stop peasants on their way to market, on suspicion of 'speculation'. In the later 1980s private plots continued to be an indispensable source of food. In 1989, though they occupied only 1.4 per cent of cultivated land, they yielded 25.2 per cent of all raw agricultural produce, including 60 per cent of the potatoes, 32 per cent of all other vegetables, 29 per cent of meat, 30 per cent of eggs, and 24 per cent of all wool. These figures were quickly seized on as evidence of real private farming potential. But private plots are a special phenomenon: a means of making a quick kopeck without having to declare profits or pay taxes, and with only the vaguest kind of quality control in the markets. In 1991, in a quickly popular experiment, the Moscow region authorities announced the distribution of 50,000 acres (20,000 hectares) for allotments.

**PRIVATE PROPERTY.** Long source of ideological conflict. Although legislation in 1990 allowed the sale of state housing to private citizens or interests, the land on which it stood remained public; and draft legislation on farm land was limited to leases. In August 1990 the spokesman of orthodoxy, Yegor Ligachev,* told *Moscow News*: 'We must not, after seventy years, go back to private property. Whatever it is, we have built socialism – perhaps distorted, but still socialism. And there is no need to return. This must not be done under any circumstances'. Not only for communists, but also for many Slavs, private property (especially land) offended a historic feeling of community and thus of humanity.

**PRIVATIZATION.** Magic word for coaxing aid from the West, where media and politicians mistakenly equate it with West European-style privatization. In the Soviet Union it usually meant giving the loss-making enterprise to the work force ('collective'), which was then expected to run it without subsidies. At the same time the enterprise might find itself cut off from the industrial network of which it was formerly part. Before the 1991 *putsch*\* there were plans to 'privatize' 21,000 retail shops, 9,300 restaurants and 12,800 service enterprises, amounting to 3–5 per cent of the total in each category. While the task of disposal was given to a new Ministry created for the purpose, a Law on Privatization (August 1991) for the first time allowed foreigners to become direct private owners.

**PRIVILEGE.** Word used by have-nots for anything suggesting a tolerable life. In 1991 an apartment of 40 square metres for a two-child family was a 'privilege', as was 'real meat' sausage or a packet of aspirin. A campaign against privilege, launched in 1987 as the corollary of one against corruption, quickly descended into demagoguery, thanks to shortages caused by the economic crisis. But in 1991 there was still some public acceptance of the idea of privilege as a reward for work for the government, as opposed to that for the Party or the Komsomol.\*

**PROCURATOR.** Personage once vilified as Moscow's instrument for imposing Soviet law on defenceless republics. When successive republics came to declare their sovereignty\* or autonomy, one of their first acts was to nominate their own procurator to enforce the supremacy of the republic's laws. Previously republic procurators were nominated by Moscow.

**PRODUCTIVITY.** Declining value – down 2 per cent in 1989–91, 8 per cent in 1990–91, and an officially estimated 15 per cent in 1991–92.

**PROPAGANDA.** In Russian, simply the propagation of information; not used pejoratively as in the West.

**PROPISKA.** Residence permit serving a system of population control denounced since 1988 as an infraction of human rights. Without the correct one in his Soviet identity document, a person could be charged with breaking the passport\* law. The system prevented people uprooted by ethnic confrontations from finding new homes, and even complicated the settlement of military families repatriated from Eastern Europe.

**PROSTITUTION.** In March 1988 the director Sergei Baranov gave a restricted showing of his film *How do you do?* It showed intimate scenes of prostitutes and their foreign clients in Moscow's National Hotel, and included interviews with call-girls at a work camp near Leningrad. Until a year before, the Soviet Union had denied that prostitution existed. When the press broke silence, it transpired that many prostitutes were young, rich and fluent in several languages. Prostitutes in Moscow and Leningrad started working under 'protectors', another milestone on the road to a Western-style economy.

**PROVOCATEUR.** Invention available in Russian political debate as long as anyone can remember. In a society given to polemic,* yet unable to tolerate contradiction, anyone putting forward an unusual idea is liable to be called a 'provocateur'. And since, by definition, the provocateur is the agent of someone else (an enemy who is all the more dangerous for remaining 'out there' in the shadows), it is reasonable enough to want to put him away.

**PRUNSKIENE,** KASIMIERA (1943–    ). Ex-Party nationalist (and economist) who resigned as Lithuanian prime minister on December 22, 1990, over parliament's rejection of government moves to raise food prices. Her more realistic approach to negotiation with Moscow, as to the reform of the economy, put her at loggerheads with Landsbergis* and the Sajudis* legislative caucus.

**PSYCHIATRY.** Branch of medicine converted into a Brezhnevite weapon of repression. In 1983 the USSR withdrew from the International Psychiatric Association to avoid expulsion for the use of psychiatry against dissidents. In July 1990 a reformist law purportedly ended the possibility of abuse and guaranteed respect for the civil rights, dignity and welfare of all patients. In cases of commitment to a mental institution, the last word would rest with a tribunal, assisted by a magistrate if necessary. In addition, patients were entitled to know the nature of their illness, to choose their own doctor and to discuss treatment with experts. In previous years psychiatric abuse had caused the confinement of 71,000 people, according to a 1988 article in the Party journal *Kommunist*.

**PTU.** Initials standing for technical and trade schools. In the 1980s their exposure as places for lumping together blue-collar workers' children, petty delinquents and the children of 'problem' families killed the myth of social mobility.

**PUBLIC TRANSPORT.** Service stripped of subsidies, causing tripled fare increases (February 1991). A first round was silently accepted by a population travelling daily across vast city distances in overcrowded Metros and decrepit buses. People found it harder to cope with January

1992 increases (200 per cent for rail, 300 per cent for air travel, the latter expected to rise still further due to rocketing fuel costs).

**PUBLISHING.** State-reserved field until opened to a flood of private ventures by the Law on the Press.* In 1992 Moscow pavement vendors offered a high-priced selection of Agatha Christie, Graham Greene, bibles, sex manuals and books explaining how to succeed in business.

**PUGO,** Boris Karlovich (1937–91). Former Latvian KGB chief and head of the CPSU Party Control Committee, appointed Soviet Interior Minister in December 1990 in succession to Bakatin.* His nomination, with Gromov's,* marked a departure from Bakatin's more flexible handling of the secessionist problem. In 1991 he was perceived as the instigator of OMON* attacks in Latvia and Lithuania, and the partner of Kryuchkov* in allegations to the Soviet and Russian parliaments of plots to subvert Soviet society by the CIA. In August he emerged as one of the principal *putsch** leaders, with authority over Ministry of the Interior* forces intended to take control in Moscow and Leningrad. When the attempt collapsed on August 21, he committed suicide.

**PUSHKIN,** Aleksandr Sergeyevich (1799–1837). Living voice for modern millions – like the vast crowd in Leningrad, spontaneously commemorating his free spirit on the 150th anniversary of his death in a St Petersburg duel. In Moscow, with *glasnost*, Pushkin Square became the city's *agora*: the platform successively of refuseniks, early democrats, the founders of Memorial,* and partisans of Yeltsin. When meetings were accused of stopping the city's traffic, orators moved to the nearby pavement in front of the offices of *Moscow News*.

**PUTSCH.** Threatened cataclysm that became a fiasco, achieving in three days what could have taken fifteen years (Yakovlev's* estimate). At 6 a.m. on August 19, 1991, Soviet radio announced that Gorbachev had been incapacitated and government taken over by an 'emergency committee' headed by Vice-President Yanayev.* Other members were Kryuchkov,* Pugo,* Pavlov,* Yazov,* O.D. Baklanov (deputy chairman of the USSR Defence Council), V.A. Starodubtsev (chairman of the USSR Peasants' Union*) and A.I. Tizyakov (president of the Association of State Enterprises). In fact Gorbachev was under arrest at his Crimean family holiday *dacha*, where the day before he had been visited by a *putch*ists' delegation calling on him to hand over power. He had refused, and found his telephone cut. The amateurishness of what followed suggested that the plotters had fully expected him to comply. They also misjudged the readiness of the army to obey orders and the willingness of a hungry and frustrated population to accept the return of an authoritarian regime.

Early on Day One (Monday), troops acting on Yazov's orders occupied Moscow 'key points' – but not the all-important Russian parliament building known as the 'White House'. From the Kremlin, the committee issued decrees taking over state functions, closed all but eight newspapers and imposed censorship on the media. But it made no effort to cut telephones, make arrests or perform most of the other essentials associated with a 'coup'. This laxity permitted Yeltsin to hurry to the White House, where, defying a ban on demonstrations, he was joined by a large crowd ready to defend the building. Outwitting censorship, staff of the independent radio 'Moscow Echo'* set up a makeshift transmitter, and journalists produced a stop-gap *Moscow News*.* Western television chains used satellite aerials to broadcast hourly commentaries whose content found its way back from abroad to the general population. Outside Moscow, coal-miners called for a general strike (but received only a patchy response). Only one republic leader welcomed the *putsch* – Mutalibov in Azerbaijan – and only two foreign governments, China and Cuba (plus the PLO).

On Day Two, army and Ministry of Interior troops occupied more points in Moscow, and moved into the Baltic capitals to occupy broadcasting stations. It was meanwhile announced that Pavlov had resigned from the emergency committee for health reasons (according to witnesses later, he was confused and drunk). The news heartened large demonstrations in Moscow and Leningrad, where Sobchak* had persuaded the local commander to keep his forces in their barracks. In Moscow, crowds defied an 11 p.m. curfew order, barricading approaches to the White House with trucks and buses. About midnight an armoured column advancing through the city was stopped and fire-bombed, and in firing by soldiers three young men were killed.

On Day Three (Wednesday), it was announced that important military units, including part of an armoured division, had gone over to the opposition. Soon afterwards Yeltsin announced that he was sending emissaries to Gorbachev, and the *putsch*ists took flight. A group reached Vnukovo airport and flew to seek Gorbachev's pardon, but were arrested on arriving in the Crimea. In the afternoon troops headed out of the city, newspapers resumed printing, and the presidium of the Soviet parliament nullified the emergency committee's decrees. At 9 p.m. Gorbachev announced that he was back in control and returning to Moscow.

The *putsch* was the act of political hard-liners; not of the army, which was brought in as an auxiliary. The real leaders, Kryuchkov and Pugo, were determined to undo both the decree of July 25 depoliticizing the armed forces and the KGB, and the new union treaty,* giving a large measure of independence to the republics, due to have been signed on August 20. Their error was not to have understood the changes that had taken place in Soviet society as a result of *perestroika* and the creation of real parliaments. (It was widely observed at the time that had the attempt been made two years earlier, before the 1989 elections, it could well have succeeded.) The consequences of the *putsch* were enormous. It discredited, for ever, the authority of the Communist Party, where most of its supporters were to be found. It dissolved at a stroke the ties still holding secessionist republics.* And by gravely weakening the position of Gorbachev vis-à-vis Yeltsin, it led directly to the break-up of the Soviet Union at the end of the year.

# Q

**QUALITY CONTROL.** See 'Gospryomka'.

# R

**RADIO.** Medium once centrally controlled by Gostelradio,* now by republics. In Russia it is organized in four services; 'Spiritual Values' (cultural and aesthetic programmes); Radio Mayak (news and politics); Radio Orpheus (classical music); and Yunost (inter-state youth broadcasts). There are also numerous commercial stations. In 1992 the Russian broadcasting authority set up a Moscow-based collaborative programme with the BBC World Service.

**RADIO LIBERTY.** Cold War weapon with a problem of conversion after detente and the opening up of the Soviet media. With Radio Free Europe (beamed at Eastern Europe, including the Baltic region) the CIA-backed station employs a largely émigré staff of 1,700. The two stations broadcast in twenty-two languages. In 1990 Radio Liberty was allowed to set up an office in Moscow.

**RAIKOM.** Party committee of a *raion*.*

**RAILWAYS.** Vital industry on a shaky track (60 per cent worn-out in 1991). Shortage of rolling stock, similarly defective, has slowed down energy production, contributed to the food crisis (two-thirds of the 1990 sugar-beet harvest never reached the refineries) and piled up mountains of goods at frontier stations. The huge system (with 12 per cent of the world's mileage, 25 per cent of world passenger traffic and 9 per cent of freight) works with obsolescent equipment, insufficient staff, and the frequent threat of blockades.*

**RAION.** Administrative unit corresponding to a district in cities, consisting of a group of villages in the countryside. It has its own council and forms part of a region (*oblast**).

**RAPE.** Word excluded from polite conversation until 1986, when it was first uttered by *Pravda* in connection with the trial of a group of youths accused of taking girls home and 'treating them rough'. (The paper accused the Komsomol* and police of sitting at their desks instead of going out to talk with such young people.) A rise in rape was first blamed on the showing of foreign films, then on alcoholic parents, drugs and mental illness. Only in

1990 did discussion turn to sexual backwardness, particularly in the case of juvenile gang-rapes.

**RASHIDOV,** SHARAF RASHIDOVICH (1917–1983). Uzbek political leader and close friend of Brezhnev. As republic First Secretary for twenty-four years he was notorious for a reign of corruption and stagnation.

**RASPUTIN,** VALENTIN GRIGORYEVICH (1937– ). 'Country writer',* sometimes called 'Siberia's Faulkner', for whom the end of the Russian countryside would be the end of a civilization. He has taken part in nearly every big ecological campaign, turning anti-Western wherever he sees Russia falling prey to Western values – a tendency that has caused him to play a leading role in the development of a chauvinist outlook within the Union of Russian Writers. In 1989 he joined the short-lived Presidential Council.* His books include *Poslednyi strok* (The Final Stage), 1970; *Zhivi i pomni* (Live and Remember), 1974; *Proshchanye a Materoi* (Farewell to Mother), 1976; *Uroki frantsuzskogo* (Lessons in French), 1982; and *The Fire*, 1985.

**RATUSHINSKAYA,** IRINA BORISOVNA (1953– ). Dissident poet and religious believer, now living in London. In 1986 she was allowed to emigrate after seven years' imprisonment for 'anti-Soviet agitation'. Her poems, written from the age of 17 and distributed in the USSR and abroad, criticized the docility of the people, Soviet education and the communist view of history. She was one of those given back their Soviet citizenship in 1990.

**REASONABLE SUFFICIENCY.** Principle of defence first suggested by Gorbachev during a visit to France in 1985. In 1987 it was given place in a communiqué following a Warsaw Pact summit in Berlin. Still needing formal definition, it suggested that Soviet aims are not aggressive, and that, while defences must be capable of stopping aggression, they must not present, or seem to present, a threat to others. See 'Defensive defence'.

**RED.** Chosen colour of the international socialist movement, now out of fashion. The red flag was hauled down over the Kremlin on December 25, 1991. 'Red Square' has nothing to do with communism and dates from long before the Revolution. The Red Army was renamed the 'Soviet Army' after World War II.

**REFERENDUM.** New democratic toy first adopted by Gorbachev in March 1991 to test support for his proposed new union treaty.* Six republics (the three Baltic states, Moldavia, Georgia and Armenia) refused to participate. Others, like Russia and the Ukraine, attached questions of their own. To the loaded question – 'Do you or do you not approve a revived Union treaty?' – 76.4 per cent answered 'Yes' and 21.7 per cent 'No'. In Russia, two-thirds answered 'Yes' to the question 'Do you want the [Russian] president to be directly elected?' (a victory for Boris Yeltsin, who needed a popular mandate for his opposition to Gorbachev and 'centralism'). A Leningrad referendum changed the city's name to St Petersburg.

**REFUGEES.** Wanderers uprooted by ethnic disturbances. In 1991 they numbered 800,000, unsettling life in eight republics and half the regions of Russia. Their arrival aggravated housing and jobs shortages, led to increased crime, and provoked other ethnic conflicts. In the places they left there were serious problems arising from the loss of professional skills. The worst affected area was Central Asia.*

**REFUSENIKS.** In Russian, *otkazniki*. Originally and accurately, Jews* refused exit visas and administratively persecuted by being sacked from their jobs, expelled from universities, called up for the army and other tricks. The Western word 'refusenik' was later applied to all Jews kept waiting for visas. For Gorbachev's first two and a half years, the treatment of refuseniks remained a bar to improving relations with America. The last act of persecution, at the end of 1987, was to accuse them of deliberately sustaining tension in order to prove that the Soviet Union was anti-semitic. It followed the refusal of a Jewish scholar, Iosif Begun, who had finally been given a visa after sixteen years, to leave without his son, also a refusenik. Jewish emigration has differed from other forms of emigration (German, Armenian) by its size, its repercussions on the Middle East situation, and the long history of anti-semitism in Russia and Ukraine. From 1988 emigration was permitted freely. In 1989, Moscow refused Zionists who wanted the institution of direct flights to Israel in order to stop emigrants with Israeli visas deserting to other destinations in Vienna. (The flights were eventually started in October 1991.) It also rejected Arab demands for action to halt the exit of Jews liable to be settled on the West Bank.

**REGISTRATION.** Administrative act punctuating every citizen's life from the cradle to the grave. Registration is required for birth, marriage, change of residence, military service, study, employment, parenthood, retirement and burial. In 1990 'registration' acquired a new technical meaning when the Law on the Press* and the Law on Association required the registration of newspapers and organizations independent of Party or state.

**REHABILITATION.** Way to the reversal of Stalinism, beginning in 1987 with the reinstatement, both political and legal, of Bolshevik leaders shot in the 1930s purges. The rehabilitation of the leaders was followed by a review of the cases of all people 'illegally punished' between 1923 and 1953. The work, including the opening of mass graves, was done jointly by the KGB and an independent panel of investigators. In 1988–90 the investigators directly examined 800,000 dossiers on more than one million people. According to the KGB, a total of 3.6 million had been unjustly sentenced and 800,000 shot. A rehabilitation bill passed in 1991 covered everyone illegally condemned between 1920 and 1988. The state was expected to spend R1.5 billion a year in compensation, on the basis of R80 for every month spent in captivity by each person.

**RELIGION.** Historic foe of communism, absolved when Gorbachev saw the need of allies in his campaign to moralize Soviet society. Absolution for the foremost adversary, the Orthodox, was finally given by a law of 1990 recognizing freedom of conscience and extending the church's rights. The same law also ended restrictions on religious education (which did not stop churches complaining that there would still be no religious teaching in state schools). Similar freedom was extended to other churches and to the Muslim and Buddhist communities. Religion has since assumed a public role that surprises many Westerners. One day priests bless a Memorial* monument, the next day the site of the new stock exchange. Official speakers refer to the church's cultural role and some communists even praised it for being 'in fact close to the communist ideal' (of solidarity, family feeling, etc). When in 1987 Gorbachev argued for a separation of church and state, he meant that the state should stop interfering in church affairs. But in 1991 it was the church which threatened to intervene in state matters, with the creation of Christian and Islamic political parties (something unprecedented in Russian history).

**REMONT.** Simply 'repair'; but with shops, museums, clinics and similar facilities, notice of *remont* often means indefinite closure. *Kapitalnyi remont* (complete renovation) leaves no chance of a reopening this century; *profilaktitcheskyi* (prophylactic) *remont* is used for the cutting off of hot water each summer; ordinary *remont* can mean anything from a broken lift cable to non-delivery of vegetables.

**REPRESSION.** The first comprehensive figures for victims of Stalin's repression were published in 1988 by Roy Medvedev* in *Moscow News*. They exceeded previous Western estimates. Using information gathered over many years, he gave the breakdown as follows: 1929–32 (years of collectivization*), 10 million deported, of whom 2–3 million died; 1937–38, 5–7 million arrested, of whom 1 million were shot; 1939–40, 2 million deported from territories annexed under the German-Soviet pact; 1941–46, at least 10 million arrested and mostly imprisoned; 1944, 3 million deported from the Crimea, North Caucasus and Lower Volga, of whom 1 million died in transit; 1947–53, 1 million subjected to less massive forms of repression.

**REPUBLICS, THE.** In February 1992 the Independent Republics forming the Commonwealth of Independent States (CIS)* were Armenia, Azerbaijan, Byelorussia/Belarus, Moldavia/Moldova, Kazakhstan, Kirghizia/ Kyrgystan, Russia, Tajikistan, Turkmenia/Turkmenistan, Ukraine and Uzbekistan. A twelfth former Union Republic, Georgia, had not yet joined. The independence of the Baltic Republics outside the Union had been recognized in 1991. The status of a Republic, a sovereign or independent state with the option of joining, on its own terms, a confederal successor to the former Union, was approved by the Congress of People's Deputies in September 1991. Those Republics having within their borders more than one national group and thus containing auton- omous republics* and autonomous regions* often face difficulties when the smaller units demand independence in their turn. From the forming of the Union in 1922, Union republics – all having frontiers with the outside world – always had the theoretical right of secession; but it was not until 1987 that some proposed the exercise of this right. While the Communist Party dominated both Union and republic governments there was no serious clash of purpose. But with assertions of 'autonomy' or 'independ- ence' from 1989 onwards, big differences developed over the implementa- tion of economic reforms and over the ownership of capital investments (factories, transport) and natural resources. The 1990–91 argument over the shape of the new Union treaty was essentially as to whether the basis of power should rest with the centre, which would assign parts of it to the Republics, or with the Republics, which could surrender part of it to the Union. Accelerated by the *putsch*,* the answer found at Minsk* and Alma-Ata* was neither. The Republics simply became independent states in a centre-less Commonwealth.

**REPUBLICAN PEOPLE'S PARTY OF RUSSIA.** Largest Russian patrio- tic party, formed in April 1990 by a merger of the Leningrad National Patriotic Centre and the Monarchist* Russian People's Party. Allied to 'Democratic Russia',* it claims to have 20,000 members pledged to its goals of reform and republican sovereignty.*

**RESEARCH INSTITUTES** (foreign policy). Entities established by the Twentieth Congress to provide the Party with expert analysis. During the Khrushchev and Brezhnev periods, staff were recruited from the Party elite but given a degree of academic independence. Institutes like IMEMO* and ISKAN* produced ideas that were later adopted and developed under Gorbachev, causing them to be described in a moment of enthusiasm as 'power houses of New Thinking'. In 1991 alumni in prominent positions of influence included Vladimir Petrovsky, Yevgeni Primakov,* Georgi Shakhnazarov* and (in semi-retirement) Aleksandr Yakovlev.*

**RESTAURANT.** The autumn of 1987 saw the appearance of Moscow's first foreign restaurants, braving the problems of bulk importation, customs, bureaucracy, vandalism and theft. The first was Indian, followed by an

Italian and a French river-boat restaurant (later a casino), the 'Alexandre Blok'. By 1991 nearly all were for hard currency only, which did not prevent their chief clientele being Soviet *bizinesmen*.*

**REVOLUTION.** Word adopted by Gorbachev to give his reforms a new dimension, at the same time evoking Lenin. First publicly used in his 1987 Murmansk speech, in which he spoke of 'a revolution without shooting'.

**RIGHT-WING.** See 'Wing'.

**RIVERS.** Different things to many people: carriers of industrial waste, life-blood of agriculture, pawns of planners, and on the Chinese border a contested demarcation line, the Amur, finally agreed by both sides in May 1990. In 1986, after protests by ecologists and writers, particularly Rasputin* and Zalygin, the Party's Twenty-seventh Congress* killed a grandiose plan for turning round the northern rivers (Volga, Sri-Darya, Don, Kuban and Terek) to irrigate yet more thousands of unwanted hectares of Central Asian cotton.* Five million roubles had already been sunk in the scheme, which was conceived before World War II. In 1990 the Volgograd region stopped the funding for another grandiose hydrological project, a second Volga-Don canal.

**ROADS.** Invitations to bravura and anarchy – Russian weaknesses that, with the state of the highway, haphazard maintenance and alcohol, help to explain the appalling accident figures. In 1991 *Pravda* reported that more people were killed in road accidents in the Soviet Union than in the United States, even though the country has many times fewer vehicles. Fourteen per cent of Soviet casualties died (compared with 1.2 per cent in America and 2 per cent in Germany), due mainly to poor ambulance services and the inability of the police to provide basic first aid or cutting equipment. Wide variations in personal wealth make penalties for driving offences arbitrary: a month's average pay and six months' suspension for drunken driving, jail for a second offence; minor sums for crossing a red light or speeding. Smaller fines are collectable on the spot and, despite a clean-up, still often go into the policeman's pocket.

**ROCK.** Western decadence that captured the young in the 80s, as jazz had in the 60s. The Party's resistance was the same each time. The first Soviet rock groups had to borrow guitars and do without studios. Ignored by Melodia, the state recording company, musicians gravitated to Riga and Leningrad, cities in touch with abroad; then invaded old-fashioned industrial centres – Sverdlovsk, Vladivostok, Barnaul. The Twenty-seventh Congress* put a stop to the war being waged against rock by the cultural bureaucracy; and within eighteen months 'rockers' on motorbikes were terrorizing Moscow's midnight streets. By the end of the 1980s, the

Soviet Union was the scene of poor-man's Woodstocks, using music so outmoded that no one would have dared to put it on in the West. The borrowed culture did as much to transform Soviet society as five years' debate about the nature of democracy, and led to rock groups celebrating the defeat of the 1991 *putsch** in front of the Russian parliament.

**ROMANIA.** Post-war satellite that has not forgotten the Soviet annexation of Bessarabia and northern Bukovina. In 1940 these two territories became part of the Moldavian* Soviet Republic, under secret clauses of the 1939 German–Soviet Pact.* In the 1970s Ceaucescu's Romania embarked on a remarkably independent foreign policy, while remaining a member of the Warsaw Pact.* When the family and the regime were overthrown in the December 1989 revolt, the events were reported calmly by the Soviet media. In June 1990 Romania became the first East European country to sign a bilateral treaty with the Soviet Union, setting a precedent for the kind of relationship Moscow thought (optimistically) to establish with former members of the Warsaw Pact and Comecon.

**ROMANOV,** GRIGORI VASILYEVICH (1923–   ). Former Party First Secretary in Leningrad, notorious for having commandeered a Hermitage dinner service for his daughter's wedding party. In 1985, he unsuccessfully competed with Grishin* and Gorbachev for the succession to Chernenko, and in July was sacked from his Politburo and other posts.

**ROSTROPOVICH,** MSTISLAV LEOPOLDOVICH (1927–   ). The world's leading cellist, deprived of his Soviet citizenship in 1974. In 1990 he returned in triumph to give a concert in Moscow, having once said gloomily that *glasnost* was 'not for me'. The same year saw restoration of his citizenship. In 1991 his appearance on the barricades defending the Russian 'White House' was used as a reproach to more reticent Soviet public figures.

**ROTARY** club. Association once officially called a 'capitalist conglomerate, using charity to justify the exploitation of the proletariat'. In 1990 it was accorded respectability with the founding of the first Rotary Club of Moscow. The Soviet organizers (Foreign and Foreign Trade Ministry officials) told Western guests that they now realized that 'business can have a human face'.

**ROUBLE.** Paper currency, whose multiplying exchange rates (five separate ones in 1992) testify to its progressive depreciation. Each new 'more realistic' rate, up to and including the 1991 special 'tourist rate' (thirty times more generous than the official rate) was promptly matched by the black market. For Soviets the blow came in February 1991 when R100 and R50 notes were called in overnight in a move to defeat the black market. People received smaller notes, but only up to the value of a month's salary. Above that, high-denomination notes could be paid into savings bank accounts, if shown to have been legally acquired. But as withdrawals from savings accounts were temporarily limited to R500 per month, the half-baked currency reform struck many as more like a confiscation. While it savagely hit small savers, the black-marketeers had already turned most of their wealth into property or *valuta** and came out relatively unharmed. Nor did it achieve any of the advantages normally associated with a currency reform, such as bringing hidden goods into the shops. In the first eleven months of 1991 the amount of money released into circulation went up by 340 per cent. See also 'Convertible rouble'.

**ROUND TABLE.** Magic words suggesting that if differing parties can get round a table, wisdom will emerge. Alternative to referral to a commission as a means of postponing difficult decisions.

**RUKH** (Movement of Ukrainian People for *Perestroika*). Name taken by the Ukrainian Popular Front, an organization that began by demanding cultural autonomy but was soon demanding Ukrainian sovereignty. Its second Congress, in October 1990, removed the word *perestroika* from the title. The meeting, attended by 250 delegates including visitors from twenty-four countries with Ukrainian communities, was opened by the head of the American-based Ukrainian Autocephalous Church. Unexpected guests were the president of the Ukrainian parliament, Leonid Kravchuk,* and the former First Secretary of the Ukrainian Communist Party, Pyotr Chelest (who had been expelled for nationalist deviation). Rukh emerged from the Congress with a new face, proclaiming as its goal the 'restoration of Ukrainian independence', if necessary by extra-parliamentary means. From then on it was dominated by secessionist West Ukrainians. Leading figures include the national poets Ivan Drach and Dmitro Pavlychko.

**RUMOUR.** Source of information once ascribed to the muzzling of the press; but *glasnost* has only added to it. Any crumb of official information is liable to be seen as the tip of an iceberg. The press itself publishes 'news' based on rumour. Among typical items are 'authentic' sightings of unidentified flying objects, advance warnings of impending shortages (the report becomes self-fulfilling), and genealogical trees showing Raisa Gorbachev to be the niece of the late President Gromyko.

**RUSSIA.** Sentimental notion far transcending the political entity known as the Russian Federation, strongly shared by the 25 million Russians living outside it. The romantic notion of Russia took a political turn after the ending of the Union, with arguments about the definition of Russia. Did it mean the Russian Federation, or the Russian nation? There was even a new word coined – *Russianin* instead of *Russkyi* – meaning the 25–30 millions of people of Russian origin living in independent or autonomous republics.* The debate divided political forces, including the Russian

Democratic Movement, whose Travkin* wing was close to the position of the Russian Vice-President, Rutskoi* (arguing for holding the Federation together, by coercion if necessary), while Afanasiev* was ready to let regions like Tatarstan* go their own way.

**RUSSIAN FEDERATION.** Formerly the Russian Soviet Federative Socialist Republic (RSFSR); otherwise simply 'Russia'. Largest of the fifteen former Union republics in terms of area (three-quarters of all Soviet territory), population (147 out of 290 million), and natural resources (90 per cent of all Soviet oil and 70 per cent of all known gas reserves). It also produces half the Union's energy and half its meat. As well as Russians (82 per cent), the population includes a hundred or more smaller nationalities dispersed over sixteen autonomous republics,* six autonomous krais,* forty-nine autonomous regions* and ten autonomous areas. Two large components, Siberia* and the Soviet Far East, contain three-quarters of all former Soviet mineral reserves, including oil, gas, coal, diamonds and gold. The North Caucasus, Volga and Amur regions, southern Siberia and the Russian Far East were the former Union's granaries.

Its mosaic of peoples and natural resources, plus the struggle for power in its far-off capital, Moscow, make Russia more susceptible to fragmentation than any other republic. On a slightly reduced scale, it has all the problems of the former Union, which it defied in 1990 by proclaiming its sovereignty. After encouraging other Union republics to defy Moscow, the Russian leader, Boris Yeltsin,* faced declarations of sovereignty, and claims to natural resources, from autonomous entities in his own Federation. But none of this deterred the Russian parliament, in which Yeltsinite 'democrats' narrowly outnumbered conservative communists, from trying to force the pace of economic reform by promoting a 500-day plan for transition to the 'market' by the whole Union. When the Soviet parliament declined to play, Russia said it would go it alone but later pulled back. In 1991 the biggest deterrent to Western credits and investment was eased by an apparent truce between Yeltsin and Gorbachev and Russia's participation in the Novo-Ogarevo* agreement. In June 1991, Yeltsin (until now only head of parliament) was elected president by a decisive popular vote. But he faced a huge task in fulfilling bold promises to right the economy as well as dealing with explosive ethnic issues in the Caucasus, Tataria and other parts of his far-flung domain. Later, the identification of the RSFSR with the defeat of the August 1991 *putsch** prompted claims to Union leadership that worried other republics and even some Russians. Their concern increased four months later when Yeltsin's Russia took over the rights and duties of the Soviet Union. The West originally welcomed the take-over, especially as regards arms control and debt repayment, but at the same time resisted the idea of Russia playing too dominant a role in the Commonwealth of Independent States.*

**RUSSIAN NATIONAL MONARCHIST PARTY.** Party founded in 1991 on the basis of the Russian Monarchist Movement. In 1991, the chairman, Aleksei Brumel, proclaiming himself 'regent', offered Yeltsin the title of 'Grand Duke' for his defence of Russia at the barricades.

**RUSSIAN POPULAR ALLIANCE.** Group founded on the initiative of the Rossiya group of deputies with the aim of creating an organized opposition to the Russian leadership on current economic policy. Its first congress in December 1991 decided to form a shadow cabinet under Sergei Baburin, a prominent conservative deputy. It proclaimed attachment to the keystones of European conservatism: God, the family, the state and private property.

**RUST**, MATHIAS (1968– ). Mad German pilot with a footnote in history thanks to landing his tiny Cessna near Red Square. His exploit, in May 1987 (while Warsaw Pact leaders were meeting in Berlin, and Soviet frontier guards celebrating Frontier Guards' Day), exposed the armed forces to ridicule. It also gave Gorbachev a useful pretext to get rid of 'dead wood', including the Defence Minister, Marshal Sergei Sokolov. After serving less than half the four-year sentence imposed by a Soviet court, Rust was released in 1989 at the time of the Moscow visit of German Chancellor Kohl.

**RUTSKOI**, COL. ALEKSANDR VLADIMIROVICH (1947– ). Vice-President of Russia (and former pilot in Afghanistan). Before election he was leader of the 'Communists for Democracy' movement (7 per cent of Party members) founded in April 1991, and of a broader all-Russian socio-political movement called 'Civil Accord'. Both were created in the hope that a debate within the Party might prevent its disintegration. In August 1991 his key part in organizing the civilian defence of the Russian parliament gained him promotion to Major-General and a platform for launching a Democratic Communist Party of Russia.* Four months later he complained of 'undemocratic tendencies on the part of the Russian leadership', an over-hasty transition to a market economy, and 'lack of human sensitivity' on the part of the Young Turks surrounding Yeltsin – with whom he had virtually no communication. In February 1992 Yeltsin put him in charge of reforming agriculture, a favourite method of burying political opponents.

**RYBAKOV**, ANATOLI NAUMOVICH (1911– ). Leading writer of the *glasnost* period, thanks to his epic *Children of the Arbat*, describing the repression of the 1930s through the medium of a group of young people living in Moscow's Arbat* street. The book became the centre of a battle between reformers and conservatives over the rewriting by novelists of the history of Stalin's time.

**RYZHKOV,** Nikolai Ivanovich (1929–  ). Broken Prime Minister, earlier the third musketeer (with Yeltsin and Ligachev) in a trio descending on Moscow from the Urals. From 1950 to 1975 he worked in heavy industry, becoming director of factories in Sverdlovsk. In 1975 he became deputy minister for machine-building and heavy transport, and in 1979 vice-president of Gosplan.\* In 1981 he was elected to the Central Committee and next year made a Secretary. In 1985 Gorbachev brought him into the Politburo and made him Prime Minister in place of the octogenarian Tikhonov. After a modest start he showed an unexpected flair while organizing Armenian earthquake relief. But his handling of the central problem of the reform of the Soviet economy was hesitant and disappointing. Radical opponents not yet daring to call for Gorbachev's resignation demanded Ryzhkov's. From the end of 1989 his resignation was predicted daily. In December 1990, when a change of functions reduced the role of Prime Minister to mere management of the presidential cabinet, he conveniently suffered a heart attack and resigned. In June 1991 he trailed far behind Yeltsin as one of five candidates for the Russian presidency.

# S

**ST PETERSBURG.** Leningrad's old name restored to the city by the Russian parliament in September 1991 as a result of a 54 per cent vote in a referendum held on June 12 that year. See also 'Leningrad'.

**SAJUDIS.** Name, meaning 'Union', taken by the Popular Front* of Lithuania,* launched by Algirdas Brazauskas, First Secretary of the Lithuanian Communist Party. After victories in the 1989 and 1990 elections, it formed an 'independence' government under Kasimiera Prunskiene* as prime minister, with Vytautas Landsbergis* as president. The movement's unity was rudely tested by the Soviet blockade* but stood up less well during subsequent negotiations with Moscow and arguments over the economic plan for 1991. At the end of 1990 a split occurred with Mrs Prunskiene's resignation, but was prevented from going further by the February 13 attack on Vilnius TV station by troops of the Soviet MVD. Leadership now devolved almost exclusively on Landsbergis; but behind the bold front presented by defiance of Moscow there were stirrings of opposition, by a handful of new parties (Christian, Social Democratic, Agrarian) and − perhaps more importantly − Mrs Prunskiene and other ex-communists who saw the need for something more than patriotic exhortations. In December 1991 the Third Congress of Sajudis voted to turn what had been a broadly based independence movement into a proper political party. At the same time it took a turn to the right by banning from its membership former communists or adherents of the Lithuanian Democratic Labour Party (the Communist Party's successor). The three priorities were 'honest work, family and love of the fatherland'.

**SAKHAROV,** ANDREI DMITRIEVICH (1921–90). Nuclear physicist ('father of the Soviet H-bomb') and greatest of Soviet political dissidents. He first collided with authority (Khrushchev's) through his growing concern with the dangerous effects of nuclear tests, later extended to other environmental issues. His next encounter was in 1968 with publication abroad of his essay 'Progress, Peaceful Co-existence and Intellectual Freedom', calling for the convergence of the Soviet and American social systems. In the 1970s he put himself even more deeply at risk by helping victims of repression, often regardless of their different viewpoints. His most powerful alliance was with Solzhenitsyn,* with whom he helped to found the Moscow Helsinki Monitoring Group. In 1975 his courageous defence of his principles and his fellow dissidents won him the Nobel Peace Prize, received on his behalf by his second wife, Yelena Bonner.* Though forbidden to travel and relentlessly harassed by Brezhnev's KGB, he still kept his title and privileges as an Academician. (Fellow Academicians would have created a dangerous precedent for themselves if they had voted to expel him.) In January 1980 he was banished to Gorky, a closed city where he could no longer be visited by Western journalists. He remained in forced residence until the famous December 1986 telephone call from Gorbachev, calling him (and Bonner) back to Moscow. Back in the capital, he took his place among democrats, continuing to attack all that he found wrong (including Reagan's 'Star Wars'* programme) but superbly ignoring the struggle taking place for moral leadership of the remaining dissidents. Not wanting to claim rights for a single category of citizen, he declined to sign a petition for Jewish emigration and was accused by refuseniks of having 'sold out'. Elected a parliamentary deputy in 1989, he sided with the Inter-regional* group, helped to found Memorial,* and showed himself a critical ally of Gorbachev. His place in history was best summed up by Zhores Medvedev*: 'For the dissident movement, disorganized and repressed as it was after the Soviet invasion of Czechoslovakia in August 1968, the appearance of Sakharov was a salvation. Soviet official propaganda had always treated political dissidents as minor figures who were victims of foreign ideological services. When Sakharov joined the human rights groups in Moscow, the whole movement took on a new lease of life.' His posthumous memoirs, published in 1990, underlined a deep difference of thinking between Sakharov the scientist and Solzhenitsyn the religiously inspired Russian patriot.

**SAKHAROV DEMOCRATIC MOVEMENT.** Movement formed to defend human rights 'for all'. The adoption of Sakharov's name for recruiting purposes was deplored by his widow and friends. In 1991 its co-chairmen were Vladimir Vorinin, Aleksandr Lebedev and Galina Amineva.

**SAMIZDAT.** Literally 'self-publishing'. System for the clandestine circulation of dissident literature, adopted in the 1970s. Usually the work was typed on thin paper with a maximum number of carbon copies, then distributed and copied by others. In the later 1980s *samizdat* lost its *raison d'être* with the appearance of independent presses and non-official newspapers.

**SANITARY DAY.** Day of closure of shops, bakeries etc., for cleaning and disinfestation. Unannounced and frequent.

**SARCOPHAGUS.** Concrete coffin isolating the burned-out Chernobyl* reactor. Hastily built at great risk to the workers, it was designed to prevent the escape of radiation. But by 1991 radioactive dust escaping through gaps in the concrete blocks threatened to shorten its useful life. About the year 2010 it will be necessary to surround it with a new sarcophagus. The problem is that the marshy subsoil is barely capable of supporting the existing weight. In 1988 'Sarcophagus' was the title of a play about Chernobyl by the Soviet journalist Vadim Gubarev.

**SAVING.** Virtue of necessity in a land of empty shops. At the end of 1990 there were R380.7 billion in the state savings bank, R42.9 billion more than at the start of the year. In 1991 a further R211 billion was thought to be in notes under people's mattresses. Total savings increased by 10 per cent in the first six months of 1991, not because of the increase of interest rates (from 2 to as much as 10 per cent, in November 1990) but from fear of another currency reform.

**SAVISAAR,** EDGAR ELMAROVICH (1950– ). Estonian prime minister, elected 1990. He managed to resist growing nationalist pressure following the independence proclamation of Lithuania, aware of the realities in a republic economically dependent on non-Estonians. His caution caused an open row with Rein Otsason, head of the state bank. In January 1992 he was replaced by a technocrat, Tiit Vahi.

**SAVOY HOTEL.** Expensive symbol of Western luxury restored under its old name in the former 'Berlin' hotel; one of the earliest big joint-ventures, between Intourist* and Finnair. Preparing for his first visitors, the Finnish director made a point of engaging only untrained staff rather than Soviet hotel workers.

**SCHNITKE,** ALFRED GARIEVICH (1934– ). Vanguard composer of the new Soviet music, others being Edison Denisov and Sofia Gubaydulina. After a furore over his First Symphony (1975), he went unperformed until the second half of the 1980s, when mounting popularity led to a 1990 Schnitke festival in Gorky (then still closed to foreigners). His works include 'Poems of Penitence for the Millennium' and 'The Story of Doctor Johannes Faust'.

**SCIENCE-FICTION.** Literary genre killed by *glasnost* – an undeserved fate since it helped to defeat censorship. Gaining respectability under Khrushchev, authors such as Ivan Efremov, Ilya Varshavsky, Anatoli Dnepov and Sever Gansovsky cast a spell over a whole reading generation. Science-fiction became a screen behind which its authors attacked tyranny under Brezhnev. Two writers – the brothers Arkadi and Boris Stugatsky – went beyond their cover and paid for their 'negative' attitude with several years of harassment. *Glasnost* removed the political fun, and in 1991 most science-fiction had descended to the level of children's books.

**SECESSION.** Constitutional right of Union republics, first taken seriously in 1989 by Estonia, Latvia and Lithuania, subsequently by Georgia and Moldavia.

**SECOND ECONOMY.** Euphemism for black and 'grey' markets in services, manufacturing, trade, education, health, farming and transportation.

**SECRETARIAT** (of the Central Committee). Body charged with the daily work and political management of the Party, including nominations to posts. The once powerful Secretaries, with particular responsibilities — agriculture, propaganda etc. — were elected by plenums.* By order of the Twenty-eighth Congress,* one of their new tasks was to develop contacts with 'new political forces' (i.e. other parties). The intention was overtaken by the 1991 *putsch.**

**SECT.** Old sore of Russian and Muslim society. During the years of anti-religious propaganda, belonging to a sect was a way to protest at the submissiveness of the religious authorities. The granting of religious freedom did nothing to end the phenomenon; on the contrary, an explosion of religious movements matched that of political forces. With freedom of travel, people's fascination with the exotic and young people's thirst for new experiences made the Soviet Union fertile ground for foreign recruiters masquerading as tourists (in 1987 there were fifteen arrests of 'Children of God' alone). The authorities were ambivalent. Having up to 1985 imprisoned, and up to 1987 persecuted, inoffensive Pentecostalists, Baptists, Seventh-Day Adventists and other protestant groups with an estimated total of three million adherents, they fell over themselves to register strange Orthodox and other sects, including many regarded with the deepest suspicion in the West.

**SECURITY COUNCIL.** New body created by Gorbachev in 1991 to advise on all kinds of security problems, external or internal. It was initially concerned with problems arising from ethnic disturbances. Members included Yanayev,* Pavlov,* Bakatin,* Bessmertnykh,* Kryuchkov,* Primakov,* Pugo* and Yazov.* After the *putsch** leading liberals, including Yakovlev* and Shevardnadze,* humiliatingly declined to serve as replacements.

**SECURITY GUARDS.** New profession created by the rise in crime. The first security guards co-operative claiming to have quasi-police powers was registered in September 1990. Several politicians, including Yeltsin* and Gavril Popov,* ostentatiously engaged private bodyguards rather than accept protection by the KGB.

**SELF-EMPLOYMENT.** Novel concept established by the Law on Individual Economic Activity.* Until May 1987 anyone not state-employed or belonging to a creative union was liable to prosecution for anti-social activity. To avoid arrest, dissident writers, artists and musicians took jobs as boilermen or cleaners.

**SELF-MANAGEMENT.** Magic wand for conjuring up shop-floor zeal for reconstruction. Workers were given the right to choose their leaders at brigade or factory level. The first, much publicized experiment was in 1987 at the Riga minibus factory. But four years later most workers and managers, used to directives from above, were still reluctant to make decisions.

**SEMIPALATINSK** (pop. 317,000). City and region of Kazakhstan, situated in the restricted military area known as the 'polygon', used from 1949 for Soviet nuclear tests. *Glasnost* brought hair-raising accounts of the carelessness attending early tests, and the medical effects on participants and nearby communities. This caused local people, then the Kazakhstan parliament, to demand a closure. In February 1989 protestors meeting in Alma-Ata founded the 'Nevada' anti-nuclear movement. This secured a two-thirds cut in the number of tests and the transfer of the most powerful to Novaya Zemlia.* The military resisted closure of the polygon, which had cost 4–5 billion roubles to construct. In September 1991 it was closed by the Kazakhstan government to demonstrate the republic's mastery of its environment, and the closure celebrated with a benediction by Muslim clergy.

**SEX.** Activity so discreet that it long had no place in the arts or conversation, except when discussed 'between men'. Which left Soviet society ill-prepared for a sudden flood of articles, books and films on the subject. In 1986 it was still the height of daring for a director to show an unmarried couple (fully covered) in bed. In 1987 newspapers were deluged with letters from readers shocked by the new 'frankness' of television, with bedroom scenes, drunken parties and 'loose' girls smoking in the streets. A year later audiences were packing cinemas to see 'Little Vera' wriggle topless on top of her casual boyfriend. And in 1990 street-vendors displayed photocopied Western 'sex manuals', generally compilations of the 'hotter' passages, with illustrations helping to fill space, and the reader's imagination, while saving on translation.

**SHABASHNIKI** (moonlighters). Before co-operatives, workers using their spare time (and often state materials) to plug holes in the official economy.

**SHAKHNAZAROV,** GEORGI KHOSROEVICH (1924– ). Personal adviser to Gorbachev; as an Academician and lawyer, already associated in Andropov's time with a group round Burlatsky* that considered how Soviet legislation could be adapted to the creation of a more open society.

**SHAKHRAI**, SERGEI MIKHAILOVICH (1958– ). Lawyer appointed Russian deputy premier with responsibility for the Ministry of Justice, the State Committee for Nationalities, and 'other matters' (December 1991). His concentration of powers was regarded with suspicion by opponents of Yeltsin.

**SHARES**. See 'Joint stock company'.

**SHAPOSHNIKOV**, COLONEL GENERAL YEVGENI IVANOVICH (1942– ). Former commander of the Soviet air force, appointed Defence Minister, August 1991, following the failure of the *putsch*.* His refusal to obey orders from the *putsch* leaders contributed to their downfall. A fighter-pilot by training, he was appointed deputy air chief in 1988 and then elected to the Central Committee, where he made a number of speeches on the priority of economic reform. As commander (July 1990) he pressed for better training and more efficient and economical use of material. Relative youth, professional dedication and democratic leaning stamped him as one of the growing circle of military reformists. His rejection of the *putsch*\* caused him to be identified as a nominee of Yeltsin. On December 30, 1991 at the second (Minsk) summit of the Commonwealth of Independent States* he was chosen as interim C-in-C of the former Soviet armed forces – a confirmation of members' early incapacity to agree on a common defence policy.

**SHATALIN**, STANISLAV SERGEYEVICH (1934– ). Economist and Academician. In 1990 he gave his name to the 'Shatalin Plan' – drawing features from the 'Five Hundred Days Plan'* of Gennadi Filshin* – for a transition to a market economy. After a parliamentary debate enforced changes to make it less radical, it bore so little resemblance to the original that Shatalin disowned it. Disappointment took him to the United States, where he discussed research projects with American universities – a path trodden by other reformers. Back in Moscow, in July 1991 he joined Travkin* in forming the United Democratic Party but left after disagreements five months later.

**SHATROV**, MIKHAIL FILIPPOVICH; real name, Marshak (1932– ). Dramatist who soared above the stagnation of the Brezhnev years with his anti-dictatorial play *Dictatorship of Conscience*. Its 1986 production by Mark Zakharov had all Moscow talking and was still drawing full houses four years later. In 1988 his new play, *Onward, ever Onward*, started arguments among intellectuals over how far writers should go in interpreting history. The play showed Stalin in dialogue with 1917 Bolsheviks who were later to become his victims. Shatrov was accused of falsely portraying Lenin and using the founder of the state as a mouthpiece for his own ideas. In 1989 his *Peace of Brest* was equally controversial.

**SHCHERBAKOV,** VLADIMIR IVANOVICH (1949– ). Chairman of the General Confederation of Trade Unions until 1991, when Gorbachev appointed him to head the Soviet Committee for Work and Social Questions (when reform appeared to be leading to unemployment), then Deputy Prime Minister and Minister of Economy and Forecasting (when the so-called anti-crisis programme had to be defended at home and abroad).

**SHCHERBITSKY,** VLADIMIR VASILYEVICH (1918–1990). First Secretary of the Ukrainian Communist Party, 1972–89, and over the same period a full member of the Soviet Politburo. A protégé of Brezhnev, he continued in power for seven years under Gorbachev, thanks to his formal acceptance of *perestroika*. Another reason for his long survival was the difficulty of finding a suitable Ukrainian replacement; the Shcherbitsky 'mafia' controlled key Party positions, and it required the shock of the 1989 parliamentary elections to effect a change.

**SHEVARDNADZE,** EDVARD AMVROSIEVICH (1928– ). Foreign Minister who helped change the world, and stunned it by his sudden resignation in December 1990. Son of a teacher, member of an obscure Georgian ethnic minority, he worked as a Komsomol* activist before joining the Communist Party *apparat* and rising to become, in 1965, Georgian Interior Minister. In 1972 he took over as Georgian First Secretary, winning acclaim for his courage in attacking corruption. Shared interests in their Komsomol days had brought him into contact with Gorbachev, and in July 1985 Gorbachev nominated him foreign minister in succession to Gromyko. His appointment was taken as evidence that Gorbachev wanted to conduct his own foreign policy, and for this reason had entrusted the post to a grey figure as inexperienced as himself. Shevardnadze quickly shattered the picture, impressing everyone with his clear thinking and courtesy.

After reorganizing the Foreign Ministry* and taking various other initiatives, he directed efforts towards ending the war in Afghanistan and to establishing relations with countries previously excluded from Soviet interest in Asia and the Middle East. But his greatest importance was in the trust he inspired in Western leaders during the difficult process of ending the Cold War. This caused old-guard communists to accuse him of betraying Soviet security and selling out Soviet interests in Eastern Europe. Shevardnadze accused them of 'McCarthyism'. At the Twenty-eighth Party Congress in 1990 he left the Politburo in a move in line with Gorbachev's separation of government from the Party. But no one, including Gorbachev, was prepared for his abrupt resignation as foreign minister in December 1990. In remarks later, he left little doubt that his decision was due to the accumulated weight of attacks on his integrity by the military and hard-liners – and a feeling that in his moment of need he had been deserted by the President. Unwilling to return to his native Georgia (now ruled by Gamsakhurdia,* whom he had once gaoled for subversion), in February 1991 he became head of a new independent foreign policy institute, the Soviet Foreign Policy Association.* The following June he launched a new political movement, the Movement for Democratic Reforms,* but its founding conference was upset by the August *putsch*.* His relations with Gorbachev were badly compromised when, during the *putsch*, he accused Gorbachev of possible connivance at his own arrest. Later he attacked him for having appointed the *putsch*ists to leading state positions, and refused an invitation to join the President's security council. Although he said he would never work with Gorbachev again, he relented so far as to join his Consultative Council on reforms and in November 1991 was invited to return as Foreign Minister. The appointment lasted only a few weeks. Brushed aside by Yeltsin's take-over, Shevardnadze sounded numerous alarms about the dangers of dictatorship and social disturbance. In January 1992, having three months earlier recalled attention to his Georgian nationality by condemning Gamsakhurdia,* he offered his mediation in the situation following the latter's ousting.

**SHIELD** (*Shchit*). Association of servicemen founded in 1989 by reformist parliamentary deputy Major Lopatin.* At its creation, 'Shield' gave its objectives as accelerating *perestroika* and *glasnost* in the army, and securing parliamentary control over the army and the KGB. In 1990 it campaigned for urgent steps to provide proper housing for the families of officers repatriated from Eastern Europe, and exposed the scandal of eighteen dachas being built for high-ranking officers at a cost of 210,000 roubles each, when 280,000 military families were without homes. In 1990 it took on a more political character under the radical chairmanship of Vitali Urazhstev, registering volunteers for the Russian National Guard.*

**SHORTAGES.** See 'Deficit'.

**SHORTER-RANGE INTERMEDIATE NUCLEAR FORCES (SRINF).** Weapons with ranges below 'intermediate' but above 'battlefield' range, e.g. the Soviet SS-12. After long negotiation they were eventually brought within provisions of the INF treaty.* The move covered weapons which the Soviets had deployed above existing levels in the mid-1980s to counter US Pershing-2 and cruise missiles in Europe.

**SHORT-RANGE NUCLEAR FORCES.** Weapons for the immediate battlefield, not to be confused with SRINF (above). After protesting successfully against NATO plans to modernize the US 'Lance' missile, in

May 1989 Gorbachev announced the unilateral withdrawal of 500 Soviet short-range nuclear weapons in Europe. An offer to withdraw all nuclear weapons from Warsaw Treaty countries if NATO reciprocated was overtaken by German reunification, the Pact's collapse, and consequent troop withdrawals. In September 1991 the Soviets came under pressure to destroy all their stocks, mainly consisting of the 150-km range SS-21, as a result of a unilateral undertaking by the United States to do the same.

**SHOSTAKOVICH,** DMITRI DMITRIEVICH (1906–1975). Composer restored to national eminence after being shunted between honour and disgrace by a tone-deaf artistic *apparat*. In 1936 he was denounced for his 'dissonant' opera *Lady Macbeth of Mtsensk*; in 1948 his works were banned for 'formalism'. After ups and downs and compromises (he joined the Party in 1960), he was given a posthumous national ovation in 1986 on the eightieth anniversary of his birth. The celebrations, reported by the media, even the army newspaper *Krasnaya Zvezda*, included a performance of his Fifth Symphony, which had once been denounced by *Pravda* as 'vulgar, primitive and crude'.

**SHOSTAKOVSKY,** VYATCHESLAV ANDREEVICH (1937– ). Historian and head (until 1990) of the Moscow Party High School. He was one of the initiators of the Democratic Platform,★ calling on adherents not to leave the Party before the Twenty-eighth Congress★ in order to retain use of the technical means (presses, offices, funds) for disseminating ideas. He resigned within hours of Yeltsin★ and, losing his job, became a leading figure of Democratic Russia,★ then the Russian Republican Party.

**SIBERIA.** Semi-continent holding Russians in masochistic thrall with its evocation of political repression combined with the freedom of nature, merciless winters and flamboyant autumns. It now acts as a magnet to young people disgusted with materialism and the dehumanization of Soviet cities, who see in Siberia a moral and natural kind of purity. Since the mid-1980s Siberia has come to see itself as a special and separate place, turned more towards Asia than towards Europe and in reach of self-sufficiency by the year 2000. All that is needed is to raise rural development to the basic standard of the region's new towns (150 built from nothing in only fifteen years). Siberia can also call on huge natural resources, a vast territorial expanse, a sturdy farming tradition (Siberia never knew serfdom), and an important local intelligentsia bequeathed by Tsarist deportations and the wartime evacuation of western cities. In 1990 representatives of eight *oblasts*★ and *krais*★ conferred with the elected president of the Kemerovo region (see 'Miners') and agreed on a programme of co-operation. Plans for study included a Siberian common market, a 'kind of Siberian parliament', and a Siberian television service. In 1991 a proposal to set up a Siberian Republic based on Novosibirsk ran into opposition from allies of Yeltsin.

**SILAYEV,** Ivan Stepanovich (1930–    ). Gorbachev man who went to serve Yeltsin but later came back to the centre. An engineer by training, in 1985 he was appointed a Deputy President of the Soviet Council of Ministers (government) with special responsibility for mechanical engineering. In 1990, disappointed by the slowness of Gorbachev's economic reforms, he joined Yeltsin and was elected prime minister of the Russian Federation. After the 1991 *putsch*\* he accepted the dual post of Soviet prime minister and chairman of the Committee for the Operational Management of the USSR Economy,\* and soon afterwards resigned as prime minister of Russia, pleading that he had too many responsibilities. After the dissolution of central structures by Yeltsin in December 1991, he was appointed Russian representative to the European Community.

**SINYAVSKY,** Andrei Donatovich (1923–    ). Co-defendant with Yuli Daniel in the 1966 trial that launched the dissident movement. Arrested for publishing their writings in the West, Sinyavsky was sentenced to seven years and Daniel to five. Afterwards Daniel remained in Moscow, living modestly by translations. Sinyavsky emigrated to Paris, briefly returning to Moscow in 1990 to attend Daniel's funeral and give a number of interviews to the Soviet press. As a dissident he used the *nom de plume* Abram Terts.

**SLAVS.** Within the former Soviet Union: Russians, Ukrainians, Byelorussians.

**SMALL PEOPLES.** Ethnies with a low population factor. In 1988, sensing threats to their cultural survival, a number sent representatives to a meeting at Nalchik in the Caucasus. There they formed an Association of Small Peoples, with a Kabardian president (Sergei Tokhtabiev) and a Nanai (Far Northern) vice-president, the ethnologist and deputy Evdokia Gaier. The association aims to defend national cultures by promoting economic autonomy wherever small peoples are at risk from development plans. Development can kill their traditional way of life by causing the destruction of fisheries, abandonment of villages, and so on. At the same time they are often excluded from jobs in the newly imported industries because of their lack of qualification or interest. A spiral results, causing labour to be imported from other regions, and they become minorities in their own country.

**SOBCHAK,** Anatoli Aleksandrovich (1937–    ). Mayor of Leningrad/St Petersburg. Elected a deputy of the Supreme Soviet (parliament) in 1989, he at first refused to stand in the 1990 Leningrad local elections so as to give all his time to parliamentary duties and his work as an academician. Later, when the Democratic Bloc was unable to choose a mayor, he agreed to stand. Once in office, he found himself caught in a trench-war with the city Executive Committee (*Ispolkom*\*), which remained in the hands of

Party conservatives. He was also exasperated by sterile debates among his own supporters, who accused him of 'hidden authoritarianism'. In 1991 he was thought to be waiting in the wings for a political chance elsewhere. An opening came with the August *putsch*,* when he astutely obtained authority from Yeltsin to take over the city's defence. He then gave legal orders to the military (who were only too glad to receive them) to stay in their barracks. Following the breakdown of the Union, he actively developed relations between the city and neighbouring republics, encouraging some Westerners to see him as a presidential alternative to Yeltsin.

**SOCIAL CONSUMPTION FUNDS.** Cash reserves for welfare purposes (workers' housing, creches, holiday camps, sanatoria etc.), formerly accumulated by enterprises from profits and state grants. Their applied value came to about 30 per cent of the worker's pay, or more in the case of large families. They were used by enterprises to conserve and stabilize their work force. But in 1990 the rules were changed. When they became autonomous, enterprises cavilled at 'useless' expenditure and in many cases came to the conclusion that fear of unemployment would be enough to ensure workers' loyalty – to the dismay of economists like Aganbegyan,* who had assigned social funds a regulatory role in maintaining the living standards of people affected by reforms.

**SOCIAL DEMOCRATIC PARTY OF RUSSIA.** Party founded by Russian deputies Oleg Rumyantsev and Aleksandr Obolensky in May 1990, with a pledge to 'fight the return of totalitarianism, including the installation of a presidential regime'. Its 5,000 members are mainly skilled workers and members of the technical intelligentsia. Described as a social-democratic party of the West European type, in 1991 it had the strongest representation of any non-communist party in the Soviet and Russian parliaments (70 and 50 seats respectively).

**SOCIALISM.** Ideal abandoned by a population knowing its consequences; an over-reaction according to intellectuals who remain faithful. Thus Aleksandr Yakovlev* in October 1990: 'At the risk of seeming out of step I must declare my conviction that total nihilism towards everything socialist is no less dangerous than total self-satisfaction and self-glorification. What we need is not emotion but knowledge of the real state of things, of our actions and motives, and whether we have progressed or not. Only when we have the answers will it be possible to give life to socialist ideas. Socialism is inevitable, of that I am sure, in the not so distant future. But it is asking for disappointment to expect it tomorrow.'

**SOCIALIST PARTY OF THE RUSSIAN WORKING PEOPLE.** Party founded in December 1991 by former communists contesting the legality of the Communist Party's dissolution. It claimed to be the Party's democratic heir – a title claimed by six others. Its founders included Roy Medvedev.*

**SOCIOLOGY.** Science that became scientific only when it was recognized that the Soviet Union was not a society in the state of 'advanced socialism' proclaimed by Brezhnevite ideologists who in the early 1970s dismantled the Institute of Sociology. Most sociologists continued working under different labels (demographer, philosopher, economist) or chose politically acceptable themes such as the current state of the working class or the aspirations of young Komsomols.* Under Andropov,* the importance of knowing what people really think and want was recognized by the KGB, which called for volumes of sociological information, albeit for purposes quite different from those of the sociologists. With *perestroika*, the authorities again needed to know more about the country they wanted to reform. In 1989 the Institute of Social Sciences was separated from the Academy of Sciences and made an autonomous centre, while Tatiana Zaslavskaya* was appointed head of a new Centre of Public Opinion.

**SOKOLOVSKY,** MARSHAL VASILI DANILOVICH (1897–1968). Military theorist responsible, in *Military Strategy*, for the doctrine prevailing throughout the 1970s and 1980s that any future central war would be fought with nuclear weapons and that the use of conventional forces would be confined to the opening. He was contradicted in 1985 in a revision of doctrine by the then Deputy Chief of the General Staff, Gen. M. A. Gareev.

**SOLITUDE.** New social malady particularly affecting young women just arrived in the city and young divorcees. In 1987 *Komsomolskaya Pravda* opened a 'lonely hearts' column to help set up meetings among the country's millions of involuntary single citizens. Most requests showed a desire to form a traditional family, with a 'strong but gentle' husband and a 'good mother and housewife'. Women almost invariably sought 'non-drinkers' – a self-description frequent among the qualities offered by men.

**SOLOMENTSEV,** MIKHAIL SERGEYEVICH (1913– ). Member of the Brezhnevite 'old guard' whose conditional support of Gorbachev quickly evaporated. Opposed to rehabilitating expelled Party dissidents, he was retired from the Politburo in September 1988.

**SOLOVETSKIYE** Islands. White Sea home of a famous monastery until 1921 when it was turned into a prison for counter-revolutionaries, then for fallen Party members and other political offenders. Most Soviets first heard of it in 1989 through the film *Solovetsky Power*. In 1990 the supreme court, dealing with the rehabilitation of victims of Stalinism, took up the case of a mass execution of prisoners there in 1941.

**SOLZHENITSYN,** ALEKSANDR ISAEVICH (1918–   ). Leading writer of the years of repression, exiled from the Soviet Union by Brezhnev; later self-exiled from the rest of the world by his choice of seclusion in Cavendish, Vermont. Solzhenitsyn served as an artillery officer in World War II, and was sentenced in 1945 to seven years' camp for an intercepted letter disparaging Stalin. Camp life in Kazakhstan was the setting for *One Day in the Life of Ivan Denisovich*, published by Tvardovsky in *Novy Mir*★ in 1962. Among later novels, *The First Circle* derived from his time as a radio operator in Marfino 'special prison', and *Cancer Ward* from his treatment for cancer in Tashkent in 1954. After Brezhnev's fall, publication of *The First Circle* was stopped by the Writers' Union; and *Cancer Ward*, though accepted by *Novy Mir*, was never published. In 1968 Solzhenitsyn protested at his ostracism in a widely publicized letter to the Writers Union, which next year expelled him. A year later, in 1970, he was awarded the Nobel Prize for Literature. Together with Sakharov,★ Solzhenitsyn became a figurehead of the 1970s dissident★ movement, until publication abroad in December 1973 of the first volume of *The Gulag Archipelago* caused his arrest and deportation. Joined by his wife, Natalia Svetlova, and children, he lived for two years (1962–64) in Zurich. Solzhenitsyn's other major work, *The Red Wheel*, is a cycle of historical novels beginning with the publication in 1972 of *August 1914*, set amid the debacle of the Russian army in East Prussia. He gave all royalties from *The Gulag Archipelago* to a fund for persecuted persons.

In exile, Solzhenitsyn dismayed admirers by his authoritarian philosophy. This first appeared in a 'manifesto' published in 1973, in which he criticized the liberality and permissiveness of Western society. In 1990, in a 16,000-word essay on the changing scene, published in the Soviet Union by *Komsomolskaya Pravda*, he omitted all mention of Gorbachev or reforms and proposed instead a paternal autocracy rooted in Orthodox religion and Russian nationalism well in line with his increasing Russian chauvinism. He favoured dismembering the Soviet state and creating a greater Russia from Russia proper, the Ukraine, Byelorussia and the Russified parts of Kazakhstan. Later, in an essay in a special edition of *Literaturnaya Gazeta*, he suggested that the three Baltic republics, the four Central Asian republics and Moldavia (if drawn to Romania), should not merely be allowed to leave the Union but should be *obliged* to do so. But he stressed that membership of the Greater Russia he envisaged should be voluntary; if the Ukraine wished to become separate, there must be no coercion. The same applied to small peoples★ in the Russian Federation. When told of the restoration of his citizenship by the August 1990 presidential decree, Solzhenitsyn said he had no intention of returning as long as the charge of treason remained against him. The charge was lifted a few days after the defeat of the 1991 *putsch*.★

**SOTHEBY'S.** British auction house jointly responsible with the Ministry of Culture for the first public sale of paintings in the USSR. The auction, in

June 1988, involved avant-garde pictures of the 1920s and the works of twenty-nine contemporary artists. The prices fetched by a number of pictures, like 'The Line' of Aleksandr Rodchenko ($300,000), raised wild hopes among lesser artists; they caused recrimination among painters whose works had not been selected, and the break-up of an artistic community until then united in poverty. Seven of the 119 works, including a canvas of Glazunov,* failed to reach reserve price. The total raised was £1,852,500.

**SOUTH AFRICA.** Ultimate case of an about-turn in relations with the Dark Continent. In 1989 sources let it be known that Moscow would encourage a settlement between the Soviet-backed African National Congress (ANC) and the government of President de Klerk. For the first time white South African journalists were invited to visit the Soviet Union and were given briefings. Still keeping the other line open, in August 1990 Yanayev* received Joe Slovo, secretary-general of the South African Communist Party, to reaffirm support for the ANC in its fight against apartheid. Meanwhile, Moscow signed a utilitarian contract with De Beers (see 'Diamonds') and Soviet officials spoke lightly of the value of trade embargoes. In November 1990, the Foreign Ministry put an end to speculation by saying that Moscow was ready to normalize and develop relations (including diplomatic) with South Africa once it was sure that the dismantling of apartheid was irreversible.

**SOUTH KOREA.** Trading partner and development model finally seen by economic reformers as an easier proposition than Japan. Events moved quickly. In June 1990 Gorbachev met President No-Tae-u in San Francisco; in September the two countries established diplomatic relations; in December, Foreign Minister Shevardnadze apologized for the 1985 downing of the KAL Boeing, and No-Tae-u paid his first official visit to the USSR. Finally in May 1991 Gorbachev made a point of stopping off in Seoul on his way home from a rather barren visit to Tokyo. In 1991 trade between the Soviet Union and South Korea approached $1.4 billion, helped by a South Korean $1 billion loan. And the road to Moscow international airport became fenced with advertisements for Goldstar television, Samsung computers and Hyundai cars.

**SOUTH OSSETIA** (pop. 99,000, before 1990–91 troubles). South Caucasian territory formerly an autonomous region of Georgia. The principal city is Tskhinvali. The region is permanently open only to the South (Georgian) side of the Caucasus. The only road to North Ossetia* is cut for more than half the year by weather, having been opened in 1989–90, when the Ossetians (like the Abkhaz*) began to fear assimilation by separatist Georgia.* When Georgia learned of plans to declare South Ossetia independent, it instituted a blockade* and in December 1990 arbitrarily suppressed its autonomy. Incidents led to full-scale fighting and the shelling by Georgian troops of Ossetian villages. By the time the mountain road closed for the winter of 1991–92, 70,000 South Ossetians had taken refuge in North Ossetia, 250 had died, 480 had been wounded, 112 had disappeared, and 84 villages had been 'purged' of Ossetians. Still blockaded by a force of 10,000, the territory reaffirmed its independence and wish to join North Ossetia as part of Russia.

**SOVEREIGNTY.** Grand but hazy status, formally defined as freedom from external control, with supremacy of local over Soviet law. By 1991 it was claimed by all Union republics,* numerous autonomous republics* and several autonomous regions,* usually as the preliminary to another equally ambiguous status – 'independence'. In most cases it still signified an intention of staying within the Union under a new formula, if this could be devised. But five republics – Estonia, Latvia, Lithuania, Georgia and Armenia – opted for full independence, outside.

**SOVIET.** Literally 'council', a small or large unit in a pyramidal power structure reaching from the village to the Kremlin. Local and regional soviets were assisted by permanent commissions* supposedly chosen according to members' interest in specific subjects. With the transfer of power from the Party to the soviets in 1988–89, there was often a confrontation with the local executive committee (Ispolkom*), composed of Party bureaucrats whom it was nevertheless necessary to retain for the work of administration.

**SOVIET OF NATIONALITIES.** Second chamber of the former Supreme Soviet,* consisting of 271 deputies elected on the basis of national quotas: eleven per Union republic, four per autonomous republic, two per autonomous region, one per autonomous district, regardless of the size of population. It met separately and was concerned only with nationality questions. After the 1991 *putsch** it was replaced by the Soviet of the Republics (see below).

**SOVIET OF THE UNION.** Main chamber of the former Supreme Soviet,* consisting of 271 deputies elected by districts based on the number of inhabitants. After the 1991 *putsch** its acts became subject to the veto of a new upper house, the Union of the Republics. With the approaching break-up of the USSR it had increasing difficulties in finding a quorum and finally dissolved itself on December 31.

**SOVIET OF THE REPUBLICS.** Upper house of the Soviet parliament created after the 1991 *putsch** with a membership of 20 deputies from each republic, chosen by republican parliaments from among their members. It had power to veto acts of the hitherto top chamber, the Soviet of the Union.*

**SOVIETSKAYA ROSSIYA.** Daily newspaper of the Russian Federation, caught up in the latter's parliamentary power struggle. In September 1990, when titles came to be registered,* the recent creation of a separate Russian Communist Party called for a readjustment of its ownership by three 'proprietors' – the Russian parliament, the Russian government and the Soviet Central Committee. Its control became an issue in the fight between the Russian president, Yeltsin,* and the conservative First Secretary, Polozkov.* Violent speeches were made in the Russian parliament, where the pro-Yeltsin faction demanded the dismissal of the *Sovietskaya Rossiya* editor, Valentin Chikin, but eventually got cold feet. Circulation, 3.6 million in 1985, reached 5.2 million in 1988 (the year of the notorious Nina Andreeva* letter) before falling back to 4.2 million in 1989. In 1991, deprived of funds from its former owner as a result of the *putsch*,* it was re-registered in the name of the editorial staff, as a paper 'for honest communists of the Russian Federation'. Funds were provided by a firm belonging to Andrei Zavidya, running mate of Zhirinovsky* in the 1991 Russian presidential election. In October the same year the Russian government began proceedings against it for having 'allowed publication of calls for the overthrow of the existing regime by force'.

**SOVINCENTER.** Moscow international conference and exhibition centre, adjoining Mezhdunarodnaya (International) Hotel.

**SOVKHOZ.** See 'State farms'.

**SOYUZ.** Conservative group formed in December 1989 during the debate on a new Union treaty.* It gave its aims as 'to maintain the Union, a strong centre, and common laws and language'. But it also 'guaranteed equal rights for all republics in a "market" economy – even if the future belongs to collective property', as the founder, Yuri Blokhin, slyly put it. Soyuz denied any connection with the 1991 *putsch*\*: a denial somewhat muddied by the declaration of another leading member, Colonel Alksnis,* that the attempted coup had been 'only a rehearsal'.

**SPACE.** New 'world' conquered by Soviets at colossal cost, later to be regarded less enthusiastically in a wave of self-denigration. On the thirtieth anniversary of the launching of Sputnik (October 4, 1987) people were told how Sergei Kovalov, the 'father' of the space programme, had recognized the importance of a 1948 paper by mathematician Mikhail Tikhonravov, whom others had treated as a 'Jules Verne confusing dreams and reality'. In 1953, the two men designed the first intercontinental ballistic missile (ICBM), in which Tikhonravov saw the basis of future space-launchers. The principal Soviet 'cosmodromes' were at Baikonur (Kazakhstan), Kapustin Yar (near Astrakhan) and Plesetsk (near Arkhangelsk). In 1991 Baikonur was declared Kazakhstan property. In 1991, the disappearance of a central budget put the whole Soviet space programme in jeopardy. The only hope of rescue lay in an agreement between the three republics directly involved in space operations: Kazakhstan (launching sites), Russia (control and training centres), and the Ukraine (construction of launchers), or in co-operation with the West. At Minsk in December 1991 presidents of the new Commonwealth signed an agreement on joint activity in space exploration – which did not stop Ukraine from announcing plans for a Ukrainian 'space expedition'. The agency Glavkosmos* (in charge of commercial aspects) was meanwhile desperately trying to sell everything marketable to foreigners, including the Mir* space station.

**SPECIAL ECONOMIC ZONE.** Status claimed by a number of cities or regions under the impact of economic reforms. In 1988, when the idea originated, the Soviet government instanced three possible zones: one in the Baltic region (the Balts refused, fearing once again to lose control over their own development), one in the Pacific area to attract the Japanese (who nevertheless declined to invest as long as the Kurils* question was not settled), and a third at Odessa to attract trade with Turkey and the Mediterranean. In 1990–91 the Russian parliament accepted declarations from the Altai *krai*, the regions of Kemerovo and Novgorod, the city of Zelinograd, the Jewish autonomous region of Birobidzhan, Leningrad, Dubna, Sheremetyevo airport and many other cities and localities. Similar moves were made in other republics, regardless of the existence of such accepted criteria as an adequate infrastructure, production outlets, and a plentiful and motivated labour force.

**SPECIAL SCHOOLS** (*spetsshkoly*). Schools specializing mainly, but not exclusively, in foreign languages. In 1986-87 Yeltsin attacked them as a preserve of the 'Party elite'. Many educationalists would like to apply their expertise to the benefit of ordinary schools and bring foreign languages within general reach.

**SPECULATION.** Operation defined by a law of October 1990 as the buying of goods at state prices to sell at higher prices. The measure, imposing fines up to R5,000 (more for big operators), was deemed necessary to protect consumers in a time of shortages during transition to the market. In the previous nine months speculation was said to have increased by 30 per cent and some prices to have trebled. Much of the business had passed from individual speculators to criminal organizations able to rig prices.

**SPETSFOND.** Depository of books 'not for public reading'. In 1988 newspapers interviewed Vladimir Solodin, an official appointed the year before to supervise a revision of the 'Index'. Solodin told them that 4,000 books had already been freed and issued to public libraries. Among them were the works of Bukharin.* The restricted books were kept in special library sections accessible only to readers with permission from a very high level. More than 90 per cent, including nearly all foreign works, were being released, said Solodin; only 500 out of the 6,000 the commission had had to review would remain reserved for use by specialists, because they 'contained military secrets or inflammatory, anti-state or anti-semitic material'. Included also were several post-revolutionary pornographic works.

**SPORT.** National activity overtaken by commercialism. In 1987 clubs were allowed to carry advertising on sports gear to help them buy equipment abroad. The same year saw the first 'independent' professional football (at Dnepropetrovsk). Previously all teams were affiliated to official organizations such as trade unions or the army, which provided facilities and paid the players. Chess, skating, tennis and similar champions demanded an end to their dictatorial control by the State Committee for Sport and by sports federations, including the right to dispose of their prize-winnings and an end of hypocritical amateur status. In 1992 the future contained uncertainties, for professional and local clubs alike: the former now faced taxes on their 'gates', while the latter had for the first time to pay for the use of fields and buildings. As more and more facilities come to be owned by co-operatives, there are mounting protests at the end of free leisure activity. At the same time the break-up of the Union could put participation in first-class international sports events beyond the reach of many poorer republics.

**SRAM** (Short-range Attack Missile). Guided missile launched from aircraft as an alternative to gravity bombs.

**SS.** Wartime Nazi military elite, including several regiments recruited among Soviet minorities. In the late 1980s these were presented by some Baltic and Ukrainian nationalists as heroes fighting Soviet occupation. In July 1990 the Lithuanian government was obliged to order cancellation of a meeting of former SS in the Brauska district. In Estonia the Heritage Society organized a gathering of 'all the liberators of Estonia, regardless of their allegiance', with substantial support from the 'progressive' press. The government forbade the demonstration — a move attributed by *Independent Estonia* to pressure by 'Soviet occupation forces'. The Estonian Jewish community expressed itself somewhat differently, as did Russians who remembered what the SS had done to the people round Pskov and Novgorod. During World War II the Waffen SS in Estonia numbered 11,000 men. In Ukraine, a monument was erected to the SS 'Halychyna' division which operated in the sub-Carpathian province.

**SS-20.** Missile scrapped under the Intermediate-Range Nuclear Forces (INF)\* treaty. The last was destroyed in June 1991.

**STAGNATION** (*zastoi*). All-embracing code word for corruption, political repression, declining investment, technological backwardness, and general demoralization in 1964–83. 'Years of stagnation' meant the Brezhnev period.

**STALIN,** born YOSIF VISARIONOVICH DZHUGASHVILI (1878–1953). Tyrant first confronted by Gorbachev in his speech on the seventieth anniversary of the October Revolution. The speech set the crimes of the 1930s against Stalin's achievement in industrialization and as a war leader. It led the press to publish figures of Stalin's victims. Next, in July 1988 at the end of the Party conference,* Gorbachev announced plans for a Moscow memorial to all victims of Stalinist repression – 'to render [them] justice is our political and moral duty.' The declaration was hailed as a victory by activists who before the conference had gathered 30,000 signatures for such a memorial, and as a blow to conservatives, who saw themselves pilloried as Stalinists in the press. On March 5, 1988, the thirty-fifth anniversary of Stalin's death was marked by the first overtly 'anti-Stalinist' street demonstration. It was brutally suppressed by the police, largely through lack of experience in handling an unauthorized event. Succeeding months saw the first official re-evaluation of Stalin's reign, the rehabilitation of the Bolshevik leaders shot in the 1930s, and the first criticism of Stalin's conduct in the war. Some depicted him as betraying communism, some as a natural product of Lenin. The debate was notable for the publication in 1988–89 of four numbers of *Nauka i Zhizn* ('Science and Life') entirely devoted to links between Marxism and Stalinism. Under the title 'The Sources of Socialism', the philosopher Aleksandr Tsypko studied how and why the Marx-Engels-Lenin-Stalin quartet became a trio after the 1950s. At the end of 1990 a hitherto unknown Union of Stalinist Soviets circulated a petition calling for a celebration of the 111th anniversary of the dictator's birth.

**STANKEVICH,** SERGEI BORISOVICH (1954–   ). In 1991 Vice-President of the Moscow City Council. As a junior university lecturer with a Party card he was elected a Soviet deputy in 1989 with the backing of the radical Electors' Club. In parliament he became active in the Inter-regional* group, and in 1990 was elected to the Moscow city council. As vice-chairman – having opportunely left the Party at the same time as Yeltsin – he used his fluency in English to develop Western contacts, travelling widely abroad and acquiring the image of a 'promising young Soviet'. The image did not conceal his ambition for higher office, towards which a step was his appointment in September 1991 as a counsellor of Yeltsin.

**'STAR WARS'.** See 'Strategic Defence Initiative'.

**STAROVOYTOVA,** GALINA VASILYEVNA (1946–   ). Rare case of a Soviet woman gaining popularity through politics. A Russian by birth, she was elected as an Armenian deputy to the Soviet parliament after accompanying Sakharov* on a remarkable fact-finding tour of Nagorno-Karabakh.* In parliament she became an important supporter of Yeltsin, and was seen by some as his tactical counsellor and political muse.

**START** (Strategic Arms Limitation Treaty). The longest and most complex arms negotiations ever undertaken, 1982–91. The treaty, valid for fifteen years, was finally agreed in time for signing at the July 1991 Moscow summit. It provided for the Soviet Union and the United States to cut their combined stock of 23,000 nuclear warheads by nearly one third, bringing it to the level that had existed in 1982. Over eight years, Soviet warheads would be reduced from about 11,000 to about 7,000, and American warheads from about 12,000 to about 9,000. The Soviet cuts entailed approximately halving the number of warheads carried by Soviet land-based intercontinental ballistic missiles and the halving of the force of 308 'heavy' SS-18 missiles, armed with ten warheads, considered the most threatening weapon in the Soviet arsenal. The treaty also contained novel verification provisions (for close-range inspection of warheads, weapons factories and delivery vehicles) and a promise to exchange data recorded during missile tests.

**STATE BANK OF THE USSR (GOSBANK).** Villain of union republics complaining of 'financial colonialism'. It changed shape while going along with reforms. In 1987 five other banks were set up to take over from it in dealing with different branches of industry: Promstroibank (Bank for Industrial Construction), Agroprombank* (Bank for Agricultural Production), Zhilsotsbank (Bank for Housing and Social Security), the Savings Bank (for personal loans), and Vnezhekonombank* (Bank for Foreign Trade). The five were financially autonomous and alone responsible for their operations, which left the State Bank an organ of co-ordination, printing money and directing state monetary policy. But the move was only a half measure, because Gosbank continued to guarantee loans to the economy, and the new banks, although autonomous, remained *de facto* state banks. (In January 1992 they were absorbed by Russian counterparts, pending distribution of their assets among republics.) When in July 1990 the Russian republic 'nationalized' the Russian banking system, Gorbachev signed a decree reforming the State Bank further. Henceforth its function was limited to maintaining the rouble exchange rate and controlling exchanges between banks inside the country. All other activities became autonomous, decentralized and privatized. In the autumn of 1991 all banking activity remained under the joint direction of a new Council of Gosbank and the state banks of Union republics, while leaders discussed the possibility of a central bank as part of a new economic union. In December 1991, Yeltsin brought Gosbank under Russian control, leaving other republics to study their own banking systems.

**STATE COMMITTEE.** Equivalent of a major government ministry.

**STATE COMMITTEE FOR THE ENVIRONMENT.** Office created in 1987 without funds or staff under the only non-communist minister Nikolai Vorontsov, a biologist. For a population of 290 million the Soviet Union had only 5,000 food monitoring stations (of which less than 1,000 could detect pesticides). The only law was the 1989 Law on Ecology, which could not be enforced for lack of technical equipment and of co-ordination among republics. Nevertheless, 150 cases came to court, concerning, among other things, the pollution of the Volga, factory emissions in the Urals, and fish poaching in the Caspian Sea. Environmental protests caused public demonstrations long before food shortages and election campaigns, making the 'Greens' a nationwide movement. Pollution was blamed for the low level of life expectancy* and an increase in cancer and infant mortality.* In 1990 ecologists and intellectuals warned that under the pretext of developing the economy the USSR could be made a Western dumping ground for dangerous industries.

**STATE COUNCIL.** *De facto* government set up under interim arrangements approved by the Congress of People's Deputies after the defeat of the 1991 *putsch.** It consisted of the heads of ten republics (Russia, Ukraine, Byelorussia, Kazakhstan, Turkmenistan, Uzbekistan, Tajikistan, Azerbaijan, Kirghizia and Armenia) provisionally remaining in the Union, under the chairmanship of President Gorbachev. It acted in conjunction with an interim economic committee (the Inter-Republican Committee for the Operational Management of the Economy), and was answerable to the continuing Supreme Soviet.

**STATE FARMS** (*Sovkhozy*). Farms employing workers on a fixed wage, under an appointed director (as opposed to an elected one on collective farms). In 1991 *Sovkhozy* still accounted for 45 per cent of cultivated land, and their equipment was generally more modern. In January 1991 a presidential decree called for inventories to be made of state farms so that land could be distributed to private farmers. See also 'Farmer'.

**STATISTICS.** See 'Goskomsat'.

**STEPONAVICIUS,** Monsignor Julijonas (1911–   ). Lithuanian Catholic archbishop of Vilnius allowed to resume his function in 1988. The Soviet decision, coinciding with a sudden moderation of activity by Sajudis,* gave rise to suggestions of a deal between the Vatican and the Kremlin.

**STOCK EXCHANGE.** See 'Bourse'.

**STRATEGIC DEFENCE INITIATIVE (SDI).** Longtime nightmare of Soviet defence planners and US taxpayers; a space-based system for intercepting incoming attack missiles. Americans feared spiralling costs, Soviets insecurity if America, safe from attack, became capable of a nuclear 'first strike'. The SDI (or 'Star Wars') project was announced by Reagan in 1983, and denounced by Andropov. After failing to obtain US cancellation at the 1985 Geneva summit, the Soviet Union in May 1986 called for measures to strengthen the ABM treaty,\* which, on a strict reading, prohibited the system. While argument continued, it became evident that Congress would never vote the funds beyond the laboratory stage. By the end of 1990 'Star Wars' had sufficiently lost importance to enable a strategic arms treaty (START\*) to be signed at the US-Soviet summit in Moscow in July 1991.

**STRIKES.** Strictly capitalist phenomenon until 1988 (the Soviet Union admitting only to rare 'incidents', which were treated with the utmost severity). In 1988 Armenians used a general strike to demonstrate their anger over events in Nagorno-Karabakh.\* In summer 1989, miners in every Soviet coalfield went on strike with political and social demands; strike committees became alternative local governments, a classic component of reformist blocs.\* In 1990, faced with the multiplication of strikes, Gorbachev limited the right to strike in vital sectors. But within eight months strikes hit 1,700 factories and work centres, causing the loss of 10 million work days and direct industrial losses of R1 billion.

**STROIBAT.** Construction battalion; part of the armed forces but not counted in force totals – a typical cause of disagreement with the West. Ferociously depicted in a novel of the same name by Sergei Kaledin (unpublished until *glasnost*), the *stroibat* was reserved for recruits unfit for normal service. In fact, recruits were given back-breaking work in terrible climatic conditions. The system was ended in 1990.

**SUBMARINES.** The first Soviet nuclear-missile submarines were deployed in the late 1950s and in 1991 carried 20 per cent of all Soviet strategic warheads, compared with a US figure of 50 per cent. But even during the 'Cold War' only 15 per cent were liable to be on station at any one time. *Glasnost* revealed a long history of accidents. The 1989 'Komsomolets' disaster, costing forty-two lives due to radioactivity released by an engine-room explosion, unleashed a campaign of protest at the navy's indifference to safety questions. Deaths were blamed on insufficient training, absurd orders and counter-orders, and the poor state of rescue equipment.

**SUFFICIENT DEFENCE.** See 'Defensive defence'.

**SUICIDE.** Phenomenon of society publicized by *glasnost*. Newspapers cited cases of self-immolation by girls and young women in Central Asia, generally in connection with forbidden or forced marriages.

**SUKHAREV,** Aleksandr Yakovlevich (1923– ). USSR Procurator-General, appointed 1989. Previously Deputy Minister of Justice of the Russian Federation. In 1990 he was replaced by Trubin.*

**SUKHOI.** Design bureau for advanced fighter planes. At the 1990 Le Bourget air show, Sukhoi and (French) Aérospatiale announced a $1 billion joint project for a 15–20 seat business jet. Sukhoi chief Mikhail Simonov said the prototype could fly in three years and series production start in five. Most of the $1 billion work would go to the Soviets. Western commentators were sceptical.

**SUMGAIT** (pop. 223,000). Azerbaijan oil-city north of Baku, scene in March 1988 of the first ethnic massacre. A mob drawn largely from the Azeri sub-proletariat of a city thrown up around highly polluting industries set on the more affluent Armenians, killing at least thirty-two. The massacre began an unending chapter of Azeri-Armenian clashes.

**SUMMITS.** Increasingly occasions for signing what has already been agreed. Soviet-US summits since 1985 were: Geneva, November 1985 (Reagan-Gorbachev), their first face-to-face meeting, and proposals for ending the Cold War; Reykjavik, October 1986 (Gorbachev-Reagan), breakdown of a near-accord on nuclear disarmament because of Star Wars;* Washington, December 1987 (Reagan-Gorbachev), signature of the INF* treaty; Moscow, May 29–June 2, 1988 (Gorbachev-Reagan), a public relations exercise for the US elections and Gorbachev's domestic standing; Malta, December 1989 (Bush-Gorbachev), shipboard meeting setting the agenda for START* negotiations; Washington, June 1990 (Bush-Gorbachev), agreement on German reunification; Moscow, July 1991 (Gorbachev-Bush), signature of START.

**SUPREME SOVIET** (parliament). Former Soviet legislative organ consisting of two chambers, the Soviet of the Union* and the Soviet of Nationalities,* each of 271 deputies serving five-year terms. Under the 1988–89 constitutional reform, it was accountable only to the Congress of People's Deputies,* which, meeting twice a year for short periods, made annual elections from among its members. This unwieldy arrangement, starting from the elections of 1989, was seen by some as a stage between the old Supreme Soviet (whose 2,250 members met only to rubber-stamp Politburo decisions) and a future Western-style assembly. Of the two houses, the Soviet of the Union was the real 'parliament'. It was composed of People's Deputies elected by territorial districts and public organizations, whereas the Soviet of Nationalities was elected on the basis of national quotas. The organization was reshaped after the 1991 *putsch** to emphasize its control by republics. It voted its own dissolution on December 31.

**SUSLOV,** Mikhail Andreevich (1902–1982). Party chief responsible for ideology. His death before the advent of *perestroika* did not save him from subsequent vilification for his part in the repression of the Hungarian uprising in 1956, the ousting of Khrushchev in 1964, the suppression of the Prague Spring in 1968, and the relentless persecution of dissidents and artists under Brezhnev.

# T

**TAGANKA.** Moscow theatre accused by critics of resting on its laurels after helping pave the way for *glasnost*. Nevertheless, it is still regularly sold out, and each new production hailed as a cultural event. The Taganka was started in 1964, near the end of the Khrushchev 'thaw'. It contrived to preserve its small island of liberalism during the years of stagnation,* when its name became inseparably linked with those of the actor Vysotsky* and the director Lubimov.* In 1975 Lubimov defied a seven-year ban by reviving his production of *Alive and Well*, taken from Boris Mozhaiev's *Life of Fyodor Kuzkin*. The furore resulted in his expulsion from both theatre and Party. It also condemned Mozhaiev to a living death artistically (his name was banned from mention and his works stayed unpublished for nearly a decade). The play was revived on Lubimov's return to Moscow in 1989. Meanwhile, the Taganka had been directed by Anatoli Efros and, after his death in 1984, by the future Minister of Culture, Gubenko.*

**TAJIKISTAN** (pop. 5.1 million). Former Union republic bordering China and Afghanistan, mainly agricultural, with a population 59 per cent Tajik, 23 per cent Uzbek and 10 per cent Russian. In October 1990 depressed living standards, exploited for religious purposes by itinerant mullahs, provoked rural immigrants to riot in the capital, Dushanbe.* Latent friction between Tajiks and Uzbeks, mainly over market prices, caused the violence to take an ethnic turn, in which, however, the chief victims were Russians. The immediate occasion of the riot was a congress being held, despite a ban by parliament, by the Islamic Renewal Party. Fearing trouble, local clergy kept their distance. Groups of youths, including university students, besieged the platform to broadcast a rumour that congress delegates had been arrested. A crowd then set on the Russians in the city, and twenty people were killed. Blame was put on clandestine 'propagandists' from Afghanistan, but also on Iranians who had come with official permission to set up 'cultural links', i.e. open mosques and Koranic schools. A six-month curfew was imposed, and at the end of the year the Tajik parliament, still under communist control, approved the imposition of direct presidential rule. Using a hunger strike (declared illegal), members of the Democratic Party of Tajikistan successfully demanded a referendum to choose a new president. The vote went to Kakhar Makhamov, president of the supreme soviet. In September 1991 the republic declared itself independent. In December, after weeks of disturbances, in which the republic was threatened with fragmentation by provincial clans, new elections led to the installation of a less compromised president, Rakhmon Nabiyev. It then joined the new Commonwealth.* It was meanwhile alleged by local officials to be the first target of fundamentalist Muslims coming from neighbouring Afghanistan and Pakistan. The Tajik KGB, who detained ten 'foreign agents' in the first six months of 1991, said they had discovered a so-called 'Programme M' for destabilizing Central Asia and creating conditions for secession.

**TALON.** Russian name for ration coupons introduced from 1987 for items 'in deficit',* sometimes due to hoarding and rumours. By 1989 nearly all cities were selling a fair range of products (soap, meat, tea, sugar) on coupons and the system became standard for most basic goods at controlled prices during the promised switch to a market economy. In 1990 the Statistics Committee estimated that 94 per cent of cities were rationing sugar, and 53 per cent butter, meat and alcohol. In Moscow, in 1991, ninety-three different kinds of product were available only on coupons. Coupons were frequently not honoured, and customers given the option to exchange, e.g. sugar coupons for matches or meat coupons for tea. In 1992 a number of republics introduced a new kind of coupon intended to protect their internal markets in contradiction of the 'single rouble market' agreed at Minsk* and Alma-Ata.* Made a part of everybody's pay, in Ukraine and some other republics it became the forerunner of a separate national currency.

**TARASOV,** ARTYOM MIKHAILOVICH (1951– ). First *'perestroika* millionaire'. With the help of a Party card and a degree in technical sciences, he made his first fortune in 1986–87 as a scrap merchant. When his co-operative was forced to close by envious officials or rivals, he moved into international brokerage by founding a new firm, Istok. In 1990 his offices were raided by the KGB, under its authorization to investigate 'economic sabotage'. After a spell as a Russian deputy he emerged in 1992 as a London-based international banker.

**TARKOVSKY,** ANDREI ARSENYEVICH (1932–1988). Exiled film-maker who lived just long enough to see the removal of the ban on his works, thanks to Klimov's* arrival as head of the Film-Makers' Union.* In 1987 all his films were shown. Among them were *Nostalgia*, made in exile and shown for the first time, and *Andrei Rublev*, shown for the first time in its entirety. In May 1987 *Literaturnaya Gazeta* published a moving letter he had written to his father, a poet, explaining that exile was the only way to continue his work. His father feared his son had become a 'cosmopolitan' but refused to denounce him, with the result that he himself was put on the list of people 'not to be cited' in literary references.

**TASS.** Acronym for Telegraph Agency of the Soviet Union. Principal news agency, particularly for 'spot' news, in contrast to Novosti*, which always specialized in background material. After the 1991 *putsch*,* in the course of which Tass put out statements by the leaders, the director-general, Lev Spiridonov, was replaced by Vitali Ignatenko.* In 1992 it became a 'pool' for Commonwealth agencies, Russian output being signed 'Itar-Tass'.

**TATARIA/TATARSTAN** (pop. 3.5 million). Autonomous republic* of the Russian Federation, situated on the Volga. Since 1990, having earlier declared itself 'sovereign', it has sought full independence. The capital, Kazan,* was the first stop by Yeltsin* on his 'tour of Russia' in August 1990. The Tatars have a delicate relationship with the Bashkirs, who constitute an important minority in the republic but are attracted by the idea of joining their kinsmen in neighbouring Bashkiria. In 1991 the campaign for independence, backed by numerous acts of sabotage against oil pipelines in the area, led to confrontation with Moscow. In 1992 the republic's leaders said Tatarstan wanted to join the new Commonwealth* as a fully-fledged state. (See separately 'Crimean Tatars'.)

**TAX INSPECTORS.** Officials brought back in 1990 after an interval of thirty years. With the advent of private enterprise, incomes ceased to be identified with state wages, which were taxed at source.

**TBILISI** (pop. 1.158 million). Capital of Georgia, plunged into mourning on April 9, 1989 by the death of twenty people at the hands of Ministry of Interior troops armed with spades and gas. The subsequent inquiry never established who gave the order to disperse by force a peaceful crowd of demonstrators in front of the parliament building, with few means of retreat. The action set Georgia irrevocably on the road to independence – a course in which the city was to witness much greater violence when it became a battlefield between supporters and opponents of President Gamsakhurdia* in December 1991 and January 1992. At least 80 people died in the fighting. See also 'Georgia'.

**TEA.** Household necessity missing from most shops since 1980 due to the collapse of national production under Brezhnev. To 'fulfil the plan',* collective farms stripped the bushes of young leaves (needed for the next year's crop) and rushed the harvest with poorly adjusted machines. The crop never recovered.

**TEACHING.** Profession decimated by the arrival of an education 'market'. In the late 1980s, poor pay (R145 a month for a primary teacher, R160 for a secondary teacher, R210 for a university lecturer) caused thousands to leave for jobs as translators, accountants etc. with co-operatives. In 1990 Moscow was 3,000 teachers below strength. The crisis led to an attempt to staunch the loss by a 1991 pay increase (bringing secondary school teachers up to R385). In 1988, 21 per cent of the Union's 129,000 schools had no central heating, 30 per cent no running water, and 41 per cent no indoor lavatories. Since 1984 the school starting age has been six. For most children secondary education ends at 18 (but at 16 for less gifted pupils, who are sent for two years to professional schools, known as PTUs*). There have been successive attempts at reform. In 1984 teachers (90 per cent women) were told to teach more imaginatively and less by rote. In 1988 a reform of middle and higher education was intended to produce more high technology specialists. The break-up of the Union has meanwhile disrupted a uniform education system whereby 2 million teachers used regularly to teach 40 million pupils from the same textbooks and curriculum as laid down by the Ministry of Education and the Academy of Pedagogical Sciences. In 1991, public reaction to the August *putsch** obliged thousands of schools to throw out surviving Leninist teaching rituals.

**TELEPHONE.** Despair of all foreigners and an obstacle to internal commercial and industrial renewal. In 1991 a direct telephone line for international calls remained a privilege,* awarded on obscure criteria, for which foreigners had to pay in hard currency. Most Soviet factories had only one line (in the director's office) for direct calls to Moscow, though since 1990 Russian-made fax machines of variable quality have started to make an appearance. The state of the service has made telecommunications a field for joint ventures.* Moscow's first telephone directory (in fifty-three years) was due to appear in 1992. Printed in Nuremberg, with 200,000 copies in Russian and 10,000 in English, it was expected to cost R27.50.

**TELEVISION.** Battlefield for *glasnost** and prize in the Gorbachev-Yeltsin war. *Glasnost* was never as strong in TV as in the press, and had a setback in late 1990, when director Leonid Kravchenko declared that 'state television must toe the Party line'. The launching of Russian TV (June 1991) was preceded by the refusal of many Russian producers and performers to work for Gostelradio.* The scene was transformed by the August 1991 *putsch.** TV Russia was then allocated the whole of Gostelradio's second channel, of which it had had only a part; the evening news programme *Vremya* was totally revamped; and everywhere republic and regional broadcasting became more independent, often with commercial channels partly financed from abroad. In Moscow, Bakatin* promised to withdraw the numerous KGB operatives who had worked in Gostelradio. In December 1991 the remainder of Gostelradio's Russian-based facilities passed into the ownership of the Russian Federation.

**TENNIS.** Long rejected as being 'too individualist and aristocratic', tennis has boomed since being recognized as an Olympic discipline. In March 1988 *Komsomolskaya Pravda* received 267 instant responses to an invitation to young people to join a club in Moscow. The sport's popularity has increased with the international success of Soviet players like Chesnokov and Savchenko. Tennis symbolizes something chic and 'different', but private players have a problem finding courts and equipment.

**TERROR** (1). The Red terror of the civil war period, in opposition to White terror.

**TERROR** (2). The Great Terror of 1936–39, involving the liquidation, after show trials or 'summary justice', of real or imagined opponents of Stalin.★ It is estimated that 8 million people were arrested (one in every twenty) and 800,000 executed. The principal figures were condemned in three waves: (a) in the summer of 1936, Zinoviev, Kamenev and fourteen others; (b) in January 1937, Pyatakov, Radek and their 'accomplices'; (c) in 1938, Bukharin and others including Rykov, Rakovsky and Yagoda. The purge of 1938 more than decimated the Red Army, taking seven out of every ten officers, including Marshal Tukhachevsky and Admiral Orlov. More than 35,000 senior officers were shot or imprisoned. In 1987–88 all these people were rehabilitated, except Yagoda, who had been the chief executioner before himself being shot.

**THEATRE**. Cultural field switched entirely (660 theatres) to artistic and financial autonomy in January 1989, after a twelve-month trial period. As self-supporting enterprises, they might fix their own programmes, decide box-office prices, fix rates of pay, and distribute profits. They became free to conclude international contracts and open foreign currency bank accounts.

**THEATRE WORKERS' UNION**. Association formed in 1986 to replace the amorphous Theatrical Association which had been dissolved a month before. Its founding congress stressed the union's independence from the Ministry of Culture. The president, Kiril Lavrov, was an actor from Leningrad, and the First Secretary, Oleg Efremov, one of the country's most innovative directors. It became the largest creative union,★ with 56,000 members.

**THESES**. Propositions published by the leadership for discussion by the Nineteenth Party Conference in 1988. The name recalled the 'April theses' of 1917 in which Lenin set out his ideas for a Bolshevik revolution.

**TOPONOMY**. Expression of devotion to the pre-revolutionary past, a chance to settle scores with communism. In 1986, Moscow intellectuals began working on a scheme to restore historic names to streets and squares (the first change was actually to a Metro station, Lermontovskaya, renamed Krasniye Vorota, 'Red Gates', after an old association.) In 1988 the city of Brezhnev★ in the Tatar republic returned to its former name of Naberezhnye Chelny. In 1990 the cities of Zhdanov and Kalinin became

Mariupol and Tver again; and in the Caucasus, Ordzhonikidze reverted to Vladikavkaz. In August 1988, a toponomy commission was formed on the initiative of the Cultural Fund,* with a brief to study the restoration of old names, and the choice of new ones with local cultural connotations, to end the use of the Soviet atlas for a political pantheon. In 1990 the movement became overridingly political in its determination to suppress all traces of 73 years of revolution, as if it were possible to start again from scratch. A counter-movement accused it of 'historical vandalism'. The trend towards excess following the 1991 *putsch** worried even some of the reformists. Ninety cities changed their names, and in Ukraine 90 per cent of town names were subjected to 'Ukrainization'.

**TOURISM.** Invisible export once promoted for propaganda purposes, now simply a means of screwing hard currency from foreigners. At the time of the Soviet break-up nearly all foreign tourism was still controlled by Intourist.* At the top end of the market, for $330 one could spend a night in Stalin's former dacha on the Black Sea, or for $1,100 a day (plus licence) hunt elk and wild boar near Moscow. In 1988 the authorities took steps to stop so-called tourism by East Europeans, particularly Poles, who were trading on the black market. In ten months customs officers seized 400,000 television sets, 200,000 refrigerators, 50,000 washing-machines and vast quantities of subsidized foodstuffs being taken out of the country illegally.

**TRADE UNION.** Former device for passing down management decisions to workers. An overall trade union organization was chaired by Vladimir Shcherbakov.* In February 1987 Gorbachev told 5,000 union delegates at a meeting in the Kremlin that Soviet unions must pay more attention to workers' interests in the area of housing and health, and demand pay differentials that recognized the best work. The meeting was held at a time when workers felt threatened by the new accent being put on quality control (see 'Gospryomka') and on enterprise* profits. The Nineteenth Soviet Trade Union Congress in October 1990 voted to restructure the trade union organization as an independent confederation. But it had already been overtaken by the creation of an independent miners' trade union and a number of other independent unions. The Law on Trade Unions of December 1990 gave unions complete financial autonomy and declared them independent of all political and economic authorities.

**TRANSPLANTS.** Surgical operations requiring special authorization by the Ministry of Health. The first heart transplant was performed in 1968 (less than a year after the pioneering feat by the South African, Christiaan Barnard) by a military surgeon protesting at the Ministry's timid attitude. In April 1986 the Ministry and the Academy of Sciences* sanctioned a number of transplants, but in October doctors complained to *Literaturnaya Gazeta* that they were still not allowed to store the organs of donors in advance. Several days later the newspaper published news of a heart transplant, simultaneously citing the case of two doctors punished for performing the same operation without authorization.

**TRAVKIN,** Nikolai Ilich (1946–   ). One of the few workers to appear on the political scene during *perestroika*. A lifelong Party member and one-time military instructor in Czechoslovakia, in 1989 he was elected a deputy of the Soviet parliament and in 1990 of the Russian. He left the Party after the Twenty-eighth Congress* to found the Democratic Party of Russia,* where he was at once seen as a Russian 'Walesa'. His authoritarian manner, plus readiness to work with democratic communists, soon caused ruptures in a succession of alliances and lost him the financial support of Kasparov.*

**TROTSKY** Lev Davidovich, born Bronstein (1879–1940). Historical figure who refuses to go away. As co-author, with Lenin, of the October Revolution, creator of the Red Army and the most prominent victim of Stalin, Trotsky was an obvious contender for rehabilitation. But in 1988–90, the problem was how to deal with such awkward matters as his theories of permanent revolution and repression as a means of government. His name had vanished from history books, his face from published photographs. In 1987 the Soviet press took to writing a hagiography of sorts, pegged to the forty-seventh anniversary of his assassination in exile in Mexico. There were memoirs by his son and grandson, arguments about his role in history, an international gathering (the first ever) of Trotskyists in Moscow (they talked about launching a Soviet Trotskyist party). In mid-1990 the director of the Party's Marxist-Leninist Institute, Georgi Smirnov, continued to say that the central archive* would soon make its material on Trotsky public.

**TRUBIN,** Nikolai Semyonovich (1931–   ). Procurator General caught in an imbroglio over prosecuting the 1991 *putsch*ists. Returning to Moscow after the event, which found him in Cuba, he offered his resignation 'for having done nothing to prevent it'. The Supreme Soviet instructed him to continue pending a later inquiry. But Yeltsin succeeded in having the whole *putsch** investigation put into the hands of the Russian procurator, Valentin Stepankov. 'Democrats' would never forgive Trubin for pursuing the case against Gdlyan* and Ivanov.

**TRUD** ('Work'). Trade union newspaper, with reformist views and a strong interest in workers' welfare, women's rights, and the conditions of young work-people. It has the largest circulation of any daily newspaper (16.7 million in 1985, 18.6 million in 1991). In 1991 the editor was Aleksandr Potapov.

**TSAR,** NICHOLAS II. (1868–1918). Former villain, now saint and martyr. In retrospect the last of the Romanovs is seen as a peace-loving father, head of a gentle family, attended by decorous daughters and a sickly son, assassinated in 1918 by a horde of barbarians. The Orthodox church is contemplating his canonization; films portray him and his family as the first victims of Red terror; Yeltsin* is embarrassed when asked to explain why he destroyed the house in Sverdlovsk (now again Ekaterinburg) where the family passed their last days. In October 1990 the city donated the site for the building of a chapel, begun after its benediction by Patriarch Aleksei II.

**TURKISTAN/TURAN.** Old idea of a single state on the territory of the Central Asian republics, revived with dreams of Islamic unity. Discussed, but rejected as undemocratic and supremacist, by the Congress of the Democratic Movement of Central Asia and Kazakhstan in June 1991.

**TURKMENIA/TURKMENISTAN** (pop. 3.189 million). Central Asian republic bordering Afghanistan and Iran, consisting mainly of the gas-rich Karakum desert and mountains. Its people – 68 per cent Turkmen, 13 per cent Russian, 9 per cent Uzbek and 10 per cent other minorities at the time of the Soviet break-up – are more attentive to the voices of Islam than to those in Moscow or Minsk. But in December 1991, dependent on Moscow for economic support and industrial imports, it opted to join the new Commonwealth of Independent States.* The current (1992) president, Sapamurad Niazov, was elected on universal suffrage with 98.3 per cent of votes. He was previously Party first secretary and prime minister. There were no other candidates. The capital, Ashkhabad, has a population of 400,000.

**TUVA** (pop. 300,000). Southern Siberian autonomous republic* bordering Mongolia. It became Soviet in 1944 after twenty-three years of independence. In spring 1990 a wave of lawlessness forced Russian families to take refuge in Krasnoyarsk. Subsequently 1,500 Russian families left, abandoning their possessions – and at the same time leaving schools without teachers, hospitals without doctors, and factories without specialists. The Russians came in numbers in 1944 to exploit the cobalt and asbestos, which the mainly rural Tuvians had never worked. The flow was never reversed, and in the late 1980s Russian specialists were continuing to arrive when 6,000 young people (40 per cent with full secondary school diplomas) had no jobs. Tuva is a classic example of the failure of a development model leading to the birth of a Popular Front movement, demanding rights of language and religion (Lamaism). Unemployment has made the autonomous republic one of the most crime-ridden in the Union, with Russians the chief victims. In 1991 the republic declared itself independent of both Russia and the Soviet Union.

**TWENTY-SEVENTH CONGRESS** (February 25–March 6, 1986). Event marking a historical break with tradition. The Party endorsed criticism of 'stagnation'* and accepted *perestroika*; but it also gave clear evidence of the concern of the Party elite at Gorbachev's new line. Delegates had been chosen under conditions inherited from the previous period. Gorbachev's report, setting out the new policy, was not as radical as debates before the Congress had suggested it might be. There was some anti-Western rhetoric and a retreat from his radical disarmament suggestions made on television in January 1986 and tabled at Geneva. His four-hour speech referred to creating a 'socialist market', but the meaning was unclear. On the other hand, Gorbachev did put forward the beginnings of ideas for self-employment, co-operatives and tax reform. The Congress elected a new Central Committee, but in doing so replaced only 147 members (less than half) belonging to the old one, and made only small changes in the Politburo. The most noteworthy changes were the displacement of Grigori Romanov,* the corrupt Leningrad Party boss, by Lev Zaikov, and the appointment as a candidate member of Boris Yeltsin,* the new Moscow Party chief. Appointments to the Secretariat were: Aleksandr Yakovlev,* the head since 1985 of the Central Committee propaganda department; Georgi Razumovsky, to become responsible for cadres; and Anatoli Dobrynin,* the Soviet ambassador in Washington, to take charge of the international department. For the first time since the 1950s a woman was appointed as a Secretary — Aleksandra Biryukova, in charge of trade union and family affairs. She retired in 1990, and the short-lived experiment was not repeated.

**TWENTY-EIGHTH CONGRESS** (July 3–12, 1990). Historic event by which, after seventy years, the Party voted for its end as *de facto* government. The result was a victory for Gorbachev over conservatives. Delegates elected an expanded Central Committee of 412 members, with an increased representation of liberals, including for the first time the historian Roy Medvedev* and the economist Leonid Abalkin.* Delegates also voted 3,109 to 776 for Gorbachev's nominee, Ivashko,* to the new post of deputy general secretary, in opposition to Ligachev,* who stood as 'Marxist-Leninist'. The Congress was preceded by a gathering of radical delegates in support of a so-called 'Democratic Platform',* and of conservatives behind a 'Marxist Platform'.* Gorbachev's supporters and the Congress organizers stood in the middle. In addition to arguments over the role and organization of the Party, there were heated debates over the pace of economic reform and the Soviet withdrawal from Eastern Europe. The most publicized event was the walk-out of Boris Yeltsin,* who accused Gorbachev of surrendering to conservatives on the question of an accelerated economic programme. Others who announced their resignation were the radical mayors of Leningrad and Moscow, Sobchak* and Popov.* A threatened mass walk-out by 'Democratic Platform' delegates failed to materialize, but the Congress was followed by a nationwide drop in Party membership.

**TYPHOON** submarine. Largest nuclear-powered missile submarine, first deployed in 1983. Submarines of the class carry twenty SS-N-20 missiles and are much quieter in operation than previous types. They are constructed from alloys permitting very deep submergence.

**TYUMEN** region (pop. 2.2 million). Region of Siberia yielding 60 per cent of Soviet oil. In 1990 the downturn of production and uncertainty about future development projects caused a wave of social unrest and threats of a strike. Tyumen city (pop. 425,000) was affected by job cuts in factories producing extraction equipment. Seven Western oil companies are actively interested in development rights in a field producing more oil than the whole of the United States. Until 1991 a major obstacle to concrete negotiations was the dispute between the central and Russian governments over ownership of natural resources.

# U

**UKAZE.** See 'Decree'.

**UKRAINE** (pop. 52 million). Independent republic, formerly the second largest in the USSR; rich in industrial and agricultural potential, inhabited 74 per cent by Ukrainians, 21 per cent by Russians, and 5 per cent by lesser minorities. The pace of the independence movement, beginning seriously in 1989, was set by strident nationalism emanating from the Western half, centred on Lvov. The Western Ukraine (rural, Catholic) was first occupied by Austria, then Poland. It was annexed by the Soviet Union in 1939. Under German occupation it saw collaboration with the Nazis; then came brutal Sovietization in 1945. The Eastern Ukraine (Orthodox, industrialized) has a history of association with Russia; and under the German occupation it suffered terribly. In the north and in industrial centres the populations are heavily Russianized. The divide has helped to fuel a nationalist struggle in which neither side wanted to be left behind. This is exemplified in the rise of the Rukh★ movement and in the 'war' among Russian Orthodox, Ukrainian Orthodox and Uniate★ churches. (1990 saw the reappearance in Ukraine of the Ukrainian Autocephalous Church, created under the Nazis and surviving among post-war émigrés.)

In 1989 the Ukrainian Communist Party finally dropped its 'old guard' First Secretary, Vladimir Shcherbitsky,★ and elections to the Soviet parliament took place in a pro-*perestroika* atmosphere. The next year's local and republic elections had a more 'nationalist' result; but although nationalists scored in many localities, they failed to end Communist control of the republic parliament. In September 1989 they launched a campaign to strip the Party of the power it had kept at the polls. Members took fright when Rukh and some other parties called for the Party to be proscribed, its property confiscated, and even for individuals to be physically liquidated. One anti-communist newspaper went so far as to publish a poem depicting the Russians being massacred by Cossacks and the Dnepr flowing with blood. The movement culminated in strikes and student demonstrations, leading to the resignation in October 1990 of premier Vitali Massol (replaced by Vitold Fokin). A week earlier, under pressure from Rukh, parliament had approved a declaration of sovereignty, including the creation of a Ukrainian currency, a republic army, a state of neutrality, and economic autonomy. The presidency had meanwhile been taken over by the Communist Party's popular, and independent, second-in-command, Leonid Kravchuk,* who in July 1990 replaced Ivashko* on the latter's election to be Gorbachev's deputy. Strikes and demonstrations against a new Union treaty* then helped to develop an ultra-nationalist movement, dividing moderate nationalists, and causing second thoughts about complete independence. Hence the ambiguous votes in a March 1991 referendum: 71 per cent in favour of the Union treaty and 83 per cent for a sovereign Ukraine in a Union of sovereign states. After the *putsch* of August 1991, the degree of independence became the central issue, overtaking all other debates, including that in the parliamentary opposition as to whether or not to co-operate with the communists. With an election approaching, the republic's formerly communist leaders took a duplicitous stand – negotiating an economic treaty with Moscow while simultaneously driving towards total independence. At the same time there was a sharpening of differences between Eastern and Western Ukraine, where nationalists heroically commemorated the anti-communist and anti-semitic Ukrainian Insurgent Army and Organization of Ukrainian Nationalists. The idea of a 'confederative Ukraine' (paralleling proposals for a 'confederative Russia') was raised by autonomists in the Crimea.

In December 1991 the refusal of President Kravchuk and the Fokin government to subscribe to Gorbachev's new union treaty was approved by a large referendum majority (over 90 per cent). The result provided Yeltsin* with the opportunity to liquidate the USSR by the Minsk* and Alma-Ata* agreements setting up a Commonwealth,* including the Ukraine. Ukraine (now dropping the prefix 'the' from its name) was meanwhile caught up in a rush to establish statehood. Plans went ahead to create national armed forces* under the newly appointed Defence Minister, Gen. Morozov, and, less certainly, for a national currency. Though a large Ukrainian army was contrary to the spirit of the Commonwealth agreement, nationalist fervour demanded that it should continue with an originally given target of 250,000–400,000 men. Friction with Russia arose over Ukrainian demands that former Soviet soldiers on Ukrainian territory should sign a Ukrainian loyalty oath and over a Ukrainian claim to the greater part of the Soviet Black Sea fleet. Ukraine, in turn, was obliged to copy arbitrarily announced Russian price rises. Early in 1992 some observers feared the development of armed confrontation.

**UKRAINIAN ORTHODOX CHURCH.** Independent church formed by peaceful separation from the Russian Orthodox Church in October 1990. It was put under the authority of Metropolitan Filaret of Kiev and the Ukraine. The solemn celebration in the cathedral of Saint Sophia in Kiev was interrupted by the Ukrainian nationalists and members of the Autocephalous Church, denouncing the Ukrainian Orthodox Church for 'undermining national sovereignty'.

**UNEMPLOYMENT.** Novel condition 'temporarily' affecting 8 million, according to Anatoli Kasputin, executive director of the All Union Public Fund for Protection against Unemployment, in September 1991. Of these, 2 million could be considered 'truly unemployed'. Closures of unprofitable enterprises and cutbacks in production in 1987–89 accounted for 1.6 million. At the end of the year, officials predicting a possible total of 40 million job losses revealed that three-quarters of those so far dismissed in Moscow were women with high qualifications.

**UNIATE CHURCH.** Catholic church observing the Eastern rite, and centre of West Ukrainian nationalism. Four million of its 7 million adherents live in the Western Ukraine, where Uniate membership has been a traditional way of rejecting both Orthodox Russianization and Catholic Polonization. In 1946 Stalin accused the Uniates of collaborating with the Germans and ordered the Orthodox church to absorb them. In fact he wanted to suppress a national rallying point in a region Sovietized by force. The church survived clandestinely, its priests saying Mass in apartments and forests. With *glasnost*, Uniates demanded the legal reversal of Stalin's edict. This remained a bar to the establishment of relations with the Vatican until rectified by Gorbachev in 1989 at the time of his meeting with Pope John Paul II in Rome. A final settlement was delayed by the problem of reallocating churches and other ecclesiastical property – often involving violent confrontations between congregations. (Another cause of friction was the Vatican's hopes of bringing the Eastern church under Roman authority.) The first open Mass since 1946 was said in July 1988 in the village of Zarvanytsia, site of an apparition of the Virgin.

**UNION OF SOVIET SOCIALIST REPUBLICS (USSR – 1922–1991).** As defined up to August 1991 by the 'Brezhnev' constitution, a federal union of fifteen republics, each with the right to secede, but subject (under article 75) to almost unlimited power on the part of the centre. It contained more than a hundred nationalities, the smaller ones living mostly in thirty-eight subordinate autonomous units. Despite Lenin's early espousal of self-determination in 1918, under the pressures of the Civil War, all the nationalities living within Russia were soon brought together in a highly centralized Russian Socialist Federative Republic. (Ukrainian and Georgian attempts to leave were crushed in 1921.) Uneasy at having resorted to force and worried by the possible growth of Russian chauvinism, Lenin pressed for a wider federation. This was established by the creation of the USSR in 1922, confirmed in 1924 by a federal constitution, enlarged by Stalin in 1953 as a cover for further Russianization. In 1991 the future of the Union was thrown into the melting pot as independent republics discussed alternative forms of economic and political association, the maximum being some form of confederation. It was formally and, arguably, unconstitutionally dissolved by the Alma-Ata★

declaration of December 13 setting up a Commonwealth. (See 'Commonwealth of Independent States', 'Supreme Soviet, 'Presidency'.)

**UNION TREATY.** Focus of unsuccessful attempts to rewrite relations between the centre and the fifteen union republics. A draft produced by a preparatory commission, and endorsed by a referendum★ in March 1991, proposed central control of foreign relations, defence, banking, transport and energy supplies, but the autonomy of the republics in all other matters. Secession by any republic would require the vote of a two-thirds majority. But Russia's claim to 75 per cent of the Union's natural resources, plus the refusal of six republics (the Baltic states, Moldavia, Armenia and Georgia) to take part in the referendum, doomed the prospect of the draft's endorsement by parliaments. A more liberal draft, reached by negotiation at Novo-Ogarevo★ and due to be signed on August 20, provoked the same month's *putsch*.★ A third draft, in November, was rejected by the Ukraine in its independence referendum – paving the way to Minsk★ and the end of the Union.

**UNITED NATIONS.** World organization hamstrung for forty years by Soviet vetoes, rediscovered by the USSR in 1987 as a useful foreign policy instrument. Moscow suddenly cleared arrears of contributions and joined in moves to solve regional conflicts and to promote disarmament. In December 1987, Gorbachev used the General Assembly to announce a unilateral reduction of the Soviet armed forces★ by half a million men. The first real test of Soviet seriousness was in 1990 when the USSR with other Security Council members voted for sanctions against Iraq in the Gulf★ crisis. The Soviet Union had three seats in the UN Assembly: the Soviet, the Ukrainian and the Byelorussian (agreed in 1945 because of the country's size and its major role in World War II). With the break-up of the Union in December 1991 questions arose about UN membership for newly independent republics. With the agreement of the new Commonwealth,★ Russia claimed the Soviet seat and membership of the Security Council. Other republics expected treatment similar to that of the Baltic states, admitted to the General Assembly in September 1991.

**UNITED WORKERS' FRONT.** Extreme right-wing movement formed in 1990 to oppose democratic reforms.

**UNIVERSITY.** Backwater isolated from manifestations elsewhere until 1990, when students of Moscow State University held an anniversary hunger strike in memory of the students killed in Beijing's Tiananmen Square. At the end of the year demonstrations by Kiev students caused the resignation of the Ukrainian premier. In Moscow, students demanded the resignation of the Ryzhkov★ government, the depoliticization of the army, the suppression of the KGB, and a civil alternative to military service. But nowhere – in Moscow, Kiev or even the Baltic republics – were students consistently involved in calls for political changes on a scale that might have been expected in other countries.

**USTINOV**, DMITRI FYODOROVICH (1908–1984). Civilian Defence Minister and powerful Politburo member. He was largely responsible for sending Soviet forces to Afghanistan.

**UST KAMENOGORSK** (pop. 307,000). Industrial city of Kazakhstan,* victim in September 1990 of a 'chemical Chernobyl'. An explosion sent a cloud of beryllium over the city, directly threatening the health of 100,000 people and adding to the already grave ecological situation in one of the country's worst polluted cities.

**UZBEKISTAN** (pop. 19.5 million). Former Union republic of Central Asia declared independent in September 1991. It consists mostly of desert, but to the east of the capital, Tashkent, there are fertile valleys such as the Fergana. Uzbeks are Turkic-speaking Muslims, and have twice been involved in confrontations with minorities: with Meskhetian Turks* in Fergana in 1989 and with Kirghiz in Osh in 1990. In December 1990, at Namangan, an attack by young men on a bus carrying soldiers degenerated into a pitched battle between 3,000 rioters and 1,000 military and police reinforcements. The Uzbek press made no mention of the incident, which cost eight lives (including those of five soldiers) and fifty-two wounded (nearly all military or police). No one was capable of stopping the rioters; not the government (in the hands of the president), nor the nationalist movement, nor the religious authorities, nor the Communist Party.

The nationalist movement *Birlik*, launched in 1984 by a group of writers, relaunched in 1988 to support *perestroika*, and active in the 1989 election campaign, later split into two factions, one led by Abdurahim Pulatov (a professor of mathematics at Tashkent university) and the other by the poet Muhammad Salih. Pulatov is a great communicator whose passionate speeches inflamed the crowds; Muhammad Salih is a calm man who fears that meetings ending in violence will discredit the movement. Although denouncing the excesses after each bloody disturbance, Pulatov radicalized the movement after October 1989 when the recognition of Uzbek as the republic's official language threatened to deprive *Birlik* of its *raison d'être*. Since 1989 an increasing role has been played by religion. The newly elected young mufti, Muhammad Sadyk, has won concessions from the government, leading to the opening of new mosques (up to three a week) and the construction of housing to increase the number of students in Koranic schools. In December 1991 an old Party boss, Islam Karimov, was elected President with an 86 per cent majority of the vote. One of his first acts was to pardon offenders convicted of corruption in the early 1980s cotton* scandal.

# V

**VAAP.** Acronym for Soviet state copyright agency, a cultural bureaucracy once exclusively responsible for the sale abroad of books and plays by Soviet writers and for the acquisition of titles from abroad. For years its inertia and lack of professionalism removed the Soviet Union from contact with international publishing. With the easing of restrictions in other ways, authors who had not already done so learned to bypass it. In 1991, authors became free to deal directly with foreign publishers and agents.

**VALUTA.** See 'Hard currency'.

**VATICAN.** One-time 'spider' behind a web of anti-communist conspiracies, suddenly perceived by Gorbachev as an interesting (and interested) partner. The irony was that the Vatican should receive signals from godless Soviet Russia after years of being held at bay by Orthodox Christian tsars. In 1988 Gorbachev took the initiative by freeing imprisoned believers and changing the official attitude towards religion.★ In 1989, the hatchet was finally buried at his historic meeting with John Paul II in Rome. This was followed by an exchange of diplomatic representatives. But there were delays in fixing a date for the Pope to visit the Soviet Union (which he made contingent on being able to visit Catholics in the Ukraine and Lithuania), and on settling questions concerning the Uniates.★

**VELIKHOV,** YEVGENI PAVLOVICH (1935–   ). Nuclear physicist and scientific adviser of Gorbachev. In 1989 he was widely expected to become president of the Academy of Sciences,★ but instead the Academicians chose Marchuk.★

**VETERAN.** Symbol of social conscience and model for the young. In 1988, when such things still mattered, two Unionwide bodies – the Association of War Veterans and the Association of Labour Veterans – were fused with a common aim: the defence, by personal example, of 'socialist values'. But the real veterans of the day, *Afghantsi* (see 'Afghanistan'), preferred to go their own way. Although they agreed to address schools and youth groups, they were more concerned with helping disabled colleagues, comforting bereaved families, and generally sustaining a private world that outsiders were unlikely to understand.

**VIDEO.** Electronic status symbol, heading the 1980s black market until the arrival of computers. 'Real' videos had to be foreign-made and cost about R4,000 (twenty times the average monthly salary). For poorer citizens there were 'video-salons' where a cassette and viewing cubicle could be rented for R5. The home-viewing market was swamped with copies of American soap operas, with a single voice dubbing all the parts regardless of gender. For those ready to pay there was everything from *Rambo* to Ingmar Bergman (in demand not for art but for sexual episodes).

**VIETNAM.** Late survivor of Cold War alliances and principal base for the advancement of Soviet policy in Asia. After the Vietnam war (1965–73), Moscow supported Vietnam as a counter to China's expansion in the region. In the 1980s it backed the use of Vietnamese forces to prevent the return of the Peking-backed regime of Pol Pot in Kampuchea.* But in 1991 the sharp cut in Soviet aid, with a requirement to settle accounts in hard currency, hit the Vietnamese economy hard, the Soviet Union having for fifteen years been its principal commercial partner. Some 60,000 of the 168,000 foreign workers in the Soviet Union continued to be from Vietnam.

**VLASOVITES' UNION.** Political group formed in August 1991 'to defend the maligned memory of the Vlasov army' (composed of Soviet PoWs volunteering to fight under General A. A. Vlasov on the side of the Germans in World War Two). Chairman, Yuri Surganov.

**VNEZHEKONOMBANK.** Bank for Foreign Trade long having a monopoly of currency exchange transactions between Soviets and foreigners. It was twice reorganized, in 1988 and 1990, but its grip remained intact. In February 1992, with reserves exhausted, it found itself in *de facto* bankruptcy. A rescue plan by Swiss auditors proposed dividing it into three sections – one to continue servicing the centralized external debt, one to go to the Russian Foreign Trade Bank, and the third to become an independent commercial bank.

**VOLSKY,** ARKADI IVANOVICH (1932– ). Presidential trouble-shooter, for two years emissary to the Nagorno-Karabakh* autonomous region. Later appointed head of the all-Union Committee for Operational Management of the Economy, responsible for co-ordinating work in the defence, construction, transport and communications industries. Supporter of the Movement for Democratic Reforms,* and since January 1992 head of the Russian League of Industrialists and Entrepreneurs.

**VOZNESENSKY,** ANDREI ANDREYEVICH (1933– ). Modernist once accused of pro-Westernism, recognized since 1985 as one of the country's leading poets.

**VPK.** (*Voyenno-promishlennyi Kompleks*). Soviet military-industrial commission, responsible for co-ordinating defence production. According to Arkadi Volsky,* at the end of 1991 it had 2,500 defence plants and organizations employing 7,800,000 people. Its spirit survives in a new Russian 'Arms Trade Committee', giving 'conversion' an aspect that no one in the West had foreseen.

**VYSOTSKY,** VLADIMIR SEMYONOVICH (1938–1980). Actor and singer remembered with a sometimes embarrassing intensity ever since people were free to show their feelings. His death in Moscow was overlooked by the army of foreign journalists who came only to cover the Olympic Games. Muscovites formed a ten-mile long procession and hung his portrait from black-draped balconies. In Russian memory he will always be the Hamlet of the Taganka,* but also a poet, a film star and singer whose songs were equally familiar to intellectuals, lorry-drivers and the KGB. Although not persecuted, he was boycotted by the state recording company, Melodia. Everything changed in 1987–88. In January 1988, 11,000 people gathered at the Taganka under the aegis of the Soviet Cultural Fund* to celebrate the fiftieth anniversary of his birth, Melodia announced the release of seventeen of his (previously undistributed) records, a collection of 400 of his poems appeared, and television showed a four-part programme about him. Of his up to 1,000 songs and poems, only forty-five, all relatively harmless, were broadcast before his death.

# W

**WALLENBERG**, Raoul (1912–?). Swedish diplomat still untraced despite *glasnost* and the help of the KGB. In 1990 a committee acting for his family was allowed to visit Vladimir prison, where witnesses said they saw him in 1950–60. Heir of a rich industrialist, in World War II Wallenberg saved thousands of Hungarian Jews by giving them Swedish passports. He disappeared when Soviet troops entered Budapest in January 1945. The Soviets put out contradictory stories. The 'Wallenberg committee' was allowed to question witnesses and consult archives, without any result, except that the Soviets now ruled out a theory that he had died of a heart attack in 1947. Documents handed over during the opening of files after the 1991 *putsch*★ added nothing helpful.

**WARSAW PACT (TREATY) ORGANIZATION (WTO).** Ghost of a military alliance finally laid to rest in March 1991. The Pact – originally embracing the Soviet Union, Albania, Bulgaria, Czechoslovakia, the GDR, Hungary, Poland and Romania – was signed in 1955 in response to the creation of NATO. But it never had anything resembling NATO's political structure. East European members were bound to Moscow by bilateral treaties, and WTO military headquarters were little more than an extension of the Soviet high command. To begin with, Soviet forces were stationed in Czechoslovakia, the GDR and Poland; and in 1956 they entered Hungary to crush the new Nagy government. A move towards reform was made at the Berlin summit of May 1987, when the Political Committee endorsed the new Soviet concept of 'sufficient defence'.★ But nothing could save the alliance from disintegration after the changes that shook Eastern Europe in 1989–90. In June 1990, members voted to continue the Pact organization after the impending demise of the GDR in September. But almost immediately the Hungarian parliament voted unanimously for a withdrawal, causing others to follow. Under a revision of bilateral agreements, Moscow promised to remove all Soviet troops from Czechoslovakia and Hungary by June 1991, and those in Poland and eastern Germany before the end of 1993. In 1990 the Soviet Union suggested creating direct links between a demilitarized WTO and a demilitarized NATO as a step towards setting up an all-European security body via the CSCE.★ Other Pact members made informal approaches about direct membership of NATO, but no one in the Western alliance wanted to establish a new 'frontier' with the Soviet Union.

**WHEAT**. Expensive cereal regularly wasted by muddle, causing precious hard currency to be spent on imports. A third of the bumper crop of 1990 was lost in the fields when combine harvesters were immobilized by shortages of spares and fuel. Trucks and wagons were diverted to the ports, where contracts imposed stiff penalties for delay in unloading foreign wheat from US ships.

**WING**. New political word, as in 'left-wing', 'right-wing', adopted in an attempt to clarify the confusion resulting from reforms. 'Right' now means left, i.e. communist diehards, while 'left' means people who would once have been called 'right', i.e. free-market ultra-reformists.

**WOMEN**. The Soviet Union's real proletariat, as Gorbachev admitted to an international women's congress when he said that women bore the brunt of the economic crisis (queues, shortages, want of household appliances), often without a husband to help. Women's congresses were the only time women got royal treatment. Yet there are no feminist movements such as Western women would recognize. One reason is that whereas most Western women demand the right to a job and the means of self-expression, the dream of most Russian women is the right to stay in the home. Women's magazines stress the role of wife and mother. This made a comeback in the 1980s, when society grew alarmed at the consequences of social changes, such as juvenile delinquency and drugs, blaming them on women's absence from the family. Predictions of widespread unemployment almost certainly contributed to this newfound concern for greater domesticity. And indeed by 1991 60 per cent of those thrown out of jobs by 'market' reforms were women. In August 1987 women's career prospects were helped by the unusual nomination of a woman, Zoya Novoshilova, to be ambassador in Bern. At the Nineteenth Party Conference a quarter of the delegates were women; but outside the Party the number of women on political organizing committees could be counted on the fingers of one hand. When in 1990 the Russian parliament thought (briefly) of making a woman Defence Minister, it was mainly to teach Gorbachev a lesson; deputies talked like elderly relatives giving a chance to a not very gifted youngster. At work, women mostly occupy the poorest paid jobs (as in textiles) and the dirtiest ones (as in agriculture). Even well educated women are in poorly paid sectors (medicine, teaching, culture, shop management). Although they take 48 per cent of degrees and diplomas, women occupy only 7 per cent of managerial jobs. Research in 1991 confirmed that, in comparison to men, women were more conservative, more regretful of the loss of authority by the government, and more doubtful of the success of reforms.

**WORK**. Simulated economic activity, characterized in the state sector by the workers' affirmation, 'We pretend to work, and the state pretends to pay.' In 1990, according to Goskomstat,* 200,000 skilled workers failed to turn up for work every day, causing a year's loss of 50 million man-days. But work can also be dangerous. Each year, 14,000 people die through accidents and 20,000 more become invalids. There are 700,000 registered accidents annually; and in 1991, 3.5 million people were engaged in jobs contravening safety standards. More than 7 million workers were officially categorized as 'constantly poisoned by harmful gases and dust' or subjected to radioactivity. See 'Unemployment'.

**WRITERS' UNION.** Conservative body, contrasting with the filmmakers'* union in its heyday. Instead of using their 1986 Eighth Congress to root out the past, the 10,000 writers re-elected their 75-year-old president, Georgi Markov, flanked by a new secretary, Viktor Karpov of *Novy Mir*. In 1986–87 the mood of the times obliged them to lift the cloud on many former members. Among those rehabilitated, often posthumously, were Boris Pasternak,* Nikolai Gumilev,* Vladimir Nabokov,* Anatoli Rybakov,* and Aleksandr Bek, author of the anti-Stalinist short story, *The New Rendezvous*. They also set up committees 'to study our cultural heritage', meaning rehabilitation of figures like Mandelstam* and Vysotsky.* At the end of 1987, reformers decided they had had enough when the union voted to cold-shoulder a 1988 first meeting of Russian and émigré writers in Denmark. Attacked by Karpov and conservatives for participating, Shatrov,* Yevtushenko* and Voznesensky* founded an independent association, 'April'.*

# Y

**YABLOKOV,** ALEKSEI ALEKSANDROVICH (1933– ). Marine biologist, in 1989 made first president of the Soviet division of Greenpeace. The same year he was elected to the Soviet parliament and made vice-chairman of the Committee for the Environment. He had long waged a campaign for the protection of the environment, notably opposing the vice-president of the Academy of Sciences, Yuri Ochinnikov, who wished to increase agricultural production by intensifying the use of pesticides. In 1992 he was made Russian State Counsellor for Ecology and Health.

**YAKOVLEV,** ALEKSANDR NIKOLAYEVICH (1923– ). All-round master of *perestroika* and international relations specialist (Canada, USA); a solid and sincere personality, ready to recognize the Party's mistakes without complacency. In 1973 he was appointed ambassador in Ottawa, when embassies were used as a 'Siberia' for politicians in disgrace. Returned to Moscow in 1983, he spent two years as head of IMEMO★ until Gorbachev promoted him to the upper ranks of the Party, as a member of the Central Committee,★ then, in 1986, as a Central Committee Secretary. He left the Politburo at the Twenty-eighth Congress,★ and the Party shortly before the 1991 *putsch*.★ Though he subsequently declined to join Gorbachev's reconstituted security council, he remained an informal adviser and friend. In September he was appointed a member of the President's Political Consultative Council.★ He also served as chief negotiator with independent Latvia (Shevardnadze★ performing the same duty with Lithuania, and Sobchak★ with Estonia). The same month he attended the founding of the Movement for Democratic Reforms.★

**YAKOVLEV,** YEGOR VLADIMIROVICH (1930– ). Editor-in-chief of *Moscow News*,★ 1986–91; regarded as a friend of Gorbachev until the reformist newspaper developed its own much more radical political line, resulting in open tension between them. After the 1991 *putsch*★ he was appointed director of Gostelradio.★

**YAKUNIN,** GLEB PAVLOVICH (1934– ). Orthodox priest imprisoned in 1978 with the tacit complicity of the religious authorities, whom he had criticized for 'collaboration'. Freed by the 1987 amnesty, in March 1988 he led a campaign for the resignation of the Patriarch Pimen,★ calling on him to recognize that his 'poor health did not make him the ideal person to

241

lead the renewal of the church now back in liberty.' In 1989 he was elected a parliamentary deputy, and in 1990 he founded a Christian Party dedicated to 'imbuing society with Christian virtues'.

**YANAYEV,** GENNADI IVANOVICH (1937–   ). Soviet Vice-President, proposed by Gorbachev and elected by the Congress of People's Deputies at the time of the post's creation in 1990. A former trade union organization president and Politburo member responsible for international affairs, his undistinguished candidature was a surprise, and required a second ballot. Gorbachev would have done much better with Nazarbayev.* In 1991 he emerged as spokesman and nominal leader of the eight-man 'emergency committee' directing the August *putsch*.* With others he was arrested and charged with treason. In January 1992 he was still awaiting trial.

**YASNAYA POLYANA.** Estate in the Tula region, 140 miles south of Moscow; home of Lev Tolstoy. In 1985 its dilapidation was presented as an example of the lack of concern for culture during the years of stagnation.* Steps ordered earlier (1983) had not been followed. A nearby fertilizer factory continued to poison the trees in the park and the house was being rotted by damp. In 1987 the Tula council executive committee established a protective zone to preserve the house in the state in which Tolstoy left it.

**YAVLINSKY,** GRIGORI ALEKSEEVICH (1952–   ). Disciple of Abalkin* who once thought he had all the answers. As a 'private' political economist and a deputy prime minister of the Russian Federation (1990), he drew up a 'Five Hundred Days Plan' for transforming the Russian economy. Later he worked with Jeffrey Sachs, Graham Allison and a group of Harvard-based economists on a plan for Soviet economic reconstruction with massive Western aid. The plan was put before the G-7* summit in London in July 1991, but failed to win the hoped-for instant infusion. In 1991 he was appointed deputy to Silayev* as head of the post-*putsch** committee preparing economic reform. But when his plan for setting up a preliminary economic union was overtaken by the sudden formation of a Commonwealth* and Yeltsin's government abruptly freed prices, in a move such as he himself had once advocated, he took to issuing dire warnings of social unrest, through his research institute, 'Epicenter'.

**YAZOV,** MARSHAL DMITRI TIMOFEEVICH (1923–   ). Soldier promoted to Defence Minister, less for what he was than for what he was not. When, in May 1989, Gorbachev used the Rust* fiasco to get rid of Marshal Sokolov, he needed to appoint a reliable successor without personal ambition. He put aside obvious candidates such as Pyotr Lushev (Deputy Defence Minister, who a few months earlier had stood in for the ailing Sokolov at the Victory Day parade) and Akhromeyev,* and instead chose a man lower in rank, whom he had known long before in Stavropol and who had spent his career in the military bureaucracy. During the war Yazov served as a junior officer in Volkov and Leningrad, and after the war in Central Asia. After graduating from the Frunze military academy in 1956 and the Armed Forces staff college in 1967, he was briefly deputy defence minister in charge of personnel. From the time of his appointment as Minister he consistently defended Gorbachev's disarmament policies, but at the Twenty-eighth Party Congress* made a violent attack on those who were 'undermining the prestige of the army'. In 1991 he emerged as one of the eight members of the 'Emergency Committee' directing the August *putsch*.* According to associates, it never occurred to him that officers or soldiers might disregard his orders. He was arrested and charged with treason.

**YELTSIN,** BORIS NIKOLAYEVICH (1931–    ). According to taste, the *enfant terrible* of *perestroika* or the Mussolini of the Urals. A civil engineer, he began his Party career in Sverdlovsk, where he became regional First Secretary in 1968. In 1985 he arrived in Moscow, sponsored by Ligachev* (to whom he became Brutus) and pledged to support Gorbachev (whom he soon made his fraternal enemy). Appointed a Secretary of the Central Committee and First Secretary of the Moscow Communist Party, he set about restoring order after the departure of Grishin.* But in 1988 he was stripped of his functions, including candidate membership of the Politburo, after a stormy Central Committee plenum in which he attacked leading Party figures for the slow pace of reform. As a sop he was made Minister for the Building Industry, a post without responsibility or prestige. Yet out of the debacle he managed to construct a demagogic but victorious political campaign – against privilege, bureaucracy and the laggards of *perestroika*. In March 1989 he was elected a parliamentary deputy for Moscow with an 89 per cent vote, and became prime mover of the Inter-regional Group.* After regional elections the following year he became 'president' (in fact chairman of the presidium of the supreme soviet) of the Russian republic.

It was the moment of revenge. Yeltsin lost no opportunity to undermine the power of Gorbachev, supporting anything and everything that promised a reduction of the President's powers (contacts with rebel republics, the sending of a separate Russian delegation to the IMF,* the creation of an entourage of young technicians to seduce the Americans). He constantly said that he held his power from the people, that Gorbachev was 'yesterday's man' and himself tomorrow's. In August 1990 he made a spectacular 'Russian tour', marred by the reminder – through assertions of autonomy and sovereignty* by regions or autonomous republics – that the Russian republic was a mosaic of nationalities no less than the USSR was, and his position in Russia in some ways analogous to that of Gorbachev in the Union as a whole. In November 1990 he attempted a rapprochement with Gorbachev – the first of several in a difficult relationship of rivalry yet mutual dependency. In a succession of mass demonstrations preceding the referendum on a new union treaty* (March 1991), and the vote for the Russian presidency (June 1991), Yeltsin was careful to stay away, leaving crowds to shout his name and demand Gorbachev's resignation. Elected president with a 57 per cent majority, he indicated Russia's readiness to sign a liberalized form of the contentious new union treaty, and Western governments did all they could to persuade the two leaders to work in harness.

This happened in an unexpected way, thanks to the August 1991 *putsch*.* Defying the *putsch*ists, and taking command of the forces of resistance gathered round the Russian parliament, Yeltsin appeared as the saviour of democracy. He also saved Gorbachev, who was now obliged to share decisions with him and appoint Yeltsin nominees to many leading state offices. But although Yeltsin was the hero of the day, he soon offended liberals by his overbearing attitude, and non-Russian republics by seeming to seek Russian aggrandisement. (He had to qualify hasty remarks about redrawing borders with those having large Russian populations.) Among ordinary people, the test would be his ability to fulfil promises to improve the economy and daily life. A troublesome heart condition was seen as a means of avoiding awkward confrontations; but there was no doubt that he drove himself hard physically.

After the *putsch* Yeltsin used his increased authority to undermine Gorbachev and accelerate economic reform in Russia itself. In December 1991 he used the refusal of the Ukraine to join any new form of union to call the Minsk* and Alma-Ata* meetings, setting up a Commonwealth* that deprived Gorbachev of any future role. Yeltsin's takeover of the Kremlin turned out to be less of a triumph when popular resentment followed his liberalization of prices in January 1992, and other republics, resenting his overbearing manner (and given the example of an equally overbearing leadership in Ukraine) refused co-operation in anything liable to produce Russian hegemony.

**YEVTUSHENKO,** YEVGENI ALEKSANDROVICH (1933– ). Poet turned buffoon. After personifying the Khrushchev 'thaw', with brave poems such as 'Babi Yar' and 'The Heirs of Stalin', he sought to make good a lack of inspiration by showing that he was an all-round artist. He tried the novel (the disappointing The Wild Bays of Siberia, 1981) and the cinema (*Kindergarten*, 1984), the latter marked by heavy symbolism and some facile provocations, such as showing on the screen (separately) a topless woman and a rabbi. He specialized in the role of 'audacious' poet, though his calculated audacity never went so far as dirtying his hands on behalf of colleagues in trouble with the government or the Union of Writers. At the first Moscow street demonstrations, in February 1990, he mounted the stand to read a poem which (he said) he had composed while marching with the demonstrators. Appalled by its bathos, many hearers believed him.

**YUNOST.** Cultural review of the Khrushchev renaissance, endowed with a new aura under *perestroika*, thanks to its editor, the poet Andrei Dementev. Among the most prestigious arts reviews, it fared better than others in the 1991 subscription slide.

**YURCHENKO,** Vitali Sergeyevich (1936–    ). Erstwhile diplomat and enigmatic figure of the spy game. In July 1985 he disappeared from the Soviet embassy in Rome. Two months later the US State Department exhibited him as having been the KGB's North America station chief. In November 1985 he reappeared in Moscow, claiming to have been kidnapped, drugged and interrogated. In August 1986 he said the Americans had wanted him to admit that he had instigated the 1981 attempt to kill the Pope. In September 1987, *Izvestia* scotched rumours of his execution by publishing a picture of him walking with his grandson in Pushkin Square. A similar procedure was used in the case of an émigré journalist called Tumanov, who in 1986 disappeared from Radio Free Europe, then turned up in Moscow saying he had been recruited to work for the 'anti-Soviet' radio and espionage centre by the CIA.

# Z

**ZAGLADIN,** VADIM VALENTINOVICH (1927– ). Longtime member of the International Commission of the Central Committee, considered in the West as a moderate. In the crucial foreign policy debates of the later 1980s he took a 'centrist' line, presenting Gorbachev's policy as a compromise between the ideological positions of Ligachev* and Yakovlev.*

**ZAGORSK.** Former village, 40 miles from Moscow; famous for its monastery, a favourite spot to which to take distinguished foreign visitors with whom it is not known what to do. Originally called Sergeyev Possad, after the place's founder, Saint Sergius of Radonezh, in 1930 it was renamed Zagorsk after the alias of a pre-1917 revolutionary, Wolf Lubotsky. In 1988, a priest, a retired soldier and a cultural worker formed a group to press for the restoration of its old name. The monastery of Saint Sergius and the Holy Trinity contains superb fifteenth century buildings with frescoes by Andrei Rublev.

**ZAITSEV,** VYACHESLAV. National fashion laureate officiating since 1982 from his 'Dom Modeli' (House of Models) in Moscow's Prospekt Mira. He describes his 30-year career in couture as 'aiming to make propaganda for good taste' and his workshop as a 'fashion laboratory'. In 1987 he sought to penetrate the American market, on a crest of 'Gorbymania'. So far as is known, he never clothed Raisa Gorbachev.

**ZASLAVSKAYA,** TATIANA IVANOVNA (1927– ). Social economist whose work unconsciously paved the way for reforms. After first studying physics at Moscow University, she switched to economics, then worked in industry before undertaking a Ph.D thesis in the agricultural department of the Institute of Economics. She was from an intellectual family, and field work brought her into shocked contact with the condition of the countryside after collectivization and World War II. In 1963 she met Abel Aganbegyan,* who took her into the Institute of Economics in Novosibirsk, where she led a team study of rural Siberia. In 1968, married with two daughters, she became head of the institute's sociology division. In 1973–77, as chair of a national Committee for the Development of Soviet Villages, she helped develop a statistical model that turned out to predict an acute crisis in Soviet agriculture because of low productivity and underlying social conditions. The team concentrated on an area of the

Altai* and developed ideas for socio-economic agricultural reform that were later incorporated in Gorbachev's reforms of 1986–88. In 1981 Zaslavskaya was elected a full member of the Academy of Sciences, and next year met Gorbachev during a meeting of senior scientists to discuss agricultural and food production problems. In 1983 she came to prominence when Western newspapers printed parts of a contribution she had made to a scientific colloquium, predicting a Soviet economic disaster. Zaslavskaya and Aganbegyan were reprimanded and sidelined by the Party. In 1985 she became one of the stars of *perestroika*, and by 1987 was head of the new Institute of Sociology. In December 1990 she was chosen by Yeltsin* as part of his consultative council (together with Nikolai Shmelev, Pavel Bunich and Yuri Karyakin).

**ZERO OPTION.** Policy term meaning both sides' elimination of specified weapons system. First used of intermediate-range nuclear weapons in the INF* debate; later extended as the so-called 'double zero' to cover shorter-range nuclear forces.

**ZHIRINOVSKY**, VLADIMIR VOLFOVICH (1946– ). President of the Liberal Democratic Party, taking third place – 7.8 per cent of the vote – in the 1990 Russian presidential elections. His platform included the defence of Russian minorities outside Russia and a cut in the price of vodka. He went over the top with calls for a military reoccupation of the Baltic states. Degenerating into even greater demagogy, in 1992 he offered three solutions to the current situation: another coup, civil war, or his own election as president.

**ZIL.** Customary conveyance of presidents and senior ministers. The use of a Zil limousine, with its automatic right of way, was scorned for a time by Boris Yeltsin,* who wished to appear one of the people. In September 1990, his humbler Volga was involved in a crossroads collision.

**ZIONISM.** Scarecrow used by conservatives as a screen for anti-semitism.* In 1990, a hundred Soviet and Israeli Zionist organizations put a weapon in their hands by the founding in Moscow of a Soviet Zionist Federation. Sponsored by the Zionist organization Irgun, the Federation aims to boost Jewish emigration to Israel, to organize a lobby to 'promote a Soviet policy less hostile towards Israel', and to help Zionist candidates put up for election. The event, predictably, drew protests from Pamyat* and Soviet-based Arab students.

# SUGGESTIONS FOR FURTHER READING

Aganbegyan, Abel, *The Challenge: Economics of Perestroika*, London, Hutchinson, 1988

Bluth, Cristoph, *New Thinking in Soviet Military Policy*, London, Royal Institute of International Affairs, 1990

Brown, Archie and others (eds.), *The Cambridge Encyclopaedia of Russia and the Soviet Revolution*, Cambridge University Press, 1982

Chauvier, Jean-Marie, *URSS: une société en mouvement*, Paris, Editions de l'Aube, 1990

Desai, Padma, *Perestroika in Perspective: the Dilemma and Designs of Soviet Reform*, London, I. B. Tauris, 1989

Hasegawa, Tsuyoshi and Pravda, Alex, *Perestroika: Soviet Domestic and Foreign Policies*, London, Royal Institute of International Affairs, 1990

Hosking, Geoffrey, *The Awakening of the Soviet Union*, London, William Heinemann, 1990

Kerblay, Basile, *La Russie de Gorbatchev*, Lyon, La Manufacture, 1989

Lewin, Moshe, *La Formation du Système Soviétique*, Paris, Gallimard, 1985

Medvedev, Roy, *Time of Change: an Insider's View of Russia's Transformation*, New York, Pantheon Books, 1990

Medvedev, Zhores, *The Legacy of Chernobyl*, London, Basil Blackwell, 1990

Medvedev, Zhores, *Soviet Agriculture*, New York, W. W. Norton, 1987

Nove, Alec, *An Economic History of the USSR* (second edition), London, Penguin, 1989

Schmidt-Hauer, Christian, *Gorbachev: the Path to Power*, English edition, London, I. B. Tauris, 1986

White, Stephen, *Gorbachev in Power*, Cambridge University paperback, 1991.

Readers are also referred to *L'URSS de Lenine à Gorbatchev* (Brussels, GRIP 1990), and the authors' own *Living with Glasnost* (London, Penguin, 1988)

# THEMATIC INDEX

## POLITICAL LIFE